VIDEO GAME
LEVEL DESIGN

VIDEO GAME
LEVEL DESIGN

HOW TO CREATE VIDEO GAMES WITH EMOTION, INTERACTION, AND ENGAGEMENT

MICHAEL SALMOND

BLOOMSBURY ACADEMIC

LONDON • NEW YORK • OXFORD • NEW DELHI • SYDNEY

BLOOMSBURY ACADEMIC
Bloomsbury Publishing Inc
50 Bedford Square, London, WC1B 3DP, UK
1385 Broadway, New York, NY 10018, USA

BLOOMSBURY, BLOOMSBURY ACADEMIC and the Diana
logo are trademarks of Bloomsbury Publishing Plc

First published in Great Britain 2021

Cover image: © M. Salmond. Created in Unity, assets are from Gabro Media,
Batewar, FlamingSands, LemmoLab, Studio New Punch and Redbee

A catalogue record for this book is available from the British Library.

Library of Congress Cataloging-in-Publication Data
Names: Salmond, Michael, author.
Title: Video game level design : how to create video games with
emotion, interaction and engagement / Michael Salmond.
Description: New York : Bloomsbury Academic, 2020. | Includes bibliographical
references and index. | Summary: "Explains what level design is and how
to use it to make engaging video games"—Provided by publisher.
Identifiers: LCCN 2019050852 | ISBN 9781350099500 (hardback) | ISBN 9781350015722
(paperback) | ISBN 9781350015746 (epub) | ISBN 9781350015739 (pdf)
Subjects: LCSH: Level design (Computer science) | Video games—Psychological aspects.
Classification: LCC QA76.76.C672 S26 2020 | DDC 794.8—dc23
LC record available at https://lccn.loc.gov/2019050852

ISBN: HB: 978-1-3500-9950-0
        PB: 978-1-3500-1572-2
        ePDF: 978-1-3500-1573-9
        eBook: 978-1-3500-1574-6

Typeset by Lachina Creative, Inc.
Printed and bound in India

To find out more about our authors and books visit
www.bloomsbury.com and sign up for our newsletters.

Contents

1 **Chapter One**

Getting Started: Research and Preproduction

2 The Preproduction Process

    2 Level Design Preproduction

4 Research

6 Essential Tools

8 Blocking Out, Early On

10 Production

10 Summary

17 **Chapter Two**

The Principles of Level Design

18 The 10 Principles of Good Level Design

19 Applying the Level Design Principles

    19 Principle 1: Good Level Design Is Fun to Navigate

    20 Principle 2: Good Level Design Does Not Rely on Words to Tell the Story

    22 Principle 3: Good Level Design Tells What, but Not How

    24 Principle 4: Good Level Design Constantly Teaches

    26 Principle 5: Good Level Design Is Surprising

    27 Principle 6: Good Level Design Empowers the Player

    28 Principle 7: Good Level Design Is Easy, Medium, and Hard

    29 Principle 8: Good Level Design Is Efficient

    30 Principle 9: Good Level Design Will Create Emotion

    32 Principle 10: Good Level Design Is Driven by Mechanics

33 Summary

35 **Chapter Three**

Constraints, Player Flow, and Objectives

36 Technical Constraints

37 Scale, Integration, and Proportion

42 Flow, Critical Paths, and Intensity

    42 Flow

    43 Critical Path

    44 Intensity Ramping

44 Balancing the Level

45 Varying the Level for Maximum Enjoyment

    46 Objectives

48 Summary

55   Chapter Four

The Player:
Motivations,
Psychology,
and Behaviors

56   The Door Problem
58   Motivating the Player
59   Speed, Pacing, and Distance
    59   Navigating without Maps
    60   Curiosity
    60   Landmarks
62   No Straight Paths and Maps
    as Reward
64   Foreshadowing
65   Lighting the Way
66   Summary

71   Chapter Five

The Anatomy
of Level Design

72   Breaking Down a Level's
    Design
78   Analyzing a Game's Level for
    Pacing
80   Level Design Models
    80   The Linear Model
    82   The Branching or
        Nonlinear Model
    83   The Hub-and-Spoke
        Model
    84   The Open or Emergent
        Model
85   Summary

89   Chapter Six

The Process
of Level Design

90   Level Designers Are
    Gatekeepers
92   The Iteration Process
    93   The Pitch
    95   Pass 1: Layout
    96   Pass 2: Encounters
    100   Pass 3: Core Complete
    102   Beauty Pass
    103   Final Pass: Polish
104 Summary

109   Chapter Seven

Modular Level
Design and
Environment Art

110   Why Use Modular?
111   Modular Level Design Is a
        System
113   The Grid
114   Complexity through
        Simplicity
115   Stress Testing and
        Prototyping
116   Surfaces, Shaders, and
        Materials
117   Summary

123   Chapter Eight

Designing
Nonplayer
Behaviors and
Encounters

124   Artificial Intelligence,
        Bringing the World to Life
        (Sort Of)
125   Choice Architecture
128   Adaptive and Predictive
        Systems
130   AI Director Systems
131   Emergent Behaviors
133   Summary

141   Chapter Nine

Combat Design
and Multiplayer
Design

142   Combat and Level Design
144   Breaking Down Combat
        Design
145   Detail Is Important, Even in
        Combat
148   Level Design for Multiplayer
150   Framing and Composition for
        Multiplayer
151   Multiplayer Definitions
153   Sightlines and Exploits
154   PvP No AI Required
155   Summary
155   Next Steps

163   Bibliography and Game Credits
168   Index

Level Design: Principles and Practices from the Ground Up

Welcome to the Discipline of Level Design

My book *Video Game Design: Principles and Practices from the Ground Up* (Bloomsbury Publishing, 2016) is a great primer for what goes into making a video game from start to finish. While I was researching the book, as well as teaching my video game courses, it struck me that level design was a discipline that required more depth of coverage. What interested me most about the subject of level design is that as a discipline it is often overlooked in favor of broader elements of video game design such as animation, mechanics, and narrative. Level design incorporates a large cross section of skill-sets across multiple design disciplines and yet is still loosely defined. Although it incorporates visual and spatial communication, experience design, interface design, and the tenets of iteration, testing, and feedback gathering, it is quite possible that many players would find it hard to define what level design actually is.

0.0
Legend of Zelda: Breath of the Wild, Nintendo, **2017**

"Level design is applied game design. It is both a hyper-specialized craft and a broader study of the intersection of technology, mechanics and largely intangible fun."

(Seifert, 2013)

This book addresses the shortcomings in video game design literature by examining the discipline in depth. In writing this book my approach is to examine the discipline through the lens of design thinking (a practice that draws upon logic, imagination, intuition, and system-based reason to explore possibilities when solving design problems). As I tell my students, you do not have to get a video game design BA or B.Sc. to be a game designer. Many of the people featured in this book are talented level designers who have backgrounds in art, design, literature, or computer science. That is not to say that studying game design at university is detrimental, but it does mean that if you are creative and driven you can achieve your goals of getting into the video game industry through a variety of routes. Video games are not just about art or programming or interaction or storytelling. Every game is all those aspects and this is the reason large or independent development teams rely on wide and varied skill-sets in order to make successful games.

Who is this book for? It is for anyone from a design or creative discipline who has an interest in exploring what goes into creating interactive environments and levels in video games. This book sets out to introduce and then go into depth about the discipline of level design. It will take you through small and then larger projects that will give you hands-on practical advice on making great levels for a video game. I will be talking about how I introduce level design into my courses as well as examining how industry professionals from independent video game developers to AAA (triple A) developers master and execute their craft. Level design can be a route into the industry and you do not need to know everything about game engines or get deep into game systems to be a level designer. As an example, Steve Gaynor from The Fullbright Company (*Gone Home* and *Tacoma*) began in the industry by modifying levels in the game *F.E.A.R.* using the in-game customization tools. His levels were popular and he used those designs to get a job working on the *BioShock 2* DLC *Minerva's Den* (it is also worth noting that Steve has an undergraduate degree in sculpture).

Level design is a form of "invisible design." Players can see the shooting mechanic in a First-Person Shooter (FPS) game or the jumping mechanic in a platformer game, but what the player often misses is how the design of the level makes those mechanics more interesting, engaging, fun, or terrifying. Without good level design, there is no game.

0.1

Tacoma, Fullbright, 2017. Starting with creating fan levels for the game *F.E.A.R.*, Steve Gaynor moved on to a large studio to create *Minerva's Den*, the DLC for *BioShock 2*. He then co-founded The Fullbright Company and continues to work as a game design lead and level designer on their games. *Tacoma*, seen here, takes place on a space station. The game relies heavily on level design and environmental storytelling to create a rich experience for the player.

0.2
Call of Duty: Black Ops, Treyarch, 2010. The principles of level design can be applied in much the same way across genres of video game. The level designer focuses on the needs of the game to increase immersion for the player. The Nuk3town map for the multiplayer *Call of Duty: Black Ops* is a battlefield; there is no sense that this area needs to be explored or that it tells a story to the players. It offers a variation in aesthetic and architecture but is designed to offer tactical decisions for players in fast-paced combat.

0.3
Assassin's Creed: Origin, Ubisoft, 2017. In contrast to smaller multiplayer maps in games such as *Black Ops*, Ubisoft's massive environment for *Assassin's Creed: Origins* is one enormous level. Every element of the "sand-box" space supports the narrative setting created for the game (a fictionalized narrative set in Ancient Egypt). The focus of the open-world game is to encourage player exploration. The combat occurs in discrete events that the player has to search out.

What Is Level Design as a Discipline?

As you may expect, level design is heavily influenced and affected by game design. Video games are systems usually thought of as a set of rules, entities, and behaviors, and the interdependent relationships between them make up a game. When working as a developer "game design" is the blueprint for what the game is (setting, environment) and what the player can do and cannot do in the game (physics, mechanics, interaction). The game design is the top-level structure that incorporates every other element from level design to puzzle design, Artificial Intelligence (AI), physics systems, audio design, and so on. The game design dictates and restricts the action of the player. For example, in *Fallout 4* the player cannot run super-fast or jump super-high unlike the mechanics of *Super Mario Galaxy 2*. The physics of the game design mechanics restricts the possibilities for the player to remain consistent with the rules of the game and the expectations of the player.

Canadian level designer Mare Sheppard of Metanet Software (makers of *N*, *N+,* and *N++,* 2005–2015) has designed several games and sees the role of a level designer as one that

"…explores that huge possibility space that's latent in the game design so that we can discover various arrangements of elements that produce interesting experiences for the player to engage with. To develop a deep understanding of these elements so that we can combine them in unique ways that have some depth, and to sustain the games' intrigue."

(Sheppard, 2016)

There is no one coherent model of level design for video games because the level design is dependent upon the game itself. Designing levels for a platform game is different from designing levels for an FPS game, but the foundational principles do carry over. In short, level design is all about player engagement, outcomes, and aesthetics that are informed by the mechanics and the design of the game. Although a Mario level may look and play very differently from a level in *Halo 5: Guardians,* the methodology of the level designer is essentially the same.

DO VIDEO GAMES STILL HAVE LEVELS?

As with the difference between a game designer and a game developer there are semantic arguments over what a "level" is. Early video games such as *Sonic the Hedgehog* or *Super Mario Bros. 2* had explicit identifiers for each level. The games would tell the player they were entering "World 3" or "Green Hill Zone" and they were finite and linear (although players could replay the level to get a higher score). When the player completes World 3 in *Super Mario Bros. 2* this unlocks the "next level" and the player can then move on to play World 4. Levels were very well defined.

Today video game levels are often much less explicit, but that model does still exist. In action games such as *Uncharted 4* or *Gears of War 4* there are story chapters and "book-ended" areas that the players experience in a linear fashion, which have a distinct beginning and end. The levels in *Uncharted 4* or *Gears of War 4* have clearly defined entry and exit points, often signified by doors that prevent back-tracking of the player. The flow of the levels forces the player onward as each level offers new obstacles, puzzles, or challenges. Although more common in platform games such as *Little Big Planet 3*, these linear action games follow a similar model of level flow as of those early console games (rather than using the terminology of "level" the *Gears* or *Uncharted* series use the terms *chapters* or *acts* in a more theatrical approach).

From a surface point of view the art of level design is much like that of a production designer for a film. The focus is on making the level or scene believable, immersive, and realistic from the point of view of the universe the character is in. Players often have favorite levels that they will play and replay, and gamers' discussions often focus on how they beat this or that level even though it seemed impossible at the time. As with film or television production design, the key to good level design is visual consistency. If a scene in *Captain America: Civil War* (Walt Disney Studios, 2016), which takes place in New York City, suddenly had characters ducking behind palm trees and fighting mutant-zombie-hamsters (without it being explained in the plot), that would be very jarring for the viewer and would break them out of their immersion in the film.

The same is true for level designers—it is one of their jobs to construct the world for the player that feels believable and realistic within the rules of the universe created by the game's developers, from the ruined city streets of post-apocalyptic Boston in *Fallout 4* to the whimsical and fun architecture of the *Little Big Planet* series. Working alongside environment artists, art directors, and creative directors, the level designer's role is to set challenges, control player flow, and direct decision-making, which offer the player possibilities within the designed space. You could think of the level designer as an experience designer and an architect and the environment artists (often part of the level design team) as set, prop, and visual storytellers. Steve Gaynor sees level designers as people who "take all of this stuff that everybody's made and arrange it into the experience that the player is actually going to have" (Perez, 2016).

0.4
Player immersion is key to engaging game play. Open environments such as those used in the Boston of *Fallout 4* are designed to create opportunities that challenge the player as well as communicate the tropes of the game's design and the game's world. Wandering endlessly around a desolate wasteland would become boring after a fairly short time, so the level designer creates scenarios that will engage the player. This could be conversations, found objects that tell a story, or combat events—all of which have to be consistent with the game's themes, mechanics, and systems.

Summary

Good or great level design can make a middling game much better, but it cannot save an inherently broken game. Every aspect of the game must work harmoniously to become more than its constituent parts. Few players can point to any one aspect of a game that makes it great; instead they will talk about multiple elements. As with many design practices, the creation of a video game is a multidisciplinary accomplishment; it brings together many different skill-sets. When we think about level design, it is more than just an architectural space for a player to run around in. Level design challenges the player: it persuades them, it amazes them, and it emotionally connects them to the game. Level design propels the player into a new world, one they can choose to explore and experiment with, or one that exists simply as a series of obstacles and challenges to be conquered. Whatever the player's expectations or approach to gaming, the level designer must create a coherent and consistent space for the player and be a conduit that communicates the goals of the game. Level design is about creating possibilities for the player within a system that is designed following some fundamental design practices and principles. The next chapter is an exploration of the fundamentals of level design practice.

Getting Started: Research and Preproduction

Learning Objectives for This Chapter:

1) The process of preproduction and research

2) Game engines as a level design tool

1.0
Gears of War 4, The Coalition, 2016, Used with permission from Microsoft.

The Preproduction Process

The first step is game development is preproduction. This is the phase in the process where vague ideas and early concepts start to become the game. It may be surprising to know that many games you have played started off looking or playing completely different to their final form. For example, the first *BioShock* game was originally a successor to the popular *System Shock 2* game. *BioShock* was more focused on science fiction than the setting of an ideologically fueled dystopia called Rapture. From pitch to launch took three years and a lot of changes occurred on the way toward the final game. As an example of how the *BioShock* game changed course over three years there's an in-depth postmortem on the development of *BioShock* on the website Gamasutra by Alyssa Finley;

"*BioShock* had initially been positioned as a hybrid RPG FPS. The decision to reposition the game as a focused FPS came later, after our initial production phase in summer of 2006. . . . As the game neared alpha, key people looked more closely and saw that *BioShock* wasn't on track to become an accessible and marketable game. . . . The real turning point for *BioShock* came when we had to present the game to the outside world, which forced us to carefully consider the story and takeaway message."

(Finley, 2008)

Level Design Preproduction

Research into what other studios are creating, or what the marketplace is currently saturated with, are good indicators of the plausibility of the game concept being profitable. This should not be the only marker for success, however, as the apocryphal quote from car inventor Henry Ford attests: "If I'd asked people what they wanted, they would have said faster horses" (Vlaskovits, 2014).

With preproduction underway it may be several months before proper programming and art for the game begins in earnest, but a level designer will become involved as early as possible. Much like the film industry, the game leads and directors will start with an idea and have some concept art created that sets the mood and environments of the proposed game. Once the look and aesthetic are established (this game takes place in space/haunted house/underwater) the level designer (LD) can begin to work on the broad structure of the game. The LD will ask questions such as, is the game using completely new assets or are we using existing assets? How many levels are going to be needed? Is there enough variety in the proposed environments, and will they make sense to the player? Knowing what the main goals or story of the game are, the LD will want to know how those convert into individual levels. The role of the LD in preproduction is to build a solid foundation that will become a sequence of levels that will make sense in the wider context of the game. Preproduction is the best time to solidify these goals and work out a strategy for production. Programmers and artists will be asked to come

1.1
Rocket League, Psyonix, 2015. Innovation in the preproduction phase can produce unexpected results. No one knew that combining a football game and a driving game would produce the phenomenon that is *Rocket League*. This game is based on an earlier title from the same developer *Supersonic Acrobatic Rocket-Powered Battle-Cars*. By iterating on the core idea and leveraging a core fan base, *Rocket League* developed into a popular team based multiplayer game.

up with (or more often reuse) systems and assets that can work in the broader strokes of the game's goals.

Preproduction should create a "safe space" to experiment and fail (image 1.1). There's a term that's used in the wider technology industry of "Fail Fast, Fail Often," which is a good summary of the preproduction process: it's a time to figure things out inexpensively and without consuming a lot of time before moving into production. Given that this is an experimental phase it is also an opportunity to commit to a heavy amount of research, both technical and conceptual.

"Preproduction should create a 'safe space' to experiment and fail."

Research

It should be obvious that people in the video game creation business play a lot of video games. Games are an important part of popular culture and designers across all roles in preproduction will be looking for references from all types of media. Building a reference library is as much for others as it is for you (image 1.2). If you are trying to describe a multi-layered skyscraper city in a dystopian future to someone it's a lot easier to show them a clip from the film *The Fifth Element* or *Blade Runner* than painstakingly drawing something out. Along with film and television, comic books are a useful reference when thinking about story boards for an encounter or player movement through a level. Comics break down and focus on just the most important movement; each panel has a camera angle and there is succinct action across a few frames. They create their own optimal path in story telling which is very useful for a level designer. Looking at how Batman enters Arkham Asylum in a comic-book, the motion, angles and points of view could easily translate into a player entering a tomb or foundry. Comic books show the line of sight in third person as well as points of focus (important features) and scale.

Photographic references are always useful and whenever possible they should be your own because you get the opportunity to take a photograph from multiple angles rather than just looking at Google Images. Also your own photos can have size references (how high was that wall? Put a person next to it and you will know) as well as being able to express your personal eye for detail, color, texture and architecture.

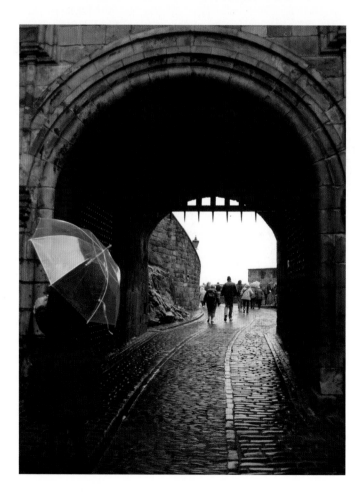

1.2
When making a medieval-inspired game if you happen to live in (or visit) a country that has good reference material, getting your own image library is essential to understanding the constructed environment, its composition and interaction with the space. How big should a castle portcullis gate be? How deep? Knowing how these real-life elements are composed (including being able to give combat designers feedback on potential enemy engagement areas) will inform your level's design.

Composition is a key skill for a level designer, you are designing unique spaces and you must be able to compose angles, buildings and assets in such a way as to complement the aesthetic of the game and to be interesting for a player. This is as true for a *Call of Duty* game as it is for more aesthetically heavy games such as *What Remains of Edith Finch*. The composition of a level's layout must make sense in the world from a mechanics point of view as well as from an environmental artists point of view. Walls that are too high will obscure important architecture or story moments. Too narrow a space in a crowded area or too widely spaced buildings that a player has to walk between can all become barriers to

an engaging game. A great looking building with important assets in it is most likely to be ignored by a player if it's too far from their most direct path. Depending on the need of the game the LD may have to incentivize the player to go out of their way. This is partly common sense and partly research; by playing other games you will get a sense of pacing distance and layout. There is no formula for this, as with many aspects of games it is somewhat subjective. Whatever the genre and goal of the game, gaining a deeper knowledge of different types of architecture, spaces and how humans interact within them will ultimately better inform your design process (image 1.3).

1.3
This is part of the gardens at Belsay Hall in the UK that could translate into part of a level's design. There is enticement towards what might be an ambush or a reward. The player has a clear and well-lit gateway or exit but there is restricted movement for the player (narrow walls) and blind spots on the left and right. This is a study in how real-life environments can inspire a level designer.

Essential Tools

Tools will vary dependent upon the studio; some use in-house level editors, others use off the shelf solutions and some studios may use a hybrid between the two in their workflow. As with most design industry practices, there's no one way to do anything—it's whatever gets the job done and done right.

Early level prototypes could be created using different tools than the ones used in the final game's production. For example, the developers of *Journey* used Adobe Flash and Java to create prototypes before using PhyreEngine for the final game (image 1.4) (PhyreEngine was developed by Sony for its console platforms and is open source/free). In my video game courses I have students create game prototypes in a variety of technologies dependent on their skill level. Some may create a point-and-click adventure game in PowerPoint or Adobe Edge just to get a feel for how the interactions and decision trees will work, while others use Unity and its asset store to make playable prototypes that have no consistent aesthetics but are good tests for their ideas.

1.4
Journey, thatgamecompany, 2012. *Journey* changed as it moved from preproduction to production. It was originally a cooperative (2-player)-only game but during preproduction the publisher (Sony) was uncomfortable with that focus from a sales perspective. The developers switched the game to focus on single player but retained a "drop in and drop out" 2-player function that ended up being a powerful aspect of the final game.

It is unlikely that a level designer will be involved in selecting a game engine. Instead they will be expected to create a workflow to match whatever the production team is working in. It will be up to the level designer to discuss options with other team members on how to best work with the engine and level editor. As Max Herngren (level designer at Mojang) puts it in an interview for 80.lv; "you should really strive to be the expert on the editor on your team as you will most likely be the one spending the most time in there. If you learn the tools in and out, you'll make your life a lot easier" (Sergeev, 2017).

A game engine is selected based on a lot of factors, from your team's skill base to what that game engine is capable of and if it fits your game concept. If you're creating a 2D *Legend of Zelda*-style game an engine like GameMaker might be the best choice because that is the main focus of that engine. If you're developing a *Candy Crush* style mobile game, engines such as Stencyl, Gamesalad and CocoS2d-X would work well. The standout engines for console or PC 2D and 3D games are Unity, Crytek and the Unreal engine with Amazon's Lumberyard gaining ground. Even so, there are plenty of studios that use their own bespoke or customized engines. For example, DoubleFine productions used a modified version of the open source game engine Moai to create their game *Broken Age* (Zipline, 2014), which reduced their overall costs because rather than spend time (and therefore money) building a proprietary game engine from the ground up, modifying a free engine got them into production much sooner (image 1.5). The downside was that everyone had to learn how to use this engine, regardless of whether or not they were already familiar with Unity or Unreal.

1.5
Broken Age, Doublefine, 2014.
DoubleFine Productions used a
modified open-source game engine
(Moai) as a base for their point-
and-click adventure game *Broken
Age*. The developers had a very
specific look and very specific form
of interaction going into production.
The decision to use this engine was
made very early in production. For
valuable insight into their production
process watch the YouTube
DoubleFine Channel: www.youtube
.com/user/DoubleFineProd.

WHY REINVENT THE WHEEL?

Alongside engine selection and prototyping,
preproduction is also a good time for the
team to research and think about other tools,
software, hardware and scripts that they'll need
to develop the game efficiently. An example is
the Unity asset store, which extends the Unity
game engine with a lot of plug-ins, scripts
and models that people can purchase to add
into their game. The studio Campo Santo
used Unity and its asset store to develop their
game *Firewatch*; because their production
cycle was short they were able to cut down on
development time by using already developed
scripts and systems.

For example, they used Hutong Game's
Playmaker (a visual programming plug-in for
Unity), Marmoset's Skyshop (a lighting and
skybox manager) and Sectr (which allows for
intelligent streaming of large levels or scenes
so that *Firewatch* could have a large world
that would run on a mid-range gaming PC)
(Ng, 2014). In a larger studio it is more likely
that they will use proprietary engines and
make all of their own assets, because they
have funding. Indie games are lean and low
budget, so using assets to overcome hurdles
and get the game into stores is always worth
considering.

Once the tools have been decided upon
and a workflow is in place, the LD can begin on
blocking out the rough level design. This process
is often referred to as gray-boxing, because it
usually just has lots of boxes (and they're usually
gray in game engines) that just define space
rather than geometry or aesthetic. This is not
game prototyping; at this point the programmers
will have systems in place (a climbing mechanic,
interactions or whatever) that they will be
working on as the LD constructs an outline using
simple blocks. Everyone will know what the
game is, so the LD will use gray boxes to get a
sense of the scale of the level and propose paths
through it for the player (the team will also know
if the game is first person or third). Later the art
team will be able to supply early models or the
LD can reuse assets from a different game or from
an asset store (a door is a door after all) but this is
just a sketch so simple is best.

Blocking Out, Early On

As previously stated, the first step for any LD is to create a rudimentary level design based on direction from the game leads. For Max Herngren his preproduction process is in the Unreal engine 4: "I'll be in there early on working with really primitive shapes such as BSPs" (image 1.6) (in Unreal, Binary Space Partitioning, or BSP for short, is a simple process for adding geometry to a level by defining what's solid and what's not). "I'll replace that block-out with actual assets that have been imported from whatever 3D software the environment artist is using. Most times you'll be working with something coming from Maya or Zbrush" (Sergeev, 2017).

Blocking out the level as soon as possible creates a space for the game to begin to develop. In Unreal designers use BSP Brushes to create shapes or geometry as the foundation for a level.

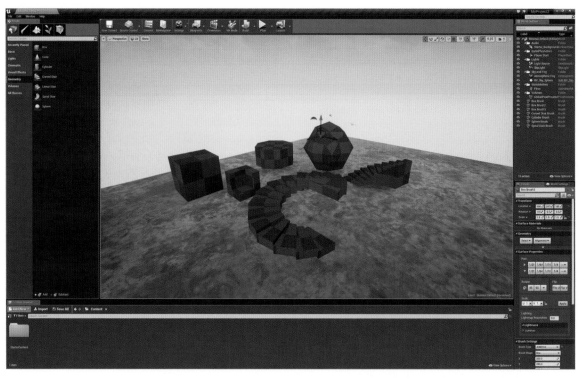

1.6
The BSP Menu in the Unreal engine and the geometry it creates in a level. Using these "brushes" a level designer can quickly sketch the layout of a level which includes player flow through horizontal and vertical spaces. Although these shapes are simple, other BSP brushes can be used to cut out, extract and merge shapes to create other assets (e.g., a wall can become a doorway).

UnReal 4 Engine 4.21 2018.

As an example of the Unreal engine's approach to rapid development, BSPs are an easy and quick method for laying out a level and then having it tested by the team. The process for the LD is to begin a level with BSPs and then test, edit, retest and so on until a solid foundation has been laid out. The advantage of the BSPs is that although they are simple and not pretty, they are created in the engine so simple first- or third-person characters can be used to navigate around them. A better-looking 3D modelled mesh (such as a building or car) would need to be created in other software (such as 3d Studio Max or Maya) by the art team and then imported, which adds a step to the process. On top of that the better-looking model cannot be edited in the engine, so if a doorway needs to be moved the mesh has to be edited in Maya and reimported, which just adds time.

BSPs are specific to the Unreal engine. When using the Unity engine an LD would use in-engine geometry to box out a level (cubes, cones, spheres and so on) and then edit them with ProBuilder and Polybrush (image 1.7), which work in much the same way as BSP brushes. It's useful to get to know at least one of these game engines and work with their block-out tools to start creating engaging level prototypes.

As soon as the layout seems to work, better-looking art assets can begin to be moved into the level along with initial lighting passes and color schemes, which become important to the player understanding and navigating the levels.

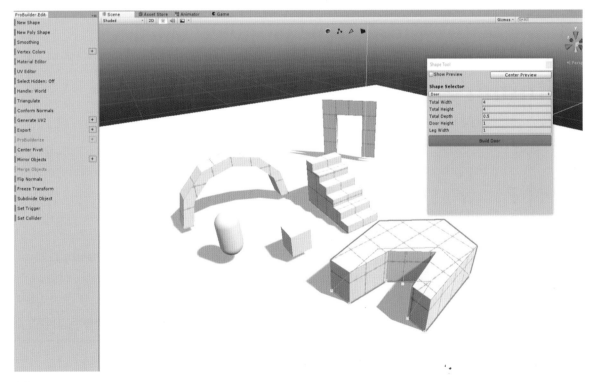

1.7
This is some geometry created using Unity's in-engine Probuilder and Polybrush tools. They work in very much the same way as the Unreal BSPs do and are an efficient and simple way of putting together a level's layout.

UnReal 4 Engine 4.21 2018.

Production

The production process is necessarily different in every studio and dependent on the ambitions of the game being produced. It can take months or years of production to create a game. As this book is an introduction to level design the focus is on preproduction and systems that will achieve success. Production itself is still an iterative process, but the idea is that a solid preproduction process enables a smooth production. Being able to create the best process that works for you or your studio is important and should not be overlooked. Speaking at the GDC conference in 2008, veteran game designer Lesley Mathieson of High Impact Games underlines this by stating that "your production process absolutely affects the design of your game, and it affects every aspect of it. This is something that everyone should be paying attention to" (Mathieson, 2008).

Most of my students just want to get on with making a game, which is understandable, but the problem is that the planning phases from preproduction to production are what make the game viable and ensure it actually gets made as opposed to falling apart halfway through. Planning and research are critical when creating a product as complex as a video game. The much anticipated game *Red Dead Redemption 2* ran into problems during its eight-year production, exemplified by decisions such as when "the top directors decided to add black bars to the top and bottom of every non-interactive cutscene in hopes of making those scenes feel more cinematic" (Schreier, 2018). That decision late in the production process added weeks or months to the production timeline with many on the team pulling long days. That is not to say it wasn't the correct decision for the game, but these decisions come at a cost and planning is the best way to lessen those impacts.

Summary

Video games are complex and very hard to make; advance planning can be a huge aid in making the process less painful. It is difficult for my students to take the time to plan when making games—understandably, they have a concept for a game and want to get on and make it. In classes my role is very much that of the project lead or director. I have to coerce students to take the time to plan and structure their game designs and go through the steps of the preproduction process. Students can be resistant to this, but as they make mistakes and missteps in the prototype phase they begin to understand the advantages of this time-tested approach to the process. There is never enough time and you can never learn enough—planning takes some of that stress out of the equation. Energy and enthusiasm are great, but spending a semester working on a project only to find out that the engine cannot do what is required of it is frustrating. Planning and research answer the question of what the game actually is; prototyping answers the question of how the game will work. Now that we have a sense of the primary steps in the process, the next chapter defines the fundamentals and principles of the discipline itself.

INTERVIEW: METANET AND THE DEVELOPMENT OF *N++*

Mare Sheppard and Raigan Burns are the cofounders of the indie game company Metanet based in Toronto, Canada. The company has completed the *N* series of games, which includes *N* (2004), *N+* (2008) and finally *N++* (2015). *N* received the Audience Choice Award at the Independent Games Festival in 2005.

How did Metanet begin?

In 2001, we formed Metanet Software. We didn't have a clear idea of what to make at first, and just started playing around with little experiments: implementing algorithms we found interesting, trying to recreate the parts of other games we loved (such as the wall-jumping in *Super Bubble Blob* and the tiny main character in *Puchiwara no Bouken*), and seeing how all the parts fit together (or didn't). We taught ourselves ActionScript (the programming language of Adobe Flash) and worked in Flash on AI and collision detection, physics and graphics. Flash was a fantastic tool since we could use vector graphics and lean on the built-in animation system, which simplified things. We wanted to make a platformer because we love them, and initially the "ninjagame" we were working on was about stealth. However, we discovered as we played around with it that because of the physics in the game, running around at top speed pulling off acrobatic moves

was much more fun. We let the game tell us what it wanted to be, and that developed into *N*.

We spent a lot of time figuring out what worked and what didn't. One of the things we cut was a grappling hook (we'd still like to build a future game around it) and made a ton of levels in order to learn what was fun. We really enjoyed playing *N* and released it as freeware in 2004, not expecting much, so we were surprised to learn that other people enjoyed it too. That eventually led to *N+*, a paid "plus" version with more levels and some new enemies released in 2008 for Xbox 360. *N+*'s popularity is what allowed us to quit our day jobs and work for our company full time. And recently we've released *N++*, which is really the culmination of ten years of trial, error and thought. We refined the concepts and added some new elements that feel like they could have been there from the start, they're such a good fit. It's the best version of the *N* game we could ever make, we're so proud of it.

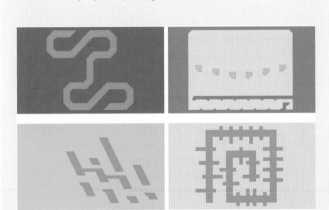

1.8a, b, c, d
Graphic design studies of levels from *N++*. There is a minimalist approach and the use of complimentary colors fixes and guides the eye around the level. The design of each level is a small work of graphic art: it has balance, symmetry, dynamism and color.

1.9
An early moodboard for *N++*, this was used to suggest and control the color palette of the game. As the game was "low-resolution," color was one method that the designers could use to guide the player as well as visually excite them.

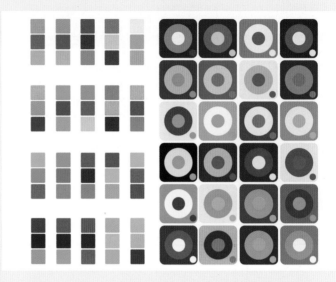

As a game designer, what do you feel are the skill sets people need coming into the industry?

It's hard to say. Neither Raigan nor I have ever worked in a bigger development studio; as such we don't really know what the norm is in the industry, but here's what we've learned running a small independent studio: being creative and adaptable is probably the most important skill, being able to learn new tools and being able to explore the limits of a game's design to find all the exciting aspects. Being patient enough to learn is also important, so you can keep challenging yourself to push further. Having a passion for what you're doing and trying to exceed your limitations is a necessary skill too. You have to be self-aware enough to realize what's working and (more importantly) not working for you, and adjust your process accordingly.

The ability to communicate with people and compromise is also important, especially when you're working on a small team. Sometimes what makes so much sense in your brain, using your references and experiences, is completely unintelligible to those you're working with. Even if you're working from the same book as someone, it takes effort to get onto the same page. Effective time management is also very useful, knowing where to best focus your efforts, what needs attention against what can be left until later.

Another factor for success is confidence, being a level designer is a bit like being an architect or a musician: you're trying to create something with a set of tools/materials you've been given. There are a lot of constraints and you have to find something useful within them. You're going to need to make

a lot of mistakes until you understand how to use those tools. You might not even recognize your mistakes until later on, when you know and appreciate more what you're working with.

In your website's bio you mention that you find inspiration from "print, industrial design, architecture, and fashion"; how do these disparate design disciplines feed into your game design?

The foundation for our game development philosophy is that inspiration comes from everywhere, and that what you create is composed of what you take in. I think the most interesting creations come from people who have a variety of influences and are interested in a variety of things, and have a solid understanding of a number of different disciplines. That lets you see patterns and corollaries, and appreciate balance in many new ways. A wide range of inspirations lets you create variety, which generates a richness and a nuance that really intrigues me. Imagining a game inspired by another game is easy. But imagine a game inspired by a painting, or the way a forest smells after a rain. How would you capture those? That's interesting to us.

This relates to another of our design philosophies, and our company motto: "backward-looking, forward-thinking." The idea of applying modern technology and techniques retroactively to add a new direction to old genres and game styles is something we find interesting to explore, as the juxtaposition of perspectives often leads to something unique. As a more concrete explanation, look at the N series. Our level design reflects balance, symmetry and our love of geometry, but at a meta level we draw a lot from music; the idea of pacing and dynamics, of different parts and movements working together. When we arrange levels we try to make sure that there are calm moments in-between the stressful ones, which lets the player rest and recover a bit (and which also makes the intense parts feel more intense). A lot of what's interesting about playing the game is in those undercurrents.

Many levels in the series were inspired by architecture, which in general is a great source of inspiration for games. Like architects, we design spaces and environments and the experience of moving through them, from the superficial shapes to the feel of a space—there's a lot to learn from architecture. Sometimes when we are walking around a city we'll see a building that would be perfect for a level, whatever would work for a parkour runner would work in an *N* level. Levels in *N* are about traversing structures in creative and often unintended ways. Brutalism (an architecture movement that lasted from the 1950s to the 1970s) inspires us a lot too, because the strong shapes and blunt angles are so powerful. We love the confident minimalism of Tokyo architecture, and especially love the work of Tadao Ando (a Japanese architect), which crops up in *N++* levels frequently.

There is also an element of dance in the levels: traversing each level is a sort of ballet, involving timing, rhythms and patterns of movement, and we've tried to think about it like this when building and analyzing the level designs. Especially in levels with rockets, the movement of the player becomes very much like a dance, and even a pas de deux.

When we released *N++* for PS4, we referenced dance in our marketing campaign in a series called *Motion++* (www.motionplusplus.com). *N++* is somewhat atypical: it features minimalist art and eschews high-resolution, realistic graphics in favour of something more abstract; we wanted to capture how it feels to be a ninja (*N++*'s main character). With *Motion++*, we wanted to complement what the game stands for with a diverse idea of what beauty is, and to show speed and agility and inner ninjas externally manifested. Our goal was to explore the influence of dance and movement and art in our platformer, to try to foreground some of the themes in *N++* that are subtle and not easy to grasp without playing the game. As creative people, what we do comes from the unique blend of inspirations and opinions and ideas that surround us and infiltrate our lives, we wanted to show how a diverse cross-section of inspiration can lead to something beautiful.

What issues and problems have you learned to avoid in game design?

Getting too focused on a fixed design, and not having the perspective or distance necessary to see when something's not working, or when there is a better direction that might deviate from the initial plan, this can be quite destructive. It's better to keep an open mind and be able to adapt to what you learn as you work on the game, rather than trying to follow the initial concept perfectly. You can never predict where something as complicated as a game design is going to go, and often you find new unexpected things as you're developing the game. It can be hard to recognize these opportunities, and you need flexibility and a lot of courage to be able to abandon plans that aren't working in order to pursue new directions.

"Motivation and energy are very important; game development is a long and arduous process."

If you panic when an idea isn't working, or when you're stuck on some aspect of the game design, that can be difficult to overcome. You have to have faith in yourself, that you will eventually figure it out or learn something that allows you to move forward, but it can be very difficult when it's been days or weeks without any progress. Avoiding this is impossible, but you can learn from it know that eventually the path will become clear. You might want to step back and work on something else for a while too, distance can be important. Working with other people is a good way to push yourself in a different direction if you're stuck on something, often just talking it over with someone is enough to help you realize a solution.

Motivation and energy are very important; game development is a long and arduous process. Staying motivated and happy, so that you can focus completely on the game and really immerse yourself in it, can be hard. This is a difficult psychological problem, but you can definitely take steps to make it easier.

1.10
Early designs for the Ninja character in *N++*.
Although some aspects of the game's aesthetics
directly link back to 8-bit games, such as
Mario, the designers needed a more fluid and
animated character.

As an indie developer, how much does the business side of being a developer impact the creative side? How do you achieve a balance between those two aspects as a small studio?

It's a constant struggle, because we just want to make games, but at the same time we can only do so if our business is healthy enough to support us. This means we often end up spending a lot more time than we'd like doing miserable work; emails, bookkeeping, copy writing, press releases, etc. While it's hard to develop enthusiasm for these mundane tasks, you definitely need to learn how to do them. There can still be satisfaction from doing a job well even if it's not something you're really interested in. Since there are two of us, we're able to trade off and help each other out as needed, but there is definitely a real overhead to running a business. Don't expect to be able to spend five days a week doing nothing but development.

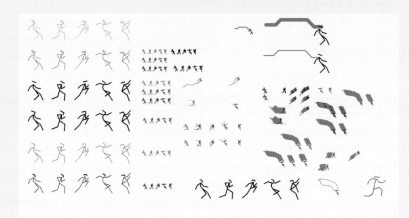

1.11
Even a simple stick figure goes
through multiple design passes.
In this image Mare and Raigan
are balancing expression and
movement against visibility and
style.

How important is level design when creating a game? Is the mechanic more important?

Game design and level design are intrinsically linked. As with the previous example, you can't say that the piano is more or less important than the song being played, both exist as parts of a whole and both are necessary to create music. The mechanics are the foundation that level design builds upon, to tease out what is fun and explore all the possibilities. On its own, they're just abstract ideas, piano keys waiting to be touched. Level design is really what makes each mechanic interesting by showcasing the opportunities each one creates; playing particular chords and sequences of notes to generate a particular sound, mood or feeling.

Level design is important, especially in the *N* series. *N++* lives and dies by the levels. If they are not interesting, the whole game suffers. In order to make the levels interesting, we need to incorporate a lot of variety, and it's important that we have a solid understanding of every little detail of the controls of the character and the behaviors of all the in-game entities so we can really get at the core of what makes the game fun to play. If your piano only has 3 keys on the keyboard, then that really limits the sort of songs you can play on it. A piano with 1000 keys would be too complex to properly play. Game design and level design need to work in harmony so that there are enough possibilities latent in the game design to allow for a variety of interesting level designs, but not so many that it makes level design (or playing the game itself) too complicated and tedious.

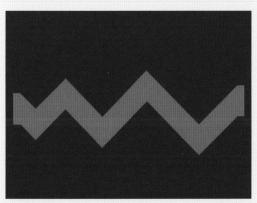

1.12a, 1.12b
These are early prototype level designs that balance interactivity with visual communication. The player is able to see an entry and exit point and create some strategy for how to get to each switch. The simplicity of the design obscures the difficulty in solving the game play problem for the player.

What are the biggest challenges when designing a level for a game?

Making sure that levels can accommodate a huge range of player skills was the biggest challenge in N++. We were able to succeed in this by layering multiple different challenges and routes onto the same level: "just beat it," "get all the gold," "get the best score," and a variety of secret challenges provide a range of challenges for a range of player skill. Ultimately, we want to design levels that are not too hard, but not too easy, so they keep players guessing and keep them engaged. This is a big challenge in level design. We find that levels for games that are skill based are harder to design, since you can't assume each player will be playing the same way. When there is more than one successful route through a level, or more than one technique of game play, designing levels is much more complicated. As a result, those levels are much more interesting for players because they're about creativity and performance rather than memorization.

Having the confidence to remove things can be difficult too. There's a tendency to add more and more, to satisfy every taste and to support every possibility players may want, but that usually just ends up making the experience muddied and cluttered. Paring back, editing, and shining a spotlight on one or a couple of things gives them much more power, and gives players much more to enjoy. Easy levels are usually the hardest to design, because you have to keep things simple while still being engaging, that is a difficult challenge. N++ rides a very fine line between frustrating and fun; every little detail is carefully thought through to keep the whole game just on the fun side. If it's too frustrating, players experience less success so what makes the game satisfying is completely lost.

The Principles
of Level Design

Learning Objectives for This Chapter:

1) Defining the principles of level design

2) Applying those principles to designing for experience and emotion

3) Introducing the psychology of level design

4) Relating the principles to immersion, engagement and interaction

2.0
Dark Souls III, FromSoftware, 2016.

As in the wider disciplines of design, there are no absolute rules but there are principles which when applied can be reasonably expected to produce good results. In the earliest days of video games the level designers were self-taught and often worked in level design because the game needed levels and someone had to design them. Sometimes that "someone" was the programmer and sometimes it was the artist; often these were the same person (Seppala, 2014). Fast forward thirty years and the scope of games has grown and with it the need for specialized designers with a deep understanding of their craft. Along with this growth of level design as a practice has been the development of the language of level design that borrows, in part, from other design disciplines and modifies it to suit the discipline.

One of the most useful approaches to learning about level design is to examine and deconstruct the games themselves. Much of what we know about contemporary level design is a mixture of looking back and looking forward. When a student starts trying to deconstruct a huge game such as *Fallout 4* or *Grand Theft Auto V* it can be overwhelming. A better approach is to look at simpler games because they are still fun to play and contain the same principles. I encourage my students to study old games such as *Pac-Man* or the first *Tomb Raider* games when starting to think about how games work.

The 10 Principles of Good Level Design

design—you do not have to use all the principles, but understanding, applying or using them as a guideline in your level design is very likely to produce positive outcomes.

The next two chapters will explore methods toward a better understanding of the practice of level design. In doing this we need to establish some definitions and methodologies. In 2013 Dan Taylor wrote an article outlining his Principles of Good Level Design for the video game industry website Gamasutra.com. These principles were based upon the 10 Principles for Good Design created by the German industrial designer Dieter Rams in the 1970s (Rams, 1976) and have been used in design practice and education ever since. Dan Taylor is a level designer at Square Enix Montreal. He has worked on games such as *Max Payne 3* and *Medal of Honor: Heroes 2*. As a veteran level designer, he was careful to point out that even though his list of principles is numbered, it is not an ordered list (which is also how Dieter Rams used his principles). For example, Principle 9, Creating emotions is no more or less important than Principle 4, Constantly teaching the player. This is key to understanding good

1: Good level design is fun to navigate.

2: Good level design does not rely on words to tell the story.

3: Good level design tells what, but not how.

4: Good level design constantly teaches.

5: Good level design is surprising.

6: Good level design empowers the player.

7: Good level design is easy, medium and hard.

8: Good level design is efficient.

9: Good level design will create emotion.

10: Good level design is driven by mechanics.

(Taylor, 2013)

Applying the Level Design Principles

Using Dan's principles as a model, we can extrapolate actionable game design practices. Connecting level design principles with other design principles in this way is an opportunity to bring in cross-disciplinary expertise, such as using architectural practice to decide where the doors, buildings and crates need to be as well as visual communication and art practice to add emotion, storytelling and intuitive navigation. For simplicity's sake, the definitions and examples that follow are taken from 3D action, RPG or adventure games.

Principle 1: Good Level Design Is Fun to Navigate

Consistent visual communication (aesthetic) creates a sense of space and connects the game's themes and mechanics to the player. The game's aesthetic and mechanics can be communicated through the players' traversal of a level if the level designer uses a consistent visual language. For example, if a player is shown that they must get to a higher level in an otherwise ground-based game, a model in the level (such as a ladder) may be outlined or given a different color or just the utility of a ladder is enough of a cue for a player: "If you put a ladder in your level, a player very likely will at some point try to use it." (Schatz, 2017) (image 2.1).

This visual cue is a convention in video game language that lets the player know that an object

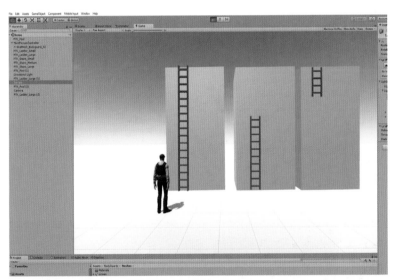

2.1

In this instance it is perhaps obvious to the player which ladder they should use, but there is no clear indicator that any of them are climbable. If the player has already encountered other non-interactive elements they may assume this is just set dressing.

Unity 2018, Assets: bodyguard by Batewar, ladder by DigitalKonstrukt.

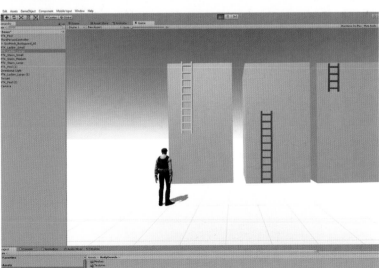

2.2

Although seemingly harder to reach, it is clear to the player that because this ladder is "different" from the others, it must be so for a reason. The player is more likely to approach and interact with the yellow ladder than the gray ones. The construct that "something different can be interacted with" is a convention that has become common across video games and has become part of the language of the medium.

Unity 2018.

is special or interactive, in this case that they "can use this to climb." This visual convention must be consistent throughout every level in every game once it has been established (image 2.2). The player's reaction to investigating a visual difference between objects comes directly from design theory. Pattern and rhythm are used to communicate visually because humans have positive associations with patterns and find them pleasing. If the pattern is disrupted (alternated) we will focus directly on the differentiation and be curious about it. The theory is that this is an ancient survival mechanism; the "different" in tall grasses could be a predator's stripes. We are drawn to patterns and we are curious when that pattern is disrupted. Level designers use this psychology to make players feel as if they have "intuitively" navigated through an area without the use of a map or signposts just by using alterations in patterns and textures. "It's the designer's job to communicate to the player when they have hit a dead end [images 2.3 & 2.4], and to encourage them forward when they are on a good path" (Kerr, 2015).

Principle 2: Good Level Design Does Not Rely on Words to Tell the Story

Level design can tell a story visually, and not just because of the setting of the game, such as "You are in space in the future" or "You are in the past because people are wearing top hats." The physical environment and art assets can be used to tell the story of what happened in this specific place or world before the player discovered it. The physical design of the level along with environmental art assets can communicate the world's back story without the need for animated cutscenes or audio voice overs. This is useful for the player who wants to feel that they are part of the world and have the environment, setting and characters tell them the story. Generally video game narrative can be defined in three ways: explicit, implicit and emergent.

Implicit narrative tells a story through the use of the physical environment and mise-en-scène, which comes to video games from the language of theater and film. For example, in *BioShock* the player is thrown into an underwater world without any context or backstory. There are audiotapes and cutscenes in the game but the initial backstory of the city of Rapture is told entirely through the level and environment design (image 2.5). The corridors are small and claustrophobic but also familiar in their use of stores, bars and human spaces. The environment is always constrained by the physicality of being at the bottom of an ocean. The art assets are also evocative of decay and the fall of the once-great city is told through posters, lighting, and textures. Any post-apocalyptic world communicates that something terrible has occurred at some point and the designers do not have to show the bomb dropping. Instead just the ruination of the landscape and the aftermath tell the story of who its populace was.

2.3
Rise of the Tomb Raider, Crystal Dynamics, 2013. In the *Rise of the Tomb Raider* game climbable or interactive areas were denoted through lighting or texturing. Ledges that are usable are subtly distinct from noninteractive models.

2.4
Uncharted 4, Naughty Dog, 2016. *Uncharted 4* uses these same changes in texture and visual hints are part of a wider language or conventions in game design. These differentiation pathways also allow for strategizing by the player when given a goal (such as an exit) and multiple paths to get to that space (is there a quicker but riskier route?).

2.5
BioShock, Irrational Games, 2007. The
original *BioShock* game is a primer in visual
storytelling through level design. The art
assets and architecture constantly reinforce
the main story and premise of the game. The
levels are crafted to promote a certain amount
of exploration and storytelling within a mostly
linear first-person shooter mechanic.

Explicit narrative tells the story of the game to the player in detail often through the use of an opening scene and the use of cutscenes for exposition. Examples of this would be in games such as *Uncharted 4* or *Detroit: Become Human*, with both games using cinematics and cutscenes to move the narrative along (image 2.7). *Detroit: Become Human* uses a flowchart in the game to explicitly indicate to a player other choices they could have made. The game's designer, David Cage, says that the flowchart is an important part of the game's structure; "Adding this flowchart was a big thing for us, because it was a way to show people [image 2.6], 'Look, this is your narrative path in the scene, but this is also all the stuff that you missed.'" As one would expect with games reliant upon explicit narratives, there are little or no grey areas narratively. In *Uncharted 4* every player will see the same ending on completion of the game unless they miss the extended scenes after the main ending (Plunkett, 2016). Games with multiple endings are also explicit narratives because there are finite combinations of endings; even in *Detroit: Become Human*, its developer says that there are over 100 combinations of possible endings. Many of those differences are subtle—which main characters survives or dies are the main endings—but it's the fate of others and the political or world structure possibilities that add some nuance.

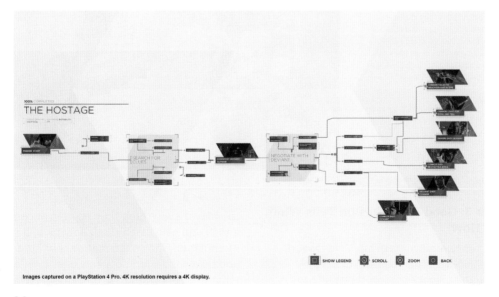

2.6
Detroit: Become Human, Quantic Dream, 2018. *Detroit: Become Human* takes the concept of explicit narrative and plays with it by adding in junction points to the main narrative structure. These decision trees add a level of replay to the game as players could choose to side with one faction and then another in a separate playthrough. The decisions are related to the mechanics and narrative rather than changes to any of the level design. Even so, the level designer would have to account for the different paths a player may be taking.

2.7
Uncharted 4, Naughty Dog, 2016.
Uncharted 4 has a linear path through its narrative and uses cutscenes to ensure the player has time to take in the level design and art (as well as being shown their goal in each level) and builds the relationship between the characters. Cutscenes are a useful device for spacing between action points and to convey meaning, a sense of wonder or to allow for exposition without the player being distracted by gameplay.

Emergent narrative occurs outside of the other narrative structures. It is best understood as narratives that are built within the player's head. Emergent narratives come directly from the gameplay and players recounting their actions. Sports games have emergent narrative: when one player in Madden NFL 16 has their team win against another team in an unexpected or highly skilled way, the recounting of the plays and the events that lead to the win become a narrative.

Another example would be massively multiplayer online games (MMO's) or any "sandbox" open-ended game where the player can create their own outcomes in the game (image 2.8). These narrative structures are sometimes referred to as emended and emergent as well as procedural where narratives are created by "accident," creating one-off events. These procedural events usually occur in open world and MMO games (Allison, 2010).

2.8
Overwatch, Blizzard Entertainment, 2016. Multiplayer games such as *Overwatch* have emergent narrative for the player or the player's team. The community surrounding the game will recount "battle stories" to each other as well as discussing tactics and talking about other players. This is as relevant a narrative as any storybook and adds a sense of connection to the game.

Principle 3: Good Level Design Tells What, but Not How

In video games a player is given a clear set of goals or objectives. It is the level designer's job to give the player the tools they need to complete that goal without getting in the way of the player's actions. The player must feel that it is they who saw the weak spots and defeated the dragon boss or found the treasure without the game holding their hand. A game will give

the player everything they need to accomplish a task and also teach them how to do it in small increments. Choice, no matter how limited, is a good way of designing a sense of "freedom" into what is a very controlled (designed) environment.

An LD should account for multiple approaches and paths toward a goal dependent upon the player's style of game play. Dan Taylor calls this "Nebulous Objectives." For example, in the game *Metal Gear Solid V: The Phantom*

Pain players are given an objective of clearing out fortresses full of the enemy (image 2.9). The level design and mechanics allow for multiple approaches to achieve this goal as well as rewards for different approaches such as total stealth or no kills. The design is a series of systems that communicate a sense of freedom to the player but are actually a set of limited options (you cannot use a crane to drop a container on enemies or use the helicopter as a sniping platform). The game does not tell the player how they should complete any mission; the systems of the game encourage improvisation and allow the player to match their gameplay style (Klepeck, 2015). *Metal Gear V* does not overtly inform the player the "correct" or "incorrect" approach to achieving success, instead the design of the levels and interfaces guide them subtly (image 2.11). For example, alert indicators are a visual cue that indicate where the guard is and which way they are likely looking—implying that sneaking up on a guard could be a tactic. There may be a well-placed sniper rifle available to a player on a higher ledge which will hint toward a possible action path. In the *Hitman* series the architecture and environment can limit the main approaches of the character or offer different points for incursion as well as the option for full assault. Other subtle limitations are the amount of damage a player can take before dying, how quickly the enemy AI reacts to an alert and so on. These are a "play and learn" approach to gameplay (also known as explorative acquisition (image 2.10)) (Graner-Ray, 2010).

2.9

Metal Gear Solid V: The Phantom Pain, Kojima Productions, 2015. The *Metal Gear* series has always balanced stealth with combat. In *Metal Gear Solid V: The Phantom Pain* there are multiple approaches to each mission. The objectives do not change, but the missions do have sub-objectives (such as "remain undetected") to encourage experimentation. The level design encourages these variations through subtle hiding spots and the placement of cover.

2.10

Hitman, Square Enix, 2016. The *Hitman* series' entire premise is based upon the "what, not the how" rule. Once the player is given an assassination target the world offers them multiple paths toward this goal. As in this image, a player can remove a target by making it look like an accident. They could also sneak up on the target and subdue or kill them but there is a risk of detection. Players may not notice the lift button at first, but earlier tutorials train the player to look for these environmental cues.

2.11
As an example of how this might be applied to a level's design, in this part of a level the player is given the goal to escape. Using the ladders as a directional element, each traversal comes with a different level of risk and reward. The blue route is the safest and would avoid detection, but that also means missing the pick up offered on the orange route. Placing two other pick ups behind the guards entices the player toward a direct approach, but that could result in their death. This form of traversal design enables the player to strategize, adding complexity. Other nudges for the player could be that the guards be more or less alert (depending on the player's earlier actions or level of difficulty), the character could be low on ammo or health and so on.

Unity 2018, assets from Batewar and Train Yard by Multiflag Studios.

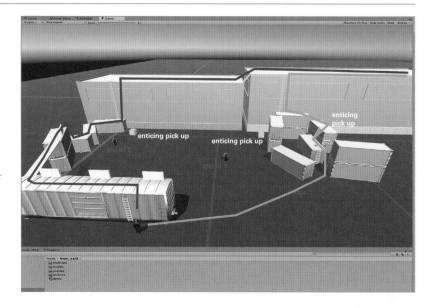

Principle 4: Good Level Design Constantly Teaches

When designers talk about "as little design as possible" this does not mean that visuals or products cannot be complex or should be minimalist. It requires that designs should be efficient and if there is a need for complexity it should be as invisible as possible for the product to work. One of the best approaches toward interface and system design is to teach the user a little bit at a time. In video game parlance, this is known as "tutorializing"' or "onboarding" (Moss, 2017).

Humans enjoy solving problems and finding patterns; it creates order in an unordered universe. If the player is always learning and completing tasks, they remain engaged. Players want to be rewarded for their actions and sometimes that reward can come in the form of knowledge and a sense of mastery. The process of onboarding usually begins explicitly with the player being introduced to the basic mechanics of the game such as movement. It can be as simple as "let me calibrate your super-soldier helmet; use the left stick to look left, look right." Having the game tell the player "well done, your helmet seems to be working" is enough positive feedback to endear the game to the player—this is part of

the onboarding process. It may seem ridiculous to the veteran player but for the new player constant positive feedback empowers them and will make it far more likely that they continue on in the game even as it becomes more difficult (Bycer, 2016).

It is also why games have tutorials that are explicit and implicit. Game designers have been playing games for many years and have played a variety of genres of games. This can create blind spots when creating a game because there is a tendency to make assumptions of who your player is. The player is not the designer. If the game does not teach the new player how the game works this is going to alienate and frustrate new players or those unfamiliar with the genre and its conventions. The onboarding process takes care of this by using tutorials within the game itself as part of the player's progress. *Skyrim* incorporated tutorials into its opening cinematics so that a completely new player could learn the basic controls systems from on-screen prompts while an interactive narrative unfolded. The veteran player would still complete the tutorials but would be more focused on the action around them; both players get something positive out of the same experience.

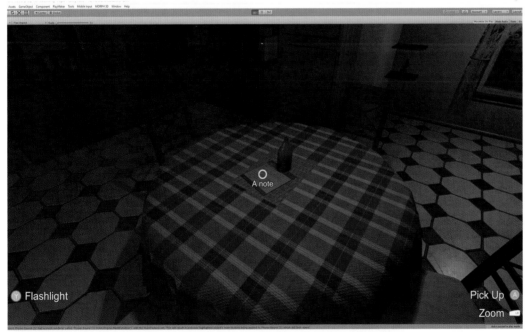

2.12a, 2.12b
The Diaries of Professor Angell: Deceased, Salmond, 2016. In my game *The Diaries of Professor Angell: Deceased* (2016)
I have used context-relevant user interface that shows the player the buttons they need to use in certain circumstances,
such as B to stop playing audio when it's playing or LB to zoom in on a document to read it. When the player faces away
from the interactive elements these on-screen prompts go away. This teaches the player the controls required to interact
with the game. An experienced player can turn these prompts off and in more advanced games the prompts themselves
are contextual; if a player successfully uses the controls they may not reappear. When a player is faced with a new control
system, the prompts will be shown.

Assets: HE Abandoned Manor by Artur G, Victorian Interiors by Andrew Pray, Brian's House by Gabro media, First Person Exploration Kit by
WhileFun games.

Beyond the obvious use of tutorials, levels should continue to teach the player in whichever ways suit the game (images 2.12a & 2.12b). This could be by mixing up the combat, adding harder or more intelligent enemies or introducing new or combination movement mechanics in order to complete a level's objective. Levels can also foreshadow events or abilities that the player will receive later in the game. This could be an opening or treasure chest that is unreachable until a player has learned a specific skill or has a new tool that allows entrance to another part of the level. Once the player has achieved a level of mastery with what they have, the game should continue to challenge them with new abilities or upgrading items (this is known as ramping) (Stout, 2015). A large part of the psychology of enjoying a video game is that we are hard coded to feel validated by the process of learning and mastering an ability, even if it's being able to customize a character to suit personal game play or getting deeper into the lore of a game's narrative.

2.13
Assassin's Creed Unity, Ubisoft, **2014.** Character customization and skill ramping is another form of tutorial. A screen that shows the player how different clothing, weapons and abilities can be used teaches them about possibilities in the game world. In the *Assassin's Creed* games (*Unity* is shown here) equipment can be swapped out dependent upon the style of play. Also, as the player gets deeper into the game they are rewarded with special items that can affect their success in the game.

Principle 5: Good Level Design Is Surprising

Surprises in design can make a product, device or graphic that much more endearing or important to the user. Surprises do not mean filling your level with cheap jump scares or enemies appearing out of closets randomly—those become routine very quickly (Remo, Sheffield, 2009). Instead, surprises can come from a variety of sources, from crafting the intensity of the level to a narrative twist or cool new ability. Using the player's own psychology and expectations against them is a useful tool for the designer. If a player has encountered five rooms full of enemies, they would expect the same in the next room. Making that room empty or very different from the others tells the player that this is not a game in which they should become complacent. A designer needs to add variety in order to prevent player boredom as well as being able to offer variants in gameplay (image 2.14).

2.14
Dishonored 2, Arkane Studios, **2016.** The "Clockwork Mansion" in *Dishonored 2* is an example of a change in gameplay and level design. The setting for the mission is a large mansion whose architecture and appearance can be reconfigured by the player (this image is of the inventor's main lab, which is actually a huge puzzle). This is the only level that has this configurability and adds another level of exploration and approaches to mission completion for the player.

A surprise or revelatory moment does not happen only in the designed and scripted areas of the level design. When a player expects, or knows what is coming next, there is a loss of engagement: "Games grow boring when they fail to unfold new niceties in the puzzles they present" (Koster, 2013).

A practical approach to pacing a level for surprise is the rollercoaster method (images 2.15 & 2.16). This comes, unsurprisingly from how rollercoasters are designed in phases to maximize enjoyment for the rider. As Alexandre Mandryka, a game designer at Ubisoft Montreal,

summarizes pacing and level design, it is focused on creating uncertainty. That is where the "fun" is for the player: "in games, it's the uncertainty that makes the experience fun. A game gives you a problem that has to bear uncertainty in how to solve it whatever the nature of the skills involved." Uncertainty and surprise when balanced with pacing make the level and the wider game more engaging for the player. Moving the player in and out of their comfort zone leads to a higher level of positive reaction from the player, but they should be individually crafted moments because a surprise is not a surprise if it occurs every ten minutes.

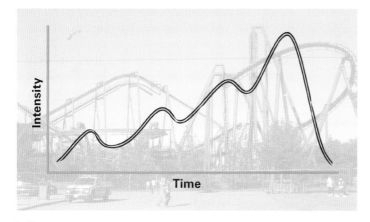

2.15
A rollercoaster is usually paced much like a level for intensity. It will build (the lift) it then dips into a hard drop and then through a series of twists turns or loops. There are "rest" areas (Brake points) which serve as two functions: a breather for the rider and as a practical safety point for the ride. The ride will then continue on, sometimes with its most intense banks and loops before returning to the station.

2.16
Pacing intensity of combat or jumps against periods of rest, exposition, or puzzle solving are an important factor in designing any level. As with a rollercoaster there is a direct correlation between enjoyment, terror, relief, and reflection. If the coaster is too long and too intense it will only please a small amount of people. If there are long periods of inaction where the rider sits with nothing to do (unless it is building anticipation such as in the lift) the experience will be more negative overall.

Principle 6: Good Level Design Empowers the Player

Empowerment and wish fulfillment are core pillars of game design. In my other videogame book I interviewed Steve Gaynor of The Fullbright Company. He said that the games he has worked on have always begun with the premise of "What wish are we fulfilling for the player?" In Fullbright's *Gone Home*, that wish was not to save the world or be a supersoldier; instead it was to be given permission to nose around someone's house without ever getting caught. Video games are escapism, and it is the game designer's job to deliver a particular fantasy to the player. This could be to become MVP for the NFL or NBA, to save the world from aliens or just to make friends with other characters. Along with being at the center of the game experience, players' actions should have a noticeable effect on the game world.

Wish fulfillment is empowering your player to be able to make their own discoveries and make their own choices. Player empowerment could come from exploring a darker side of a player's personality by making evil or morally questionable decisions or by exploring gender and sexuality. Video games can empower the player to make choices, so the world and its levels should react to those choices too, because this reinforces the role the player is embodying. Nonplayer characters (NPCs) should shy away from the evil character or smile and wave at the good character. If the game acknowledges the decisions the player is making and reflects those back at them in a meaningful way the immersion becomes deeper as the player becomes aware of their influence on the world (Schaffer, 2004).

Principle 7: Good Level Design Is Easy, Medium, and Hard

Although it still exists explicitly in some games (usually in the FPS genre) it is unusual to see games that have a difficulty selection (White, 2016). One reason this has gone out of fashion is that these selection processes can be arbitrary. The player does not know the difference between the experiences on Easy compared to a game on Hard before playing the game (Venturelli, 2016). Of course, the player can go back and change the difficulty setting, but this only works if that setting is attached to enemy artificial intelligence (AI) numbers or damage levels. For example, when choosing the "hardest" option the enemy will be able to soak up more bullets before dying or has better dodging AI so is harder to hit. On the "easy" option the enemy may just stand around in the open waiting to be shot at and one hit kills them. A more subtle approach toward the same end is to use diverging pathways that set up a risk versus reward proposition for the player, or to implement a dynamic difficulty system that reacts to the player's success and failures. *The Witcher 3: Wild Hunt* had a form of dynamic difficulty; enemies had levels or skull markings over their heads, which was a visual communication to the player that this combat might be winnable but would most likely result in the player's death. They could come back to that same scenario when more powerful and take on the enemy.

Difficulty could also be defined through choice as in *rule three*. The player can make a "hard, medium, easy" decision based on their in-game mastery, game play style, and which is directly related to their confidence level. *Far Cry 5* and *Metal Gear V: The Phantom Pain* make good use of these multiple path options (image 2.17). The added advantage of the multi-path design is that the player has more "buy-in" because on successful completion they will feel that they completed the mission using their prowess and strategy.

2.17
Metal Gear Solid V: The Phantom Pain, Kojima Productions, 2015. In *Metal Gear V: The Phantom Pain* it was far more difficult to complete a mission completely in stealth mode, being undetected and not killing any of the enemy (as seen in Figure 2.17, the character is attempting to use a silent sniper mode). The same level could be played out by wading in as a more aggressive frontal assault. In many missions the difficulty was dependent on the player's choices rather than an explicit setting at the beginning of the game.

Predetermined difficulty does have the advantage of replayability as a medium-level player may complete the game and feel ready to take on the game again on a higher setting. This is true of the different path methods, too; if the sneaky way worked once, the player who now has better armor or weapons may feel inclined to try a frontal assault and the level will feel completely different but not in as obvious a way as going from "easy" mode to "hard." To some players those settings are a badge of honor—like a black belt in karate, players can attest to their skill level by saying that they play on the more elite levels. The *Halo* and *Gears of War* franchises still use the difficulty setting in their games. As a game designer these design decisions need to be made early on as they will have a profound effect on the level design. If the environment prescribes the difficulty, then the more paths the player can take toward a goal, the more complex the level design is going to have to be to accommodate that. If the decision is to have Easy-Medium-Hard gameplay settings then the level design will be the same in each case, but the mechanics and AI will adapt to the difficulty setting and elements such as ammunition, health or power ups may be more or less frequent.

Principle 8: Good Level Design Is Efficient

A level designer should maximize all of the resources at their disposal because lean game design is good game design. Without getting too technical, a level designer could make huge levels with an enormous amount of detail that make use of weather systems, crowds of nonplayer characters (NPCs) and enemies, god rays, particle effects and high dynamic levels of detail. All of which is great until one of the game engineers looks at the enormous strain on the platform and has a nervous breakdown. A mantra of all designers is "use what you need to get the job done, nothing more." Hollywood productions do not build whole buildings; they use façades. There is nothing behind that front wall you see in the shot and interiors are built with just enough of the room and contents to sell the audience on the reality. There is a similar approach in video games when modelling level design: it is all smoke and mirrors. The reality of level design can get very technical with polygon counts and render-draw times or GPU hits, but essentially you only ever need to show the player what they need to see and do this as efficiently as possible.

One approach is to use modular game design (explored in detail in Chapter 7). Once a model is loaded into the game engine it takes up a set amount of the system's memory. If it's used again it really doesn't add much to the render times and memory because it is already in the system. If the model is turned a bit, is mirrored or repeated enough to become complex it will look sufficiently different to the player to seem new or as a continuation of that aesthetic (image 2.18) (there is a reason early 3D video games were mostly corridors and enclosed rooms: efficiency).

2.18
Fallout 4, Bethesda Game Studios, 2015. *Fallout 4's* level designers were able to create a very large open world because of its efficient reuse of resources and application of modular design. The mutant and raider forts have their own aesthetic and because of that the assets can be repeated throughout the world with multiple variations. The level designer can then add a few unique buildings or structures (landmarks) without them being a drain on limited resources.

Another approach is to use bidirectional gameplay—this is not the same as backtracking. Forcing a player to go back through a room they just cleared of zombies because they now have to find a key downstairs that opens a door they were just in upstairs is not fun. If something has changed in the room the player has to go back through, that becomes part of the gameplay. It does not have to be the enemies respawning— that feels too much as if the game has cheated the player—but different enemies, perhaps guards who have come to explore the ruckus from earlier, can be interesting and feels natural. Backtracking is often a derogatory term but can be used by level designers to encourage exploration (perhaps the player has missed the treasure/object because of the fighting/challenge) or it could be that completing one puzzle opens up a previously locked area. The sense of achievement in unlocking or finding an object will compensate for any negative effects of going back through a previously explored area and previously explored areas have already been accounted for in the game's memory usage quota.

2.19a
Figure 2.19a is an example of bidirectional play. In this level the player (Naomi) has to cross tracks in between trains and fight some guards in order to reach a control panel that will open a door that exits the level.

Unity 2018 assets from Third Person Controller from Opsive, Urban Underground from Gabro Media, and bodyguard models from Batewar.

2.19b
Once the panel is activated it also sets off alarms which attract more guards who chase her back to the exit across the same tracks (switching the trains off allows for mobile combat). The player is unlikely to be annoyed with "backtracking" in this instance as both goals have different challenges.

Principle 9: Good Level Design Will Create Emotion

Most players will respond to virtual spaces in similar, if not identical, ways as real spaces. Most of us find open countryside pleasing and calming (unless it's full of zombies); round rooms and certain color palettes are also calming and soothing. The opposite is also true: harsh angles and loud or disturbing colors (moldy greens, blood reds) can be disturbing and evoke different emotions within us (image 2.20). In addition to the use of color, the space in the level will amplify emotions.

Architectural theories are useful in video game design, because architects are trained in the use of space. For example, there is the theory of spatial empathy (Duarte, Pinheiro, 2016): because a player has experienced many different spaces in their lives (as well as in film and other media) they can empathize with their character as they react to different game spaces. Tight enclosed spaces have the same psychological effect (albeit muted) on players as they do in real life. Tight corners will make the player feel trapped, labyrinthine corridors will make the player confused and tense. Wide open spaces create a feeling of epic scale, loneliness or wonder. Spaces create emotional internal moments too—when a player emerges from a series of tight narrow spaces into a larger open space the player may experience a sensation of wonder as if leaving a cave in the spring (image 2.21). The physical architecture of a space communicates directly to the player and should be thought of as a character in the world.

2.20
Resident Evil 7: Biohazard, Capcom, 2017. Different spaces in levels have different emotional effects. Tight, narrow and dark corridors amplify feelings of tension and terror. Most of the action in *Resident Evil 7: Biohazard* takes place in a house or confined spaces. This adds to the tension because an enemy can come at the player from almost any part of the house.

2.21
The Legend of Zelda: Breath of the Wild, Nintendo, 2017. In contrast, *The Legend of Zelda: Breath of the Wild* is an open-world game with a brighter color palette and much softer edges and lighting. The game is focused on adventure and exploration filled with moments of wonder.

The general rule for designing with an emotion in mind is to start from the emotion you want the player to feel and work backwards (Bura, 2008). Emotions are surprisingly easy to get out of audiences in movies but not so easy in video games outside of happiness or fear. It is a form of manipulation to use visuals and audio cues to create feelings of disgust, apprehension, terror or happiness and most media use very similar approaches to evoke emotions in their audiences (watch a horror movie with upbeat music playing over it and your emotions are completely altered). The difficult emotions are the ones in between, the nuanced feelings we have toward other humans or situations. When we design for emotion we are really designing for emotions—plural. No game can make you happy for hours on end (not even *Mario* or *Legend of Zelda* games); instead the designer is looking for

specific emotions for particular scenes or levels. The psychology can be used to amplify emotions in the player fairly simply.

For example, if the designer wants the player to feel a sense of desperation or higher tension they could add a countdown timer. Imagine the scenes from Figures 2.19a and 2.19b: defeating the first guards and hitting the switch may have taken a minute or so. Hitting the button sets a timer that gives the player 2 minutes to get to the door before a big explosion. In Figure 2.19b there are twice the enemies, which is going to create a mixture of panic and excitement for the player. A counter adds a sense of urgency and will amplify the possibility of failure and this alters the emotional mindset of the player (Palmer, 2015). Another example would be the "cavalry" moment at the end of a level where a player has to defend an NPC/castle/treasure against a horde of enemies or a seemingly impossible number of bad guys. Right at the very last moment the drop ship appears and the player is saved. That feels really good—the ramp up of the player fighting and thinking all is lost gives way to the release of being safe and away from danger. It is good pacing as well as good emotional tuning; what the player does not know is that they were really never in any danger of being overrun. The level's designer will have set a limit of time or numbers of enemies killed that will trigger the "cavalry" coming to save them. That is very deliberate designing for emotion because it will always work even though it is a familiar trope from film and television.

Principle 10: Good Level Design Is Driven by Mechanics

Level design is the playable realization of the game mechanic or rather the mechanic delivery system. The role of the level designer is to take the mechanics of the game and make them work for the player through the world they are in. The assumption is that the mechanics of the game are developed in advance of the environment art, character design and the level design. In a perfect world they would be, but sometimes even the best plans can come unstuck as testing and feedback lead to certain mechanics being dropped or added during the development process (*Sunset Overdrive* was originally a ground-based "run and gun" game with a crafting mechanic) (England, 2017).

As with all design disciplines, communication is vital for success. In Principle 7 we looked at how giving the player different options to overcome an obstacle or work toward a goal is rewarding and efficient game design. This can only work if the mechanic lets it. It might sound obvious, but if the level designer considers a feature to be very important it's vital that is communicated to the game designer/programmer early on. They're unlikely to be able to add it in later in the process. This communication needs to go both ways; if the mechanic designer has a feature that is used for a specific purpose, such as explosive gel that can be used to blow up walls (the Batman franchise does this), could that explosion also take out unsuspecting enemies on the other side of the wall if the level designer positioned them there? Designers are always looking for solutions as well as opportunities when given tools to play with.

A mechanic will also impact the level design in other ways. For example, if flight is allowed then everything should be built so that when seen from above it seems realistic (no facades). As a designer the question would be, if a player can fly how could that mechanic be used in cool ways in the level to showcase the flight mechanic beyond just getting from A to B? Answers might include: dropping bombs, buzzing pedestrians, earning points by flying through tight spaces, and so on. That is the role of the level designer within the development team—to take the mechanic of the game and envision how it could be leveraged within the rules of the world to create a better experience for the player.

Summary

In my classes I have adopted and adapted Dan Taylor's and Dieter Rams' principles and use them as a touchpoint for my students to keep them on track with their process. Principles are not commandments set in stone, so it is important that my students understand that what works in one game may not work in another if applied too rigidly. Game design, like all design disciplines, is flexible and adjusts to the needs of the development team and the players. The most important focus for any game is to create a positive experience for the player by giving them the tools and freedoms to fulfill their fantasy. The role of the level designer is to facilitate that as much as possible. Sometimes this requires leading the inexperienced player by the hand through the early areas of the game and then having them release themselves as they master the mechanics. The balance to that means designing levels for the experienced player to be able to experiment with the world you have created for them, and giving them options for further mastery of their skill set or be able to adapt their existing style to the game intuitively. As a designer it is always worth asking yourself how many principles you are checking off in your game and how you could improve the experience for the player by adopting more of them. In the next chapter we will examine level design both from the standpoint of technical constraints as well as exploring the role of designing from the player's perspective.

Constraints, Player Flow, and Objectives

Learning Objectives for This Chapter:

1) Examine deeper aspects of the role of the level designer

2) Introduce concepts of payout, scale, and asset integration

3) Introduce concept of player flow, movement, and its effects on gameplay

3.0
The Last of Us 2, Naughty Dog, 2020.

Design is seldom a straight line and it is rare that everything goes exactly as planned. To paraphrase the German field marshal Helmuth von Moltke "No game idea survives contact with the development team." Video games are multidisciplinary and complicated; when working in a larger team plans can change based upon feedback and the design team adapts to meet new demands. The process outlined in Chapter 6 could be seen as an oversimplification of the development process. To address this as much as possible the first part of this chapter examines some of the more ethereal and technical considerations of level design.

Technical Constraints

As a level designer, it is usually part of the process to adhere to specific goals for performance that every level needs to hit to be viable in the overall game. The LD should know what these technical constraints are before developing beyond the gray box prototype: "You have to build within the framework of what your team and engine are capable of producing, and you have to keep those goals in mind even when prototyping" (Brown, 2013). The constraints depend on the game being produced but can range from the desired polygon count for models, the number of players that can be in combat simultaneously without any frame rate drop, or using scripting to avoid memory-draining loops in the level (for example if code attached to a treasure chest is constantly checking to see if the player is colliding with it or not, it would be simpler to create an active/inactive state based upon a button press). Level designers, like other designers, are problem solvers but there are some key preventative measures to consider. Simple steps when coding can avoid system slowdowns. The usual culprits here are: not optimizing scripts, not optimizing pathfinding for the player or leaving geometry in the level that the player will never see (but the GPU does) (images 3.1 & 3.2). Bethesda call this "opportunity time" (Burgess, 2013) because getting in front of problems and fixing them as soon as possible increases the likelihood of being able to ship a solid game.

3.1

This is an almost complete level in my Unity engine-based game with the stats tab selected. This shows me how my game is performing as it is being played. These figures are with occlusion culling on, so the framerate, poly/tri count and performance feedback are based upon what the camera is seeing. The LD would constantly monitor these stats in playthroughs and testing to make sure the numbers hit levels agreed upon previously.

Unity 2018. Assets: First person Exploration Kit by WhileFun games, Victorian Interiors by A. Pray, Wooden Crates by Animation arts.

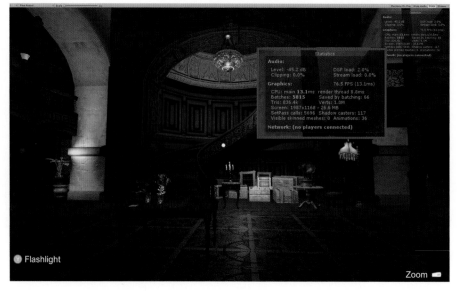

Scale, Integration, and Proportion

The degree of movement that the player can perform informs the game space and level layout directly. In first-person games such as *Overwatch* or third-person games such as *Uncharted 4: A Thief's End* the players' avatars can jump, run, dodge, and walk. For a level designer, knowing that there is a jump or a dodge/roll mechanic across all levels immediately influences the

layout and scale of the design (Principle 10, see Chapter 2). In the game *Gone Home*, although it is from the first-person perspective, there is no running, dodging, or jumping. Due to this the house layout and rooms can be much tighter on the player's character. If a player needs to dodge incoming rockets or a wave of enemies, the game space and architecture have to be designed to compensate for these styles of movement. If there is any verticality, such as climbing or a jump option, this again alters the scaling and modeling possibilities for the level (even more so if there is an enhanced jump such as in *Dishonored 2* or *Call of Duty: Infinite Warfare*).

3.3
Overwatch, Blizzard Entertainment, 2016. This is the original cast of *Overwatch* player characters, all of which must be able to traverse the maps based upon their movement mechanics and physical size. It is a challenge from a level design perspective to be able to accommodate such a range of character designs and abilities, and seamlessly integrate them into the same environment.

Let us examine the development of scale when integrating a player character into a third-person shooter game (these considerations would translate to a first-person or 2D game too). In the planning phase the design team would let the LD know the proposed scale of the main character. This is important because it informs the game's physical architecture. For example, in the *Tomb Raider* franchise reboot, Lara Croft is cited to be 5' 6" (1.68 m) (Stewart, Horton 2012) whereas Master Chief from the Halo franchise is "standing seven feet tall and weighing half a ton in his armor" (Bungie, 2004). Master Chief exists within a human universe certainly, but if you played any of the games did you ever notice having to duck to go through a doorway or bending double to fit into a warthog? Of course not, because the environments and assets are tailored to fit the size of the main character. In our game, we will set the main character at 175 cm (5' 9") and in preproduction the LD and the environment modeler would calculate the layout's scale based on that measurement (image 3.4). Even though we do not get to see the main character in *Gone Home* or *Doom* when playing, the proportions of the world are still set to the character's height (the camera's point of view) as well as a proportional width and depth. This is a critical piece of knowledge for the LD as it will avoid any strange proportions and inform the size of rooms, buildings props, and NPCs.

3.4

In this view from the Unreal Engine 4 editor we have the beginnings of scaling the level's architecture to the size of the player (in this case the Barbarian asset from the free-to-use *Infinity Blade* suite of assets). An LD should always build the level to the scale of the player. The LD will know the player and architecture dimensions from the game designers and the 3D modelers. It could be very costly in time and effort to have to rescale a level or multiple levels because of assumptions made on the size of the character (i.e. modeling a level for Lara Croft when it needs to be for Master Chief).

Unreal engine 4.16, Asset is from the *Infinity Blade: Warriors* pack.

In 3D games, knowing the physical height of a character is a good start, but the LD also needs to know the character's collision space; its height, width, and depth (think of collision as an invisible box around the player's avatar or body parts). Once this has been defined there may be variables depending on what the player is able to do for movement such as jumping, crouching, and perhaps a cover crouch. The LD would need to know how much these animations alter the dimensions of the collision box. For example, how high can the character jump? A normal human can jump about 16" to 19" (41 cm to 50 cm) or beyond 70 cm (28") (2016) if they are a trained athlete. Knowing the height of the character jump affects the scale of any obstacles that need to be jumped over or grabbed on to as well as dictating what obstacles would be unassailable (can the player jump and grab? This extends their reach by a large factor). Even with these measurements, "there is an element of 'feel' to these calculations, they do not have to be exactly mathematically correct" (Burgess, 2013); as long as the architecture and models are built to match the character size then any jumping, vaulting or cover mechanics will need to be adjusted to have

a certain amount of aesthetic look and feel to them (image 3.5). This is somewhat of an art and is based upon the player's perspective within the level and what feels right rather than being a true percentage of the character's height. Even so, making a barrier that is 200 cm high and having a normal human character be able to vault over it is going to look odd.

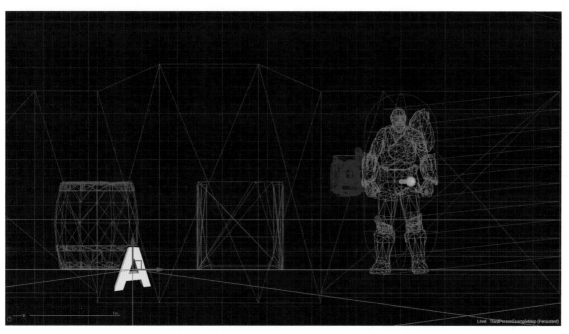

3.5
This is an orthographic view in the Unreal Engine 4 editor, which means that the view has no depth or perspective. Everything is shown on the same plane so no matter how far in the distance a model is, it is shown as the same size as everything else. In this view the gray background grid is set to 10 units, which means that each square of the grid is 10 cm. When we look at the barrel to the left we can see that it is 0.9 m and our warrior character is 1.75 m (or 5' 9") tall.

In the Unreal Engine 4 (UE4) editor the default units of measurement equate to a centimeter: 1 UU (Unreal Unit) and 1 grid unit are equivalent to 1 cm. In the game engine Unity the default is metric but flexible and instead relies on the best practices approach of the design team creating models in metric sizing in whatever software that is being used (the unit default for Max is inches, in Maya and blender it is centimeters). The modeler would then export the assets using a 1-meter cube that can be used as a proportional reference guide in Unity for scaling. It's a bit confusing but works out like this based upon the defaults:

When importing a model Unity assumes 1 meter in the game world to be 1 unit in the imported file so the modeler has to set the scale in their application accordingly

(1 meter = 1 unit even if they've been working in centimeters). The UE4 editor is more complementary as it is set to cm explicitly so its workflow makes it easier to import models from 3D applications to scale in the engine.

In Figure 3.6 I have placed two cubes that represent the collision area of the character and the height of its jump. It is important to set how high and wide architectural elements need to be from the walls, stairs, and doorways to gaps in trees or the height of barriers that block the character's movement. The LD can put together a gray box level working from this scale but the environment artist and 3D modeler will also be working from those measurements when creating assets for the game, and they need to match up as the game goes through its passes.

3.6

As a level designer, a conversation with the game designers in the planning stages will set up the dimensions of the game; this goes beyond the character and includes basic architectural proportions.

Unreal engine 4.16, Assets are from the *Infinity Blade: Warriors* pack and *Infinity Blade Grasslands*.

3.7

This side-on view shows the cube that would represent the characters' collision area, which is measured and set against architecture such as doorways and distances from objects. These cubes are only for reference in the initial planning stages.

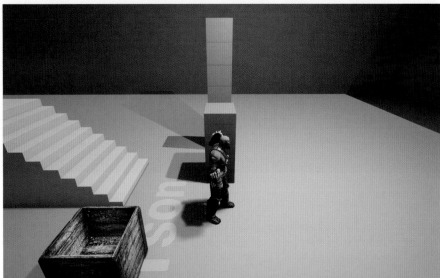

3.8

The farthest left cube represents the default jump height of the player. This will have a direct impact on the design of the level, which has to accommodate all aspects of the move mechanic into its architecture.

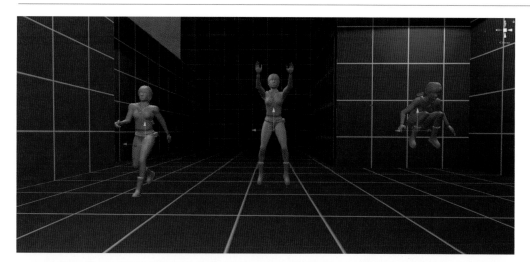

3.9
In this version of a level in the Unity game engine the adventure game character has several movement options available—from walking to reaching and jumping. These alter the size of the collision box and this must be considered into the level design because players may be able to jump, reach and grab onto a ledge, adding vertical possibilities to the game.

Unity 2018, assets from Third Person Controller from Opsive

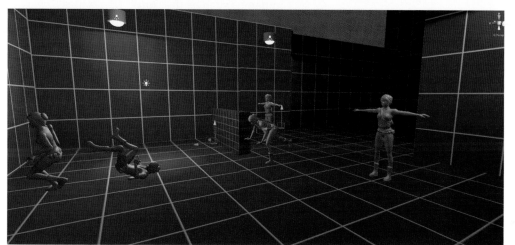

3.10
As an adventure character, a roll can take up a significant amount of space when animating. This does not mean that every space should accommodate this roll completely, but it is a consideration in combat or other encounters (if the character hits an object such as a wall they will usually switch to a tighter roll animation). The roll is part of the character's movement options so can be called by the player at any time. There may instances when it would be desirable for the roll to be "turned off" and the player has to understand the reason behind that change (for example when other actions are occurring such as pick up, fly, or climb).

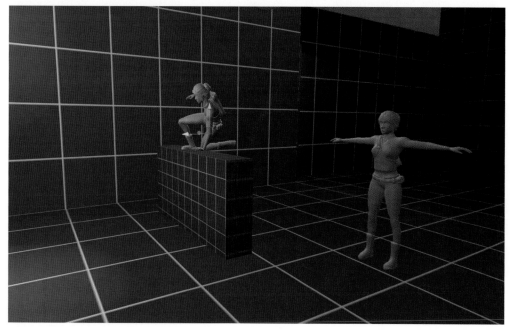

3.11
Other movement mechanics have a direct effect on the architecture. If there is a cover or vaulting mechanic the objects and walls must consistently be at the most believable height for the characters. The *Gears of War* series approaches this very explicitly; every battle arena has cover at almost exactly the same height and width, so much so that it is now part of that series' aesthetic.

Ensuring that everyone is on the same page with scale is critical in the planning stages and makes for a fluid work flow as the LD begins to place encounters and assets, as well as scaling the architecture for the player. Once a general scale has been agreed upon and can be assessed by the LD and design team the next logical step is to work on the layout of the level itself. There is no set sequence for these to occur in; some LDs may begin with the layout and then place a character and rescale, whereas others begin with a character and then start their gray box design process (Seifert, 2013). Whichever way the sequence is approached, layout is a foundation of the level design process.

Flow, Critical Paths, and Intensity

Level design is focused on delivering different levels of experience to the player in a way that feels intuitive and natural. Some players look to barrel straight through a level and others take time to explore, while others may be a mix of both styles. LDs have to create critical paths (the most direct route) as well as noncritical paths, both of which have to deliver a consistent experience. LDs may use loot to encourage exploration or hide lore in off-the-path areas of the level. In action games the balance between intensity and cool-down periods has to be carefully addressed, and the combat or puzzle design should begin to put the player in a state where they are not thinking about what they are doing physically even if the button combinations have become fairly complex.

Flow

Usually when talking about "flow" in games the focus is on the work of psychologist Mihaly Csikszentmihalyi and what is most commonly referred to as being "in the zone" when playing a game. Flow is the point in which a player achieves a balance between challenge and skill, and becomes unaware of their surroundings and reacts without thinking (this form of flow can be designed into games, and is especially prevalent in games such as the *Guitar Hero* series, *Dance Dance Revolution*, and fighting games) (Baron, 2012). An LD looks at flow from the perspective of player movement and how their avatar navigates through a level and what could impede or challenge that progress. Planning for flow is examined in all styles of game from 3D to 2D and overhead "god view" strategy games. Physical player movement is dictated by the mechanics, but it is the LD who controls the player's path and this is a key factor in any level design strategy. Good flow in a level connects directly to pacing, and when designing for flow the LD is examining how the player's movement paces the level in relation to the layout. Good player flow is dependent on good layout, the ability of the LD in feeding the player the encounter or experience when they need it. The LD has to think about how all of the spaces in the level fit together, where the player is supposed to go and how the player understands how to get to that location.

3.12, 3.13
In these two images (Figure 3.12 is from Chapter 2), in Figure 3.13 all that has been added is two pillars, one tiled and one metal. That small change is enough to interrupt the player's line of sight and makes the combat zone seem much more crowded. It does not take much alteration to affect the player's experience.

Unity 2018 assets from Third Person Controller from Opsive and Urban Underground from Gabro Media.

In his 2014 GlitchCon talk Joel Burgess (level designer for *Skyrim*) talked about the concept of bad level design or what is known as "dripping faucet design." Burgess attributes the phrase to the developer 3D Realms. In the early nineties, many shooter games followed a formula of repetition in their level and combat design. It was essentially *enter a room—shoot all enemies—exit room—repeat*; for an entire game. 3D Realms likened this level design approach to a dripping faucet at night; eventually the sound of the repetitive drip-drip-drip will drive a person insane. The designers at 3D Realms found that by simply removing enemies from one or two rooms and creating spaces of "quiet" (where no combat took place) that players began to explore the levels far more. Another by-product was that these "quiet spaces" seemed to psychologically ramp up tension in the player because it altered their expectation of what could be behind the next door. This is now an established approach to level design and is a large part of the pacing of the level. Flow will be different dependent upon the style of gameplay too. For example, the player flow of *Sunset Overdrive* or *Tony Hawk Pro-Skater* focus on continual movement. Games such as *Doom* or *Gears of War* lock players into specific combat arenas that restrict the player's movement and flow comes from the combat. Each approach to flow is dependent on the goals of the game, but all LDs will create a critical path, or idealized route through the level that every player will experience in some form.

Critical Path

Mapping out a level begins with the critical path; "The critical path is the shortest path through a level without using secrets, shortcuts, or cheats. Basically, it's the path the designer intends the player to take through the level unless she gets really clever" (Stout, 2012). Or as level designer Steve Lee says "a critical path is what the player needs to do in order to progress, but doesn't inherently mean that it's clear to the player how to do it" (part of interview in Chapter 6) (image 3.14). The layout defines the critical path and the flow is based upon that path with other explorable areas added to the level if required. The critical path puts the most important (critical) objectives, challenges, and resolutions directly in front of the player. This path is often linear as it is predicated on the player moving forward and completing game objectives as directly as possible. There would be no backtracking or wandering off into side rooms. Critical paths in open-world games are based upon objectives and missions. For example, in *Witcher 3* the main Geralt storyline is the critical path for the player in the open world. The developers were careful to give the player freedom but maintain an eye on the storyline by having the player understand that unless they complete main missions and quests, they are eventually going to hit boundaries in the game: "there are rewards in terms of faster character development . . . or you will learn certain new mechanics" (Iwinski, 2016). These factors bring the player back to the critical path.

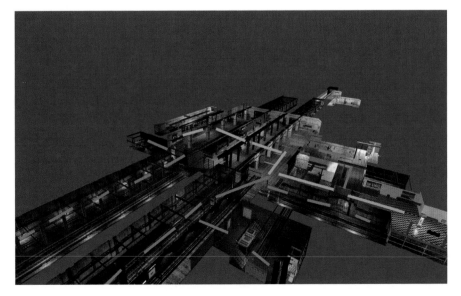

3.14

In this overview of the "subway level" the orange lines depict the critical path. This is the most direct way for the player to engage with enemies and exit the level. Ammo and health would be placed in this path. The green arrows depict secondary and tertiary paths a more exploration-focused player could take. The rewards for these paths could be narrative, collectibles, or more ammo or health.

Unity 2018 assets from Urban Underground, Gabro Media.

Intensity Ramping

Intensity or intensity ramping is the LD knowing which encounters, puzzles, or storylines are going to be in the level, but from their perspective they have to design the experience to ramp up in intensity in a way that is satisfying for the player. This could be that enemies become more difficult as the player moves deeper into the level. Or the player fails a few times against a foe, but this gives them a chance to learn how the enemies work and then the player is able to use this knowledge to display mastery of combat skills on subsequent attempts. Mike Stout (Insomniac Games, Activision) defines intensity as "the subjective difference in complexity or required skill between different parts of the same game" (Stout, 2016). Intensity can increase across levels or within a level; for example, in a combat game there could be several skirmishes with a few enemies before a final arena space that is far more intense. Or it could be that to sneak into a mansion to steal treasure there is an increasing amount of guards as the player gets closer to their goal.

When designing intensity the experience should be equal no matter the skill set of the player. In both those previous examples, a player who is a novice or a veteran would understand that the beginning of the level was easier than the end. Intensity also features into the pacing of the level as the LD will be looking at where the intensity should ramp up, then cool down, then ramp up again (this was covered as part of the "rollercoaster" design approach of pacing in Chapter 2). These ups and downs, paths, and intensity are factors in game balance. Deciding if there are too many or too few encounters, or that a mission is too easy or too hard is part of the level designer's role. Depending on the size of a studio a level designer may be working with mission or encounter designers as well as environment and combat designers. These people will have a focus on balancing the level for the player.

Balancing the Level

Balance in video games usually refers to balancing the game for the player based around the mechanics such as "is that gun too powerful or that boss too easy?" In level design balance equates to pacing and the player experience. When designing a level pacing can be quantified as with the examples of the beat charts from Chapter 5, which have a desired length of time the player "should" spend playing the level. However, if every level is set to ten minutes this would become formulaic. Predictive pacing can spoil a level's immersion by ignoring human qualities such as curiosity. Although ten minutes may be an ideal pacing timeframe there should be nothing to prevent the player from spending longer if the game warrants exploration (the opposite to this occurs in *Player Unknowns Battlegrounds*, which has multiple methods of pushing a player towards a final endpoint). The problem for the level designer is remaining objective about how long a level needs to be—play testing is the best way to arrive at a consensus as to whether the level works or not. Sensitivity and awareness of the player is important; a good LD should be conscious of player fatigue—the point in the level where the player becomes bored or turns off. Making assumptions about what fatigues a player is a trap. In a 2004 study of MMO players Nick Yee found that counter to industry assumptions, younger and male players have higher rates of attrition than older and female players (Yee, 2004). This is also why ideally testers vary across the demographic of the intended audience.

When looking for balance the LD would have to find the monotonous elements (perhaps there is too much grinding in the level) and correct them (this is from testing feedback; one person calling part of a level boring is not enough to redesign it). The LD should put themselves in the role of the player but use testers as often as possible to find out what areas need to be balanced. Watching others play a level is one of the most painful but effective approaches to testing a level for balance. When testing, the LD has to avoid prompting the player; if they are lost, telling the tester where to go does not solve the problem with the level (the LD is interested in how quickly the player got lost, if they find their way, were they really lost or just exploring?). It is hard not to assume the tester is just "not getting it" or playing "incorrectly" but that is a view based upon familiarity with the level. A new tester is the player that has just bought the game and if they struggle the game is likely to garner bad reviews. When testing at Bethesda, Burgess has this mantra; "Grab somebody and sit them down with as little setup or guidance as possible. Encourage them to vocalize as they play. Then: shut up. Don't interrupt, don't help, don't correct. Ignore direct questions unless absolutely necessary" (Burgess, 2013).

Varying the Level for Maximum Enjoyment

Pacing isn't just about how long the player will take to complete the level, it's also about possibilities. As Mare Shepard said in the introduction to this book, level design is focused on creating "spaces of possibility." Variety in level design is important and any player can point to a game where the interaction started repeating itself or became too much of a grind. It is difficult to keep a player's attention in a single player game over tens of hours, but that is the goal of the level designer. Multiplayer or player vs player (PvP) games tend to suffer less from this factor as the competitive nature of beating another human as well as an increase in skill mastery is very motivating. Multiplayer PvP matches or raids also tend to be short so the player is not focused for long periods of time, unlike a traditional action game where a level may last thirty or forty minutes.

3.15

This is an example of a "bowling alley" layout in level design and it is easy to see how a player could get bored with this quickly. With an obvious exit the player is likely to run straight towards it; variance would make them cautious or want to explore. There is little interaction and even less variety; a player could spend 2–3 minutes in this level, but there would be little point to it. A curve or turn in the passage or a visual effect would be enough to engage the player.

Unity 2018, assets from Victorian Interiors from Andrew Pray, Animation arts creative Wooden Crates.

Game designers recognized the importance of variety early on. The original *Sonic the Hedgehog* has a surprising amount of variety in its level design and pacing. We may think of the early *Sonic* games as being frenetic and always moving, but there are water levels that slow the player down considerably. There are also levels that switch from side scrolling to a third-person "Z-axis" movement, and the end-level boss fights restrict the players space to one screen, disrupting the movement options learned from other parts of the level. Changes like these work because they make sense within the context of the game and are applied consistently; the variants surprise the player but do not confuse them. It's important that level designers do not arbitrarily use an "add variety" randomizer script.

Changing up the level design must serve the wider concept of the game as well as being a tool for player engagement. Introducing a new mechanic can be as much a variety and pacing tool as moving to a different aesthetic. Roguelike games are an example of variety with consistency. The variety is that when the player dies they are permanently dead (known as perma-death) and restart the game each time with a different character. In a roguelike game the player retains the knowledge of the enemies and mechanics, but the challenge is always different. The levels are procedurally generated, which means that an algorithm dictates the layout of the architecture, items, and enemies each time the level is restarted. This can turn a fairly simple dungeon crawler into a complex strategy game simply because the player can never rely on learning the layout and enemy or power-up locations.

Variance in pacing can also come through cinematics (also known as cutscenes), which can be used to break up combat monotony and allow the player to rest or explore. *Doom*, the blueprint for fast-paced first-person combat, has in-game cutscenes for exposition and pacing, as well as areas that can be explored for collectibles after an area is cleared of demons. When thinking about variance, approaches range from the complex (procedurally generated levels that are different every playthrough) to the simple (have a brightly lit room in a horror game or an outside level that has some sunlight, which communicates a different emotion). When exploring opportunities to vary or mix up the level design it is important not to lose sight of another set of constraints: making sure the player knows what the objectives are and how to achieve them.

Objectives

When planning the layout for a level the main focus is on the player's objective: what it is, how you communicate it to the player and then show them where it is. Objectives have to be clearly defined before and during a level—if the player loses track of their objective they must always be able to easily come back to it. Video games are simulations, and unlike life, fairly direct ones. Objectives in games tend to be simple: save world, defeat boss, collect most coins and so on. How the player is able to achieve those objectives is the game and the level designer must facilitate this.

Levels contain the steps towards that ultimate "meta" goal and each successful objective that is achieved brings the player closer to that higher-level goal.

David Mullich (Disney Interactive, Activision) writes that objectives can be nuanced or obvious but should contain all or some of the following criteria:

Clear. The player should never be in a position of not having an objective. The game should always clearly communicate, explicitly or implicitly, what the player's next goal is (image 3.16). Once the player accomplishes one goal, the next goal should be immediately presented to the player.

Obtainable. Do not punish the player; make the level hard, but do not make the goals seem unobtainable. A good LD will play test for this and any player (including myself) can attest to that moment in a game when, after dying three times then suddenly it all comes together and they win. Or the player could select a different difficulty level to get past the hard part (or the game system can use a dynamic difficulty system that adapts to the player (this is covered in Chapter 2).

Concrete. Make sure your player knows if they have achieved the objective or failed at it. Most failure states are obvious, the player dies in the game. Some objectives could be more ephemeral and so it is important that the

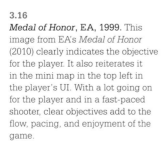

3.16
Medal of Honor, EA, 1999. This image from EA's *Medal of Honor* (2010) clearly indicates the objective for the player. It also reiterates it in the mini map in the top left in the player's UI. With a lot going on for the player and in a fast-paced shooter, clear objectives add to the flow, pacing, and enjoyment of the game.

player understands this success. For example, if the mission in the level was to collect ingredients for a medical cure the player may wander around picking up all sorts of herbs until the game tells them that they have the ingredients they need to make the cure.

Challenging. As mentioned earlier in this chapter, games are supposed to challenge the player and they should expend effort in the game to achieve a goal. This is a large part of what makes games fun. Effort and challenge should also equal reward—the more time a player puts into the game completing challenges, the better they should feel about completing those objectives. Challenge needs to be balanced too. Players gain skills in the game (even if there are no experience points or leveling up, they will get better at judging jumps or hitting targets) and this requires that the objectives should increase in difficulty in line with the player's progress.

Rewarding. There must be a direct connection between the task being completed, its difficulty and the reward delivered to the player. Rewards can be intrinsic or extrinsic. Intrinsic rewards occur in the game via loot drops, more experience points, leveling up or more story is delivered. Extrinsic rewards occur out of the game space; this could be bragging rights over your friends in multiplayer combat, telling the story in a forum of your experience in the game (this occurs in sports games a lot) or being ranked on a leader board. Having a hard boss drop rare or exciting loot after a hard-fought battle is good; gaining a million gold coins for picking three herbs for a recipe would devalue currency in the game and reduce the impact of any other coin-related tasks.

Clear objectives are key in game design and level design The player needs to understand not just what the challenge is but also how to reach it and achieve it. Unlike real life video games, constantly give the player feedback and update them on their progress and achievements. Video games are created to entertain and emotionally connect with the player as well as work across a wide variety of play styles and demographics.

Summary

As we dive deeper into some of the more technical and ephemeral aspects of level design it becomes clearer that as a discipline it depends a lot on the type of game being made. These fundamental principles cannot be applied wholesale to any one game, but they do appear in most video games (even ones from 30 years ago). The level designer has to make important design decisions based upon their experience, research and player feedback. As with most other design disciplines, level and game design are collaborative in nature with no one person being more important than another. Being able to listen to feedback from testers as well as other people in the design team is as important as being able to communicate ideas and concepts to them. Video games have an essence to them; they are all goal oriented and interactive—that is their nature. The role of the level designer is to connect all these disparate elements of the game (mechanic, architecture, objectives, combat, encounters, missions, etc.) into a cohesive and enjoyable experience. The next chapter introduces level design from the perspective of how the player thinks, and how to use simple psychology to make better levels.

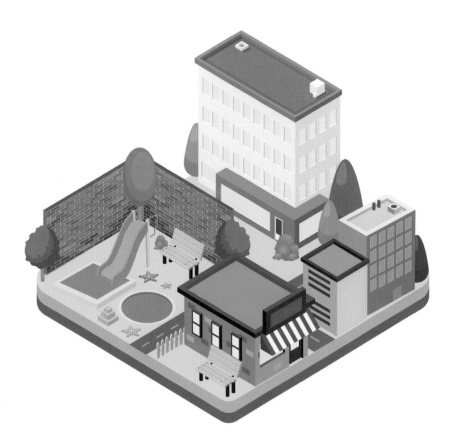

INTERVIEW: NINA FREEMAN, FOUNDER, STAR MAID GAMES

Nina Freeman has shipped many games, most notably *How Do You Do it?* and *Cibele*, which have both been finalists in the Independent Games Festival. *Cibele* was also part of the IndieCade Collection 2015 and a nominee for the Game Awards of 2015. Nina also wrote and designed *Kimmy*, which was released in 2017. Nina was level designer for *Tacoma* from The Fullbright Company.

NashCo Photography

Could you give us some background on how you got started in game design?

Undergraduate studying English Literature with a focus in poetry at Pace University, NYC—this is where I got deeply involved with writing and storytelling especially in the vignette form. I was inspired by the New York School Poets of the east coast scene of the 1970s and 1980s. I found them inspiring because they focused on personal poetry, so when I was learning to write I was writing within the context of these personal vignettes. About a year after I graduated I got really sick and this led me to decide to learn how to program again. I had been hanging out with people who made videogames and watching them make games, I did not know that small groups of people (or individuals) could make games. So I suddenly had this free time due to my illness; I began to learn to code working with friends and they introduced me to indie games such as *Dys4ia* (Anna Anthropy, 2012) and *Cartlife* (Richard Hofmeier, 2011).

I started teaching myself how to program and going to game jams, and I found collaborators who wanted to work with me. I shipped a few tiny games from the game jams. I started being more serious about games so I went to graduate school at NYU in their MA in Integrated Digital Media program. It was here that I started *Cibele*, which was the first "real" game I developed. I took a variety of courses, some related to game design, but most were in related fields.

3.17
Cibele, Star Maid Games, 2015. In *Cibele* exploring the character is achieved through the player being able to explore the computer desktop of the main character. The files, audio, and video offer an insight into her relationships, personal tastes, and thoughts.

When you develop a game such as *Cibele*, what is your approach?

Another aspect of my poetry background is it taught me to be concise. I am always looking to strip away the extraneous elements and find the core of the story idea that will communicate the concepts as clearly as possible. There is no formula, framework, or ideal length of game. My approach has always been to ask myself: what are the fewest possible pieces I can use to communicate? That transfers as much to physical space, it informs the flow of a level, how elements are placed in the level and so on. For me poetry is all about details, and so is level design. As with writing, when designing a level you have to avoid just putting in "stuff" that might confuse the player or point them in the wrong direction. As a communicator, I have to be careful that I am not adding elements to the level that I understand but only I understand. The player must understand the level too, and being as concise as possible helps with that.

3.18
Cibele, Star Maid Games, 2015. *Cibele* is a game within a game. As the player, you can explore the main character's computer and then play her favorite game—*Valtameri* (an MMO)—as her avatar Cibele. The game explores an online relationship between two players and is based upon a true story.

Why did you become an indie game developer?

For me, I only really started making games properly in 2013 or 2014 and since then everything has happened so fast. I was going to grad school but working as a programmer at Kickstarter for most of that time, and even with my master's I wasn't sure I would ever find a job in the game design industry because that is so hard to do. For a time, I thought I would continue as a software developer, they are in huge demand and so I expected games to be a side enterprise. I did want to make games full-time, but I was never sure how to make that leap. Then after *Cibele* was released into the wild I met with Steve Gaynor and Karla Zimonja and they invited me into The Fullbright Company. I was lucky that I did not have to do any real job hunting, if I had I would not have discriminated against working at a large studio at all. For me, everything is a learning experience. I'm not a very experienced game designer, and I've been lucky enough to ship games that people care about. Having a mentor who is more experienced and a person I can learn from is important and would be a big part of any career decision I made.

3.19
The main character Cibele is the avatar in the fake MMO *Valtameri* (voiced in the game by Nina), which explores online relationships, vulnerability, and life experiences.

3.20
This is the avatar of the Ichi character in the *Valtameri* MMO. Ichi is the avatar of the character Blake, voiced in the game by Justin Briner.

How do you define the role of a level designer?

The only level design job I've ever had has been at Fullbright, so that's the only experience and context I can really talk about. I have found that the role of a level designer does change from game to game and from studio to studio. At Fullbright I am one of three level designers and my focus is very much on the smaller moment-to-moment elements. Steve (Gaynor) is the lead level designer so he is designing the larger story so communicates to me what the overall communication needs are for each space. So I am designing the objects and their placement as well as footprints (maps) of some levels and thinking about how those parts of the ship (*Tacoma* is set on a spaceship) work with the other areas. For example, I designed an administrative area, and I have to think about what that means within the context of the larger level narrative. An area has to feel natural but also has to conform to the pacing that's required as well as conforming to how we want the player to encounter story beats. As *Tacoma* is essentially nonlinear (even if it was linear players rarely go where you want them to so we embrace that) so I've also focused on space design, where objects belong based on what their purpose is in the story as well as designing small interactive features so that the world comes across as lived in. That comes down to thinking about what we need in the level that will make the player feel that people really lived and worked here. More importantly we have to communicate that these specific people, the characters in the game, lived here. The level design has to constantly reengage the player with the narrative being built.

3.21
Tacoma, Fullbright, 2017. This is a production image from *Tacoma*, the Fullbright game Nina worked on as a level designer. This still shows the game being developed in the Unity game engine.

Ironically, it wasn't until I became a level designer at Fullbright that I realized I had been doing level design in my own games. I just hadn't codified it in that way. So when I was making Cibele, the desktop is the main space of the game and it's set across multiple days so each day has a new "level" with a new story beat. I would change the desktop to reflect game process and time spent in the game, which was very much level design, I just hadn't viewed it with that lens. I added small details that were not directly related to the main story but helped the space become more believable to the player. That is the level design I do for the most part—making the game world seem real.

What is your approach to researching and what forms of references do you use when designing levels?

For *Cibele* it was based on a real experience I had while playing Final Fantasy Online when I was eighteen or nineteen. I've always been the type of person who archives a lot of my life and have always been into social media so there's a lot to draw from there too. So for *Cibele* I was able to dig through my own digital archive, my old hard drives and using the wayback machine website (an archived timeline of websites) as well as other ephemera I've kept. I gathered everything I thought was relevant and then compiled it all into a clearer, more concise narrative. That was very specific to *Cibele* as it was so personal. In 2017 I released *Kimmy*, which is based upon my mom's life and for that I turned on my "research fiend" self (the game is set in the late 1960s Massachusetts) and conducted really long interviews with my mom not just about the specific story but about life in that time. In *Kimmy* I focused on my mom's specific memories of the time, so I wasn't focused on a historical record but representing her experiences. I would say the research I do for my games is very human based but supplemented by me looking up brands or culture from the period.

With *Tacoma*, Steve and Karla are writing that game so they're doing all the research. That gets very deep, from reading books on astronauts and living in isolation (such as living at the Poles), to deciding where Tacoma is in relation to the moon based on space mission research.

As a level designer you have to be detail oriented, you have to be able to look at the bigger picture then zoom down into the smallest detail such as a toilet. You have to think "does this toilet look like the sort of toilet these people would use on this space station? Who made the toilet and what does it mean that this company made it?" You have to be able to think about design from a lot of perspectives and reflect on the meaning of the object or space. I have to think in layers, from the abstract down to the very practical. Details can go from "Where does this person hide their secret diary?" to how thick the moldings on a wall should look because you're on a spaceship. It's all in service of creating a believable, cohesive environment.

As a game designer what is your process of going from nothing to a finished game?

With *Cibele* I started working on it in a prototyping course at NYU. We had a week to design and prototype a game, so that's where *Cibele* began. Originally it was a short-spoken conversation that I recorded that you would hear while you (the player) were playing with a point-and-click game. I made a chat stream and text messages that would pop up while you were playing the game too. That was created in a week and became the core design for *Cibele*. I took that prototype and found a team who wanted to work with me to develop it, and it became my thesis project. We knew we wanted the game to be point-and-click as well as keeping the audio dialog and that the game had to evoke what it's like to play an MMO. Because I had so much in place already I was able to write the script for the game in three days. The script was really an outline, it had become a block to production and we were prototyping fairly quickly so we put a lot of the dialogue in as we went along. We created a lot of "findables" (photos, emails and messages etc) in the game, which I saw as an extension of the script as they flesh out the overall experience. Those elements were being added constantly to the game as we developed it.

Also, I learned a lot about programming as I was creating the game alongside my collaborators. When you're making digital games it's really helpful to at least be able to think like a programmer. Coding is a good skill to have if you're making any interactive projects. I use visual scripting a lot now and it would be a lot harder for me to understand it if I didn't know how to code already.

What would you do differently with a game like *Cibele* now?

One of the biggest take-aways I got from *Cibele* was learning to scope a project. Going into the project I had no idea what scope was or how it applied to game projects. *Cibele* took a year and a half to make and in that time, I went from incredibly ambitious ideas of having five worlds and multiple player characters you could interact and build relationships with, and soon I realized I was trying to make a simulation of an MMO rather than a game about a relationship, which is what *Cibele* is. The team floundered for the first few months trying to think about how to create this simulation that was far outside of our time, resources and knowledge. It was a side project for me and the whole team so I had to focus it into what the game is now or it would never have been made. My ambitions were narrowed because

I really wanted to make and ship a game that people would play and that focused me a lot.

Since those early issues, I've realized how important scoping a project is if you want it to get made and ship. *Cibele* taught me to think about production and not just dream away as a designer.

3.22
This is a still from one of the video sequences in Nina Freeman's *Cibele*. Nina's game mixes between video diary and interactive gameplay to weave a story about growing up and online relationships.

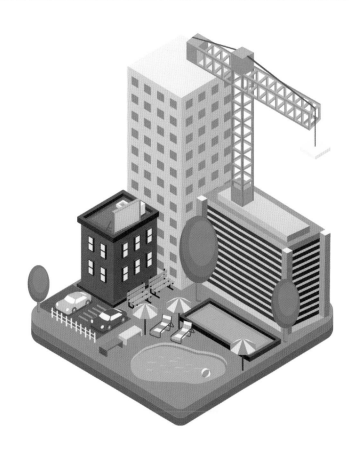

The Player: Motivations, Psychology, and Behaviors

Learning Objectives for This Chapter

1) Understand that even "simple" design decisions are complex

2) Explore how psychology is used to enhance player experience

3) Apply player psychology in level design

4.0
Horizon Zero Dawn, Guerilla Games, 2017.

In this chapter, we examine the focus of the entire game development process, the player. Knowing how the player interacts with a game, and the role of psychology, how the player can be or is motivated and which conventions best serve player needs are important. Up to this point we have examined level design from a designer's perspective: the skill sets and methodologies and their application in the development process. As the level design moves away from a mechanics-based prototype and layout into environment art and immersive aesthetics, it is important to examine the underlying motivations of the player. This chapter will begin to explore the player's mindset and look at how level design can coerce players (in a positive way) toward goals and objectives without play becoming a forced and narrow experience. We know that LDs design around an optimal path, but that is not the same as making assumptions of what an "ideal" player will do.

The Door Problem

Video games are complex systems. One approach to understanding how seemingly simple tasks become nontrivial in a video game is through what Insomniac Games' level designer Liz England describes as the "door problem": "Doors in the real world are a pretty simple premise, they open or close and can be locked and unlocked. There is visual variety, but that just about covers their use in our world."

However, when making a door in video game design it begins to look like this:

If there are doors in the game:

- Can the player open them?
- Can the player open every door in the game?
- Are some doors for decoration?
    - How does the player know the difference?
- Can doors be locked and unlocked?
    - What tells a player a door is locked and will open, as opposed to a door that they will never open?
- Does a player know how to unlock a door? Do they need a key? To hack a console? To solve a puzzle? To wait until a story moment passes?
- Are there doors that can open, but the player can never enter them?
- Where do enemies come from? Do they run in from doors? Do those doors lock afterwards?
- How does the player open a door? Do they just walk up to it and it slides open? Does it swing open? Does the player have to press a button to open it?
- Do doors lock behind the player?
- What happens if there are two players? Does it only lock after both players pass through the door?
    - What if the level is REALLY BIG and can't all exist at the same time? If one player goes through the door the floor might disappear from underneath player two.
    - Does this mean you stop one player from progressing any further until both are together in the same room?
    - Do you teleport the player that stayed behind?
- What size is the door?
- Does it have to be big enough for a player to get through?
- What about co-op players? What if player 1 is standing in the doorway—does that block player 2?
- What about allies following you? How many of them need to get through the door without getting stuck?
- What about enemies? Do mini-bosses that are larger than a person also need to fit through the door?

Someone needs to solve all of these problems and that's usually the level designer. Having a door open and close is simple enough until you realize that video game engines do not have to follow the physical rules of our world. The laws of physics have to be created and programmed, from gravity to physics and magic. When working with my students it is often this "door problem" that is the starting point for them in understanding the complexity of game design. Some of the students may simply need a door that opens when approached by a player and closes directly afterwards in a single-player game (Star Trek–style doors). That seems simple enough to implement until you break that one premise. If some doors are locked and some unlocked, how does the player know which are open? Green lights next to the door are certainly a convention on a space ship or in a modern office, but what about the medieval-styled world of the *The Witcher 3: Wild Hunt*? CD Projekt RED's solution was to use the first option—have doors open automatically when a player approaches; if the door does not open, it is inaccessible. However, *Witcher 3* is a huge open world game populated by NPCs who also go

in and out of doors. How do you prevent an NPC blocking the door to the player on entry or exit? Would it make sense to never have an NPC use a door? All of these problems need to be addressed using AI, scripts and clever workarounds.

I ran into similar door issues in my own game (image 4.1). Initially all of my doors opened both ways, but I needed to change the doors to open the same way because of some triggered events. To remedy the "step back" problem I placed an interaction trigger on the door handle and set it much further back than it would be in reality. This allows the player to open the door from a suitable distance, along with a collider that prevents the player from getting too close to the door in the first place (image 4.2). It is not the most elegant solution, but no one mentioned it as an issue during testing (testers commented on the events instead).

4.1
The green box in this image is the door handle interactive collider (an invisible box that a script knows is interactive). By having this component further from the door the player was usually best positioned to open the door and not have it collide with a door when it opens inwards. As the player approaches the door on-screen UI says "Open Door" to prompt the player's action. If the collider is actually on the door the player opens the door onto themselves which breaks immersion.

4.2
In this version the door opening is triggered by the player entering a spherical trigger. The script looks for which side of the sphere the player hits and opens the opposite way. This works well but can also be a bit jarring for the player; in this case a Victorian setting with auto-opening doors could seem incongruous, but it does solve a problem (environment is from Andrew Pray's Victorian Interiors, Unity Asset Store).

Knowing how the player thinks and building expectation on how a player might interact with a game system is important as every decision a player can make impacts the design (this depends on the game; walking simulators such as *What Remains of Edith Finch* and *Everybody's Gone to the Rapture* have reduced amounts of player freedom). Players understand their real world, but games offer a different reality. Games designers apply subtle uses of psychology to nudge the player into certain interactions.

Motivating the Player

Level designers are manipulators and I do not mean that in a bad way. This form of manipulation is in the pursuit of the most positive experience for the player. By "manipulation" I mean that the designer needs to persuade the player to go where they want them to go and perform a specific action without making the player feel that they have no choice or control over that decision. Some games offer the player no choice at all. Arcade "on-rails" shooters such as *The House of the Dead* or *Police 911* leave the player with no opportunity for movement or exploration. Although often a derogatory term, the "on-rails" shooter model has never really gone away; instead it has become

more sophisticated. In *Call of Duty: Modern Warfare 3* the designer pushes the player towards a goal with little or no option for exploration. *Call of Duty* games give the player the feeling of freedom and choice by employing some subtlety in motivating the player to progress forward in the game. For example, the level will use an NPC voice that continually urges the player to "keep moving" or "on me, up the stairs." Not much happens if the player was to just stand there, but as humans it makes us uncomfortable to ignore directions (or orders), especially in a realistic war simulation. It may not seem like much, but the psychological compulsion to stay with your team is strong and will result in players moving forward. To further motivate player movement the level designer and combat designer may use unending waves of enemies. This not only increases the tension for the player, but with limited ammunition and the reality of death from gunshots, there comes a point when standing still is not a viable option. Even having an on-screen blinking prompt that has the target or location can be enough to "bug" the player into moving towards their goal simply because it is always there reminding the player of their main mission focus (image 4.3) (this is classic UI design; it's the reason mobile phone apps tend to show unread email counts in red: it commands us to get that number down). However, not all games (or players) want mini-maps and on-screen target prompts to guide them through a game. In level design it is important that a player can use the environment to navigate without the need for UI whenever possible.

4.3
Call of Duty: Modern Warfare 3, Sledgehammer Games, 2014. On-screen interfaces guide the player through a level along with NPC shouts and environmental navigation. In *Call of Duty : Modern Warfare 3* the direct path is not shown, but the objective is persistent in the player's view. This is an extrinsic visual aid showing "Target" and "Escort." It is an overlay in the game and not part of the character's helmet visuals or part of the environment. It prevents the player from getting lost in a high-action and visually stimulating level but also reinforces the player's motivations to move toward the main goal of the level.

Speed, Pacing, and Distance

As level design has become more complex and nuanced, so too has the toolkit that level designers use in world construction, which hides the falseness of the environment. Video games, like films, have their own tropes and languages (conventions, clichés and visual shortcuts), but unlike movies the player can get lost in an open or large environment. In the real world people use a variety of visual and spatial references to avoid getting lost, or to find their way again if they do get lost. This is more difficult in a video game because those biological and psychological perceptions do not translate well onto the two-dimensional space of a screen. As an avatar in a video game the player has no proprioception, which is our brain's sense of where our body is at all times in physical space. This is part of the reason that first-person platform games are tricky to pull off: the player has no real sense of where their feet are. In third person we do not need proprioception because we can see the avatar and judge distances more easily.

Distance is another issue because video game characters do not need to perform in the same way that humans do (even if they are based upon humans). In many first-person games, players move much faster than they would be able to run or walk in real life. For example, Gordon Freeman, the protagonist in the *Half Life* games, runs at the same pace as a four-minute-mile athlete (13 mph/21 kph); Master Chief ambles at 15 mph/24 kmph and a *Quake 3* character runs at 20 mph/32 kph (Plunkett, 2015). From a level design perspective, the player will cover much greater distances in shorter time spans than we would in the real world. Designers know that if a player needs to run down the length of 5th avenue in New York City (6.2 miles/9.9 km) they want to do it in 24 minutes rather than two hours. In *Tom Clancy's The Division* the designers took great pains to faithfully recreate central Manhattan, but the game would become tedious if it took as long to run or walk between streets as it does in real life. In the game, running characters do not get tired (even when carrying a lot of equipment) and if they equip or unequip weapons they will sprint for incredibly long distances. This breaks with the "realism" of the game, but it is in service to the player who will suspend disbelief if it allows them to engage with encounters and traverse the maps faster. The LD needs to keep this in mind when allocating "time of optimal path" traversal because a player may be running for most of the level.

In first person the player will tend to be very focused on what's immediately ahead of them rather than absorbing their environment, especially if it goes past fairly quickly. Encouraging the player to walk is useful as a pacing option and it affords the player an opportunity to take in their surroundings if they want to. For Todd Howard (*Skyrim*, *Fallout*), walking is an important factor when crafting the overall open-world experience. "People will say they don't enjoy a walk from one place to another, but I don't think they know how important those few minutes of walking actually are" (Graft, 2016). Players who run through entire levels could easily miss an important item, puzzle or encounter, but it is the role of the LD to ensure that the player misses as little as possible. The player needs to know where they are going most of the time; if they do miss a critical element, they need to know that they can find their way back to it. For example, *Yakuza 0* uses the vibration in the controller along with an audio prompt to inform the player that there is something nearby worth examining. This is one instance, but there are many ways a level designer can communicate with the player using visual and psychological prompts.

Navigating without Maps

Before employing a persistent on-screen mini-map (known as an intrinsic interface) or having a map screen that players can access (an extrinsic interface) the level designer needs to consider the player who does not want to rely on any navigational aids. A player should be able to find their way through a level without any prompts. To achieve this the LD can employ a few of the techniques such as:

Curiosity. Make a world that enables curiosity and use that to steer the player (an audio prompt that leads the player to an item or a visual cue that draws them down a path).

Landmarks. We use landmarks in the real world as a method of navigation; they are useful in game worlds too (cathedrals, towers, statues) (image 4.5).

Denial and reward. The player can see the destination (a tower, mountain etc.) but the route towards it is not straight, which hides encounters and adventures (image 4.9).

Foreshadowing. Showing the player a new region, room or location in a cutscene or event (the player is able to peek through a crack in a wall and see their ultimate destination).

Lighting. Light areas equate to safety; dark areas are dangerous or impossible to navigate (also colors: darker colors in caves with lighter areas denoting a way out) (image 4.4).

Optimal path vs exploration. Show the player the most direct route to their goal, but also give them the freedom to explore appropriately.

4.4
Shadow of the Tomb Raider,
Crystal Dynamics, 2018. In this shot from *Shadow of the Tomb Raider*, it is clear to any player (even an inexperienced one) where the goal for Lara Croft is. A shaft of light (and possibly a short cutscene) is all that is required to guide the player, even though the player still has to figure out the route.

Curiosity

Todd Howard, the executive producer at Bethesda, says that the guiding principles for creating an open world game are to "build a world that piques the player's curiosity. [A world] that rewards curiosity and exploration in any way it can" (Graft, 2016). When creating *Skyrim* or the *Fallout* games, level designers and environmental artists add specific elements that draw the player deeper into the world. This could be dragons fighting in the distance or attacking an object on the ground, or it could be a small door that leads to a large underground cavern full of surprises and encounters.

The LD can also use what is known as "breadcrumbs" for the player to follow, which will lead to an encounter or exposition. Clement Menendez (*Ryse Son of Rome*, the *Max Payne Chronicles*) defines this as "influence via composition": "They are very effective at leading the player's movement in particular, almost acting as rails for him to follow. They can also lead the eye from one point to another, allowing the player to spot the most important element

and then leading him to connect that to a satellite element" (Melendez, 2017). For example, a glowing red power cable, when followed, connects to a control panel, which can be used to open a door; or perhaps an open-air duct grill emits a red or green light, inviting the player to enter it. This is using curiosity to drive the player around the level starting from the basic premise that the player knows that the space they are in is designed. As such, the player knows that there is a reason that the air duct is open or that the cable is glowing and seems to lead somewhere.

Landmarks

Model and environmental composition variety are important when creating a visually engaging level. Using the same models, colors and themes can become disorienting for the player in the same way that a hedge maze disorients a person with its monotony. As the architect of a level, the designer is looking to create models or structures that the player can use as landmarks in the environment. Some of the best examples of this come from the real-world design of the Walt Disney theme parks.

Students of Disney parks would be familiar with the term "weenie." It was coined by Walt Disney and his Imagineers to describe a structure or object that could be used to attract a visitor to an area. It serves as a navigational aid as well as a "teaser" for the content of that land. In Walt Disney World's Magic Kingdom the first weenie most visitors will see is Cinderella's castle. The castle serves as a central point in the park and can be seen from almost everywhere. It draws the visitors down Main Street into the park proper and is the main landmark of the park and serves as the hub. The Magic Kingdom employs a hub-and-spoke model of navigation, which is mirrored in games such as *The Legend of Zelda: Skyward Sword*, *Dead Space 3*, and *Alice: Madness Returns*. Other lands use weenies in the same way; Splash Mountain and Space Mountain are the weenies for their respective lands. Landmarks feel natural to players but can be expensive (in polygons) as they are unique models, so they should be used sparingly.

4.5
Uncharted 4: A Thief's End, **Naughty Dog, 2016.**
This "weenie" in *Uncharted 4: A Thief's End* is a mountain peak that serves as a destination marker and landmark, which is a continual presence in this level. The player can see the mountain from almost anywhere in the level and can orient themselves to it as well as navigate towards it. The mountain also serves as an environmental pacing element as it has presence and offers a "wow" moment, which the player is invited to observe.

Another element of visual design that the Disney and Universal theme parks use to reinforce a sense of excitement and immersion when entering a different area of the park is known as "framing." Fantasyland, Tomorrowland or the land of Jurassic Park all have clearly defined entrances. These thresholds are often open gates but serve to frame the contents of the land the visitor is going to enter. Framing gives the visitor (or in a video game, the player) a split second to pause and imagine what is ahead. The framing device also reinforces the progress of the player (if they have not been there before) and contextualizes the previous experience (entering a new space). These framing events can be designed in several ways—a large imposing entrance that is structurally different from its surroundings—or it could be achieved by using a cutscene. Other games have used "look here" button prompts that when activated control the player's camera and push their point of view towards a specific animation or building (*Gears of War* does this).

4.6
Fallout 4, **Nuka-World expansion pack, Bethesda Game studios, 2015.**
This image from the game directly parallels and parodies the Disney parks weenies and aesthetic. This familiarity helps communicate 'theme park-ness' to the player as well as giving them a destination marker.

Landmarks can be physical or geographical. Churches with spires (*Assassins' Creed*) or radio towers (*Far Cry 4*) are all large formations that orient the player. This is also possible indoors. A level designer may use a large atrium with a sculpture or fountain as a landmark within a large building (*The Last of Us*, *Fallout 4*). Because players tend to be moving fast through the game a landmark should have a strong silhouette or outline that a player can connect with at a glance. This is why towers that rise up against lower houses or structures are good visual anchors for the player.

4.7
In this image taken from my game the church is used as a navigation device for the player. The houses in this suburb are all very similar with little other than color for variation. The church is set in the center of the level, just like Cinderella's castle in the Magic Kingdom.

Unity 2018, assets from residential buildings, Gabro media.

4.8
This is the same "suburb" level but with the church in silhouette. From a distance the bell tower rises higher than any other architecture and has a strong outline. The bell tower also has the advantage of having open areas at the top, which breaks up the shape and prevents the tower from looking like a "blob" from further distances.

No Straight Paths and Maps as Reward

As explored in Chapter 2, level designers need to create an optimal path and also create exploration paths (if required by the game). Each level (or mission in an open-world game) has a clearly defined objective. As the player travels towards this place the LD will allow for breaks in the environment, which give the player options to veer off their given path. A winding road is useful because the LD can add enemy encounters, looting opportunities, and lore that are hidden from the player before they enter the environment. The downside is that it becomes easier for the player to feel or become lost. To avoid this a level designer can use subtle changes in colors, rock formations or even open spaces (a marsh or blighted field) to serve as mini-landmarks in an otherwise repetitive landscape and of course there is the use of a map or mini-map.

4.9
The Witcher III: Wild Hunt, CD Projekt Red, 2015. Signposts and distant architecture serve as useful landmarks and navigational aids in open-world games such as *Witcher 3: Wild Hunt*. As in the real world there are very few straight roads and direct routes in this game; the level designers have given the player the "trodden" more direct path option, but they can also go wherever their horse can traverse and this opens the player up to a wide variety of adventures.

Maps are another method of selling the player on the larger environment they have yet to explore and offering that exploration as a reward. In some open world games areas on the map will "open up" or become available to a player as an additional reward on completion of a mission. As a real-world analogy this makes no sense at all, but the "unlocking map" encourages the player to explore and complete tasks in discrete parts of the overall world before moving on. The extrinsic map (a screen the player has to call up using a specific button press) serves not just a navigational purpose but "teases" the rest of the world that will be available at some point to the player should they continue in the game (image 4.10). The deeper a player gets into the game the familiarity that they have with the world map is a reward, too. A map is a record of the player's progress (newly discovered areas, conquered forts, defeated enemies), and as the place names which were once unfamiliar become well known, the player will have a deeper sense of their place within the world (image 4.9). A level designer will create the map and break it up into levels, encounters and so on. The map is the bird's eye view of the world for the player; for the LD it is an intricate mechanism of multiple moving parts.

4.10
Legend of Zelda: Breath of the Wild, Nintendo, 2017. This world map view from *Legend of Zelda: Breath of the Wild* plots where the player has been and what missions or shrines they have finished. The map operates as a progress meter for the player. As the player passes through different regions the map becomes more filled out and denotes progress, as well communicating the amount of game yet to play.

Foreshadowing

Foreshadowing is used to explicitly show the player where they need to get to with a cutscene, gated objective, or a "look over there" game camera focus-point animation. It's a term used in fiction where the author will hint at a story point that will come up again later (image 4.11). In a video game the most common expression of navigational foreshadowing is a fly-through animation, which is triggered when the player enters a new environment such as a tomb or canyon. The in-game camera leaves the player's side and flies off through the level ending up at their objective, then backtracks to the player to reinforce the route. This is a useful device to ensure that the player knows exactly where they need to go to complete the level. This option should be used sparingly because it removes agency from the player and breaks the immersion. This is where communication with the LD and other members of the team is important. The LD

needs to know (or state) where intended areas of focus are, because they need to lead the player to that vantage point. If Joel and Ellie from *The Last of Us* were standing on a bridge but the focal point is obscured by a building, that is going to take some work to change.

Foreshadowing is often most used in linear narrative games, but it can be a way of ensuring the player knows their goal or objective. Another foreshadowing event can be cutscenes that show an enemy and its moves to set up expectation of how powerful they are to the player (fighting games, end-level bosses and so on).

There is a subset of navigational or narrative foreshadowing known as gated foreshadowing. This occurs when a player can see an object that is currently unobtainable, but when the player has upgraded their abilities or solved a puzzle it becomes accessible (for example, the Riddler trophies in *Batman Arkham Knight*). The player knows that this is something they will be able to get to eventually and this adds to the replay value of the level.

4.11
The Last of Us, Naughty Dog, 2013. In this in-game cut scene from *The Last of Us* (2013) the character Joel (the player) points to where they need to go (a building in the far distance). This sets the destination clearly for the player (without breaking the immersion) but is also a foreshadowing device because to get to this building in the far distance the player is going to complete encounters, combat and other cutscenes (winding path).

Lighting the Way

Lighting is important not only to add ambiance or tension to a level, but also as a navigational aid. In larger games lighting is a specialized discipline, the LD and environment artist will need to communicate where specific lights would work and their desired effect on the player. Lights can be employed to indicate a goal, a path towards an exit, or a point of interest (such as the *Shadow of the Tomb Raider* example previously). Lighting cues can be used in obvious or subtle ways depending on how much the designer wants to trust the player to figure out the connection between the lighting and their objectives. Lighting for navigation breaks down into four general use cases:

1. Exit lighting: highlighting the exit door/area for the player. This could be a consistent color or obvious to the player by having no other lit door.
2. Path highlighting: a path of torches could light the optimal path for a player, or direct their gaze towards a feature.

3. Hinting: a glinting light has become video game vernacular for a pick-up or object of interest that the player should investigate.
4. Revealing: a player could be in a dark level and find a torch and upon lighting it a precipice is revealed before them as well as a safe route to another part of the level.

These examples, if done well, should feel instinctive to the player. When testing the level its designer will take the time to examine how the lighting is guiding them in the level as well as how it is being used to manipulate player emotions (tension, relief, excitement, disgust). Level designers can rely on real world analogs as a shortcut for the player whenever possible. A red light over a door denotes a barrier to entry, a green light means the door is open. Lights can be used as a signifier that an object is interactive too. This is a convention in video games that dates back to early point-and-click games. Objects that are colored differently are interactive; this also makes sense from a usability perspective because a player may not want to try opening hundreds of chests when only three are accessible, so having specifically lit chests aids the player.

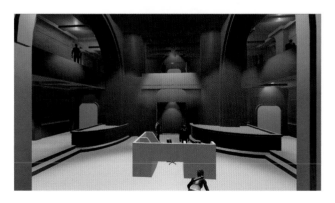

4.12
In this example (unless you are color blind) it should be obvious which door the player needs to get to. It's a mode of lighting we use in the real world and maps well into the game space in this setting. The same lighting in the level may have an action attached to it too—when the player unlocks the door the light changes from red to green and this also works as a progress guide for the player, as they'll know they have "x" number of doors to open.

Unity 2018, assets from Opsive third person controller and Republique Tech demo by Camouflaj, LLC.

Summary

Knowing what motivates a player and using visual and interactive coercion is all in the service of the experience. There is no one application of player psychology that will work every time for every player. As with real life, the designer has to paint in fairly broad strokes, knowing the most likely outcomes for most players. A level designer cannot plan for every contingency—players are always going to experiment with a game and try to "break" it by using it in unintended ways. The goal of behavioral psychology in game design is to connect the player with the game in the most intuitive way possible. The game should not get in the way of the player. By using controller and user interface (UI) conventions as well as feedback that is useful to the player, the designer can create a series of complex levels that the player does not notice are complex. To go back to Liz England's point, the player should ask "What door?"

Case Study
The *N++* Case Study: Part One (Part two of this case study is available at bloomsbury.com/level_design)

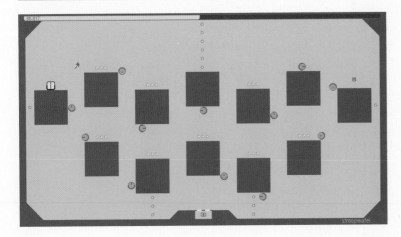

4.13
This complete level from *N++* seems simple, but from this minimal aesthetic complex game systems and game play emerge.

The Process
Our main process is iteration: just playing and adjusting the level until it feels right. We usually start with some sort of idea; we find the process influences the results. In order to naturally inspire a range of levels that are really different from each other, we try to approach level design from as many different angles as possible. Sometimes we start with an evocative level name and try to imagine what sort of level would match that name, or we draw from architecture. The exteriors and floorplans of buildings are great sources for interesting shapes. Sometimes there are happy accidents while we're working on a different level, and sometimes we just sketch with tiles until we find an interesting space to move through.

It usually takes about 15 minutes to build a rough sketch of the idea in our editor (some of the more complex levels can take a lot longer to sketch out). From there, we just try to develop it by playing it and getting a feel for the various possibilities. We may go through a variety of iterations such as:

- Swap out one enemy for another
- Adjust the tiles in an area to get rid of some awkwardness or to allow a different set of jumps
- Shift the phase/pattern of moving enemies
- Rearrange the layout of enemies
- Delete something and seeing what that changes in the level

We experiment through playing with the level to see what interesting directions there are to explore and what potentialities exist.

This process of fleshing out a rough idea typically takes another hour or so. As much time is spent playing the level and testing our changes as we put into making the edits and changes themselves. It's important to always test after making a change, because you can never perfectly predict all of the effects a particular change might make. This is like tasting your food as you're cooking.

Usually this revision is done in several shorter sessions; it can be tempting to just focus on a single level and try to crank it out all at once. We've found that it's a lot less stressful to simply play with a level, and if nothing is working, just leave it and come

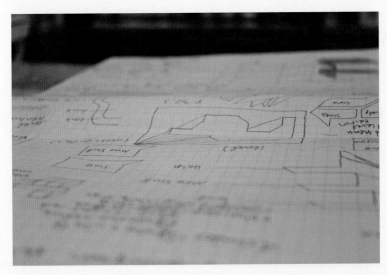

4.14
Preliminary designs begin as sketches and then move into the game engine for play testing.

back to it later. Something you learn while working on a different level might give you a new idea, or even just allowing a period of time between iterations (so that you're less familiar with the level when you return to it) can give you a new perspective. Generally we've found that performing several fast passes across all the levels is a lot better in terms of output quality than trying to get everything done in a single huge pass. You get a much better perspective when you're approaching the level across many weeks and several play sessions, and you avoid getting bored or burnt out on a particular level.

We keep a list of all the in-progress levels and iterate through this list trying to polish and refine each level until it feels "good." At this point we rate its difficulty and quality, and move it out of the in-progress list and into a "good" list; the levels in this list aren't actually finished, but their core idea/concept is solid and doesn't need more work. We then spend another hour or two developing the level: adding, removing, and moving things around in order to accommodate the multiple routes required of each level ("just beat it" vs "get all the gold" vs secret challenges). This is typically in several passes where we spend 10–20 minutes on each level, playing around with it to see what ideas come up. Sometimes we end up radically changing the level from its original version, but we always maintain a history of all previous versions so that we can easily compare and

make sure we don't ruin it with too much tampering.

Finally, once we have a sufficient number of good levels, we organize them into groups of five (called "episodes") and arrange the episodes into a grid based on difficulty. We then spend even more time playtesting, to make sure that the progression from level to level and episode to episode is fun and that there is a good varied range of situations and dynamics in terms of feel/style/difficulty without any spikes that are too rough.

We're refining levels up until the very last minute. One consequence of being relaxed with the level-making process and not trying to make each level perfect all at once is that there are always lots of little things you can improve or tweak.

Our goal in N++ is to create levels that are as different from each other as possible, to ensure that playing the game is interesting and varied and to keep players engaged. We consider:

- The general difficulty of the level; the length or duration of the level
- The types of movement required by the player (vertical vs horizontal vs a mix)
- Whether there are lots of flat surfaces or mostly angled surfaces
- The types and combinations of enemies and objects in the level
- Various types of pacing (whether the level peaks at the beginning, middle, or end)
- The types of skills required on the part of the player (timing vs

reflexes vs patience vs higher-level planning)
- The types of space in the level (wide open vs narrow hallways)
- The use of space in the level (linear or there-and-back or hub-and-spoke or branching or open unstructured space)

Our favorite N++ levels incorporate balance in terms of positive and negative space (as created by the tiles or lack thereof), position and number of objects and tiles, as well as symmetry. Repetition of pattern and shape throughout a level gives it a clean and consistent look we find pleasing and which is enjoyable to move through for players.

The Tools

The tools you use to develop the game are important; they have an impact on what the project develops into. The level editor in N++ is something that hasn't changed much since the early days of N in 2004. It's simple, it's relatively easy to use, it's quick and like the game, it's minimal as well. We designed the editor to have all the features you need to make a level, and little more so there's no clutter. We've received a lot of feedback that the editor in the N series is one of the best ever created. There's no way it would be as good if we'd used a third-party tool that wasn't built for this purpose, as it would simply be too much of a drag on our work. Having an editor that does exactly what we need it to do, as simply and quickly as possible, has been a huge boon for our productivity and creativity.

It's hard to understate the importance of good tools.

That ease of use has a big influence on our levels too, it lets you make levels without having to think about how to use the tool first. It's very easy to create and immediately test, and the process is very fluid. It would take longer to sketch a level idea out on paper than to just build it in the editor, and this way we immediately have something we can play and evaluate.

Testing

We create a lot of levels and each level takes, from start to finish, about 3–4 hours of work. After we build the first drafts, we play each level dozens of times, tweaking, refining and polishing many aspects of the design individually and then as a whole in the episode format. We need to ensure that they play smoothly, that each entity and tile is placed carefully and that there are a variety of possible solutions that accommodate a variety of players. There's a best position for everything in each level, and we keep testing and tweaking until we find it. N++ is a game that lives or dies by the quality of its levels, so testing is where the bulk of our work goes. We put in an arguably insane amount of effort to the levels, arriving at 2360 hand-crafted, precisely tuned and lovingly polished levels.

For the second part of this case study, visit bloomsbury .com/level_design

4.15
Wireframes of the *N++* user interface, which not only show how the interface works but also how the game engine is giving feedback to the player and the developer.

The Anatomy of Level Design

Learning Objectives for This Chapter:

1) Approaches in analyzing and deconstructing level design

2) Planning and prototyping a level

3) Addressing pacing and story beats

5.0
Assassin's Creed Odyssey, Ubisoft, 2018.

Now that we have established part of what motivates a player and how psychology can nudge players we will revisit what it takes to move from level design concept to prototype. As explained in Chapter 2, we know about the principles of level design. We also know to ask questions of the game designers when thinking about constraints, player flow and objectives. This chapter will examine the process of converting those early concepts into a working game. In the preproduction process key art is agreed-upon artwork that signifies the essence of the game (image 5.1). For example, with *Skyrim* it's a medieval/Viking-style warrior on top of a snowy mountain with dragons in the distance and in *Halo 5* it's Master Chief facing off with Spartan Locke. The concept art will have established a look and feel so the tone and environment will be understood by the team. Now it is the level designer's task look at those objectives, narrative elements and design overview and convert those into levels or missions.

Breaking Down a Level's Design

One approach to learning about any complex product or theory is to deconstruct it. When designing any level, even with an idea of the overall game there is a fundamental question to ask the game designer: "What are this level's requirements?" This chapter will examine how to plan a level and define the level's function within the larger game by breaking it down into its constituent parts based on the requirements of the game design. Once those needs have been addressed a level designer can add in other content or suggest other assets that will add to the experience for the player.

Using an example from a 3D action game this question could be answered in four parts:

1. The script (what story is being told in this level based upon fantasy being fulfilled?)
2. Dominant feature(s) (what is in the player's eye line, what needs to be discovered?)
3. Objectives (what are the goals, rewards, and mission needs?)
4. Build around points 2 and 3 (reiteration, honing the level, remain focused.)

(Marinello, 2014)

5.1
Halo 5, Microsoft, 2015, Used with permission from Microsoft. An example of key art from *Halo 5 Guardians*. This artwork establishes and summarizes the essence of the game, in this case the antagonism between the two playable characters, Locke and Master Chief and in the background the imminent alien threat.

These are common level design elements but as Seth Marinello (a level designer for Visceral Games) summarizes, these elements only cover the high-level concepts of good content creation;

they do not help a designer get started on making a level in real terms. The structure is too broad and vague. To answer this Marinello redefined the four-part structure in order to make it more relevant to a level designer and created his "six pillars of level design" which are more specific than the 10 Principles of Good Level Design in Chapter 2:

1. Define the primary constraints.

    These are the technical and physical constraints of the game. Defining the primary constraints informs the scope of the overall content of the level. As an example, a level may have a time constraint—players are expected to spend an hour, or three minutes, in the level (image 5.2). Knowing this, the level design will create a level to support that (smaller or larger, complex or simple). There could be a narrative constraint where characters have to meet at a predetermined location in order to move the narrative forward, which is triggered by a player's actions (for example opening a door triggers a cutscene).

    A less obvious constraint could be the number of players. Single-player campaigns or multiplayer modes work very differently even from within the same game. Solo campaigns tend to focus on narrative, exploration, character building or role play and multiplayer games tend to focus on the combat aspects. When designing a level, it may have to work for both modes (the *Gears of War*, *Mass Effect,* and *Uncharted* series do this). The game mechanic is also a form of constraint because the physics of the game dictates what is accessible and possible for the player (e.g. Can the player fly? Can the player jump? Is the environment destructible?).

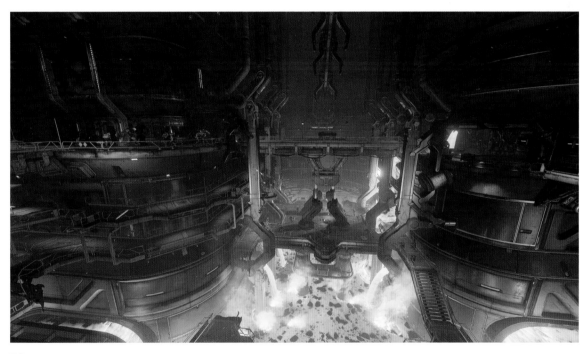

5.2
Doom, Bethesda Softworks, 2016. The foundry in *Doom* is a throwback to early level design. Although it is large the area the player can access is relatively small (a constraint). The design goal of the level is for the player to move quickly, not spend time exploring. Every enemy, health pack or power-up is more or less in the direct (critical) path of the player, leading them on to the next objective. Any deviation from that path by the player would slow the pace of the level.

2. Define and agree on each level's content.

    Which game elements have to be in every level? Which game elements do not need to be in every level? It could be that every level must contain a clearly defined start and end point (e.g. the flagpole in *Mario* games). Or if the game is combat-oriented there would have to be enemies to fight. In most action games there is a balance between combat and puzzles or narrative exposition. For example, in *The Last of Us* and *Shadow of the Tomb Raider* there are several parts of levels that contained puzzle-like elements, exposition and no enemies (image 5.3).

5.3
Shadow of the Tomb Raider, Square-Enix, 2018. In *Shadow of the Tomb Raider* (as in all the *Raider* games) the player as Lara is faced with enemies as well as physical challenges and puzzles. In this image Lara has to find the correct order of alignment of ropes and wheels to open a door that allows passage to the rest of the level. This is a unique element to this level and has to be designed to make sense within the context of the other elements of the level as well as the overall game.

A level designer needs to be aware of the level content as well as the environment because although the architecture may be designed first (based upon the concept or key art) the must-have elements should be prototyped at the same time. This enables the level designer to create with the player in mind. When designing a first-person game, health packs or ammo drops can be placed in the level early so that testers can get a feel for the pacing of the level (fewer health packs adds tension to the game, or placing enemies in front of much-needed health packs adds strategy). As the game develops, elements can be moved or removed. For example, knowing that there is going to be an aircraft hangar (because the narrative has the players escaping on a plane) level with ten enemies, some cover points, and four health packs is a very tangible place from which to begin the design (image 5.4).

5.4
The Last of Us, Naughty Dog, 2013. Setting out the cover points early on (the LD working with the combat designer) informs the pacing and layout of the level. In *The Last of Us* the levels were linear with limited exploration. This constraint focuses the player into each combat area. The LD would need to know specifics such as if there is one-button "move to next cover" mechanic because then the spacing between objects has to be precise. The LD will also be looking to add enticements for the player to move forward, placing ammo or health packs further into the level, while looking to funnel the player using obstacles such as cars or buildings.

3. Create a playable blockworld.

     Once the general requirements for what's needed in the level has been agreed upon, the next move would be to create a simple version of that level to see if the ideas work. As explored in Chapter 3, using simple geometry (BSPs, etc) the LD will create a "blockworld" which involves creating the bare minimum assets in a level that can be played as a prototype for scaling and player movement. Another prototyping method is gray-boxing, which is usually one step on from blockworlds as it can include furniture, objects, static NPCs and more architectural detail.

     Blockworld levels are akin to using LEGO bricks to make a house. It is the smallest amount of detail to give the sense of a space that a character or camera can be dropped into and move through (images 5.5a & 5.5b). A blockworld will allow a level designer to know that it might not be a great level when the player has to spend minutes walking across the level to get to a switch and then walk back again to get to a door. Blockworlds begin to answer questions of scale; are the rooms too large, or too small, does the camera have enough room to move as well as the player? How high should the ledges be? and so on. These simple prototypes also begin to reflect the emotional feel of the game: lower ceilings make for a more claustrophobic feel, higher ceilings reflect a more majestic or cathedral-like space.

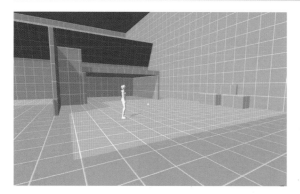
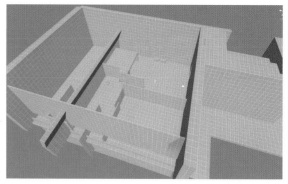

5.5a, 5.5b

Figures 5.5a and 5.5b are blockworld versions of part of a level design. This will eventually become the interior of a large mansion, but for now the LD is working on proportion and scale. There is a humanoid model in the level for scale as well as simple geometry. Figure 5.5a is the player's perspective and Figure 5.5b is the LD overview. This is the same process for outdoor environments too.

Unity 2018, assets from Opsive third person, unity standard asset pack.

4. Create level "beats."

Every level has encounters or objectives and how these are placed relies on a format known as "beats" (Rogers, 2014). In writing a film or TV show the writers use story beats to make sure that the pacing of key elements is going to work for the audience, so that they are neither overloaded or bored. A beat in a level could be that first opening scene where the player walks out of a forest and finds a castle directly in their line of sight, which will become their main objective (image 5.7). The player could then be shown the *optimal path* (most direct route that ensures the player will meet every required element in the level) by an in-game camera or animation towards that goal. Once the player begins their journey their quest is broken into beats; how soon should the player encounter an enemy or a power up? Beat one. How spaced out should the areas be that contain story items, loot, or interactive NPCs? This is beat two and so on (we examine beats and pacing a level in detail in the next chapter).

5.6

In this larger blockworld the LD has begun to pace out encounters and pick-ups. Although this is a small level the time spent in it by the player can be increased or decreased by exploration or combat. If there are more enemies, this will increase the time in the level. To increase that further the combat could become increasingly difficult. If the emphasis is on speed the ammo and health can be more accessible (critical path) and the enemies easier to deal with.

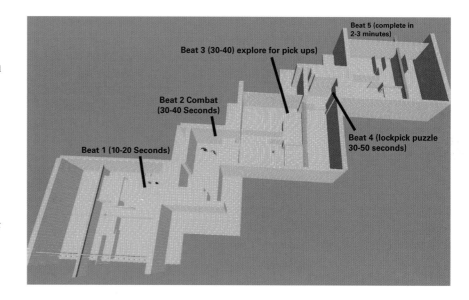

5.7
Uncharted 4: A Thief's End, Naughty Dog, 2016. Beats in a level are used for pacing out narrative, interaction, or action within a level. An example of a beat could be "this is the point in the level where we want to focus the player on a particular part of the environment because it is their next destination." In this image from *Uncharted 4: A Thief's End* the beat is used to do just that—show the player the way out and suggest a path towards it, which is used as a pacing element to break with action and give the player a problem to solve (how do I get up there?).

5. If it is not working, it has to go.

    In all design disciplines this is the hardest step. Falling in love with your design is important—it is what drives you to create it in the first place—but defending that design just because you spent time working on it can be damaging to the project. Or a director or project lead may play the level and not like it for whatever reason and you may have to justify your design choices and sometimes this discussion is a good proving ground for ideas that do, or do not, work. This is healthy and some of the best music, video games, and art have come from creative people defending their work and helping others understand why it matters (Bowen, 2010). As always it is about balance, as a designer you must remain open to the possibility that a relatively small change could define the game. For example, the original *Borderlands* title began life with a realistic aesthetic in keeping with other games of its time. As the game developed the art direction evolved to better reflect the game's quirky sense of humor and the cartoon style it has now was born out of that (Thorsen, 2010). This is where good communication within the design team and people being able to put aside egos really aids the creative process. It is also important to learn to negotiate. Rather than throwing elements away, finding a new use for them can aid the design process. That weird dip in the floor you thought you needed to get away from the boxy look was not working so instead becomes a trapdoor or part of an interesting puzzle for the player.

5.8
Borderlands, Gearbox Software, 2009. This is how *Borderlands* looked in 2008, a more gritty, realistic open-world combat game very much in keeping with the aesthetic of other shooter games of that time period but arguably lacking in personality.

5.9
Borderlands, Gearbox Software, 2009. This is *Borderlands* as released in 2009. The art style better reflects the irreverent humor, crazy names for characters and guns as well as the overall tone of the game. It also didn't look quite like any other game when it was released and subsequent sequels and spin-offs have maintained this same visual style.

These pillars are a good point of focus which offer practical advice on what needs to go into a level design. Keeping these pillars in mind will help keep you on course to creating an engaging and interesting level while being able to best communicate your concepts to the wider design team more effectively. Before going deeper into creating a level, one obvious question remains (especially if you are inexperienced): how do you know if your level design is good or not? How can you persuade your team lead or others that your level really will be engaging for a player? Having some form of analogy and data to back up your design is useful. Being able to point at inspirations and other examples of levels that do work will fortify your assertions. The only way to achieve this is through critically assessing games and being able to pick apart what makes them tick.

Analyzing a Game's Level for Pacing

A formal methodology for this approach toward a form of game analysis was suggested by Filip Coulianos, a level designer for Starbreeze Studios. Filip analyzed the games *X-Men Origins: Wolverine* and *Batman: Arkham Asylum*. In his article, Filip uses five well-known gameplay types and scenarios and logs their use as a model for pacing analysis (image 5.10).

- Puzzles: Noncombat sections where the player has to solve a logical puzzle to proceed.
- Dialogue: Noncombat sections where pieces of the story are revealed, or the player gets new weapons, tools, or resources.
- Arena: Enclosed and heavily scripted areas in which the player faces multiple enemies and/or a big boss and must kill them all to proceed.
- Roaming: Areas which the player simply travels through with enemies scattered around to keep the player somewhat on the edge.
- Vehicle ride: Areas in which the player drives or operates a vehicle.

(Coulianos, 2011)

Fillip records the occurrence of each gameplay type and time-stamps his encounters, displaying them in a color-coded chart. This is an in-depth analysis that critically and formally examines the difference between levels within the same or similar genre of game (type against type is better to analyze than putting a driving game

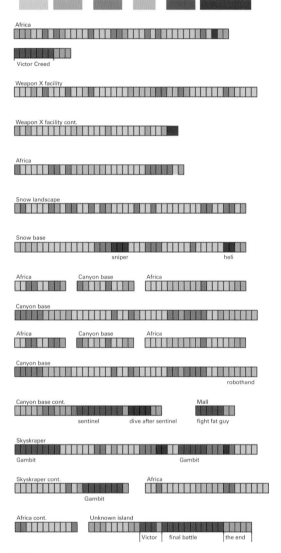

5.10

Analysis of *X-Men: The Wolverine* against *Batman: Arkham Asylum* by Filip Coulianos (2011). Both are brawler style action games, but in *X-Men Wolverine* there is a much larger focus on combat encounters and almost all of the boss fights are at the end of the game. Filip concludes that this focus on fighting becomes repetitive after a while and the game does not offer enough variation. The *Batman* game, on the other hand, varies combat against other missions and narrative.

against a platformer game). This form of analysis does go a long way towards showing that the amount of time or importance placed on aspect X over aspect Y have an impact on the player's enjoyment of the game. This form of analysis creates useful data for a level designer to be able to back up their decisions. For example, the art director may say, "We don't need to give the player freedom to roam, that distracts them from the mission" but the level designer can counter with research into successful elements of a competitor's game and argue the contrary.

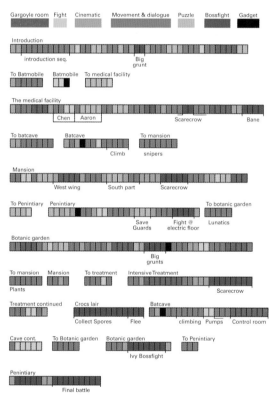

5.11
To exemplify one of the main differences between the games in Filip's map for *Batman: Arkham Asylum* there is a lot more green, which represents player roaming. The player seems to have much more freedom of movement in this game, which adds to a sense of place for the player and although there is combat, those encounters are shorter and more spaced out than in the *X-Men: Wolverine* game, which Fillip concludes to add to the critical success of the Batman game over the Wolverine one.

Filip's assessment of the data gathered from these two games is that the Batman game offers much more gameplay variance and mixes up the mechanics over those in the Wolverine game (image 5.11). He notes that although these games may have different audiences, they do share enough similarities to make a fair comparison. It is the variation, the rise and fall of the action, combat, puzzles, and roaming in *Batman* that make it the more successful game from a data-driven standpoint.

There may be people who deeply love the Wolverine game and are still playing it today. It has a metacritic.com score of 73, which is not bad by any measure whereas the *Batman: Arkham Asylum* has a score of 91. This analysis is useful to level designers because it theorizes on what could contribute to one game's level being more enjoyable for a player over another. As a caveat, it is worth mentioning that this analysis does not take into account the development time, team size, studio funding, and so on. As a level designer, "feeling" that a level is working is too subjective; you should be able to analyze and be critical of your design choices. Although part of the creative process is making judgement calls, you are always designing for the player and within the larger game. Analysis and retrospection through testing, surveys, or more formal data gathering is always recommended.

"Looking at the variation, we can see that in the chapter 'Snow Landscape' in Wolverine, the game only switches between combat and roaming back and forth, while Batman always keeps a good variation. Boss fights in Batman are also a lot more evenly spread out through the whole game, giving more interesting variation and more frequent 'wow moments' compared to Wolverine, which seems to squeeze almost all the boss fights toward the end of the game."
(Coulianos, 2011)

Level Design Models

As the analysis and research bring in tangible feedback on what designs work within the genre of the game being made, the next question to ask is, "What type of level design is best for our game?" As game genres have grown, so have level design models. Some games stick to the same model throughout while others combine them dependent upon the needs of the game. In the second part of this chapter we will explore the most popular models of level design.

The Linear Model

Linear level design is the singular path through a level from A to B to C (image 5.12). This style of level design is still common in 3D and 2D video games, from the *Gears of War* franchise to the *Uncharted* series (image 5.13), *The Last of Us, Little Big Planet,* and *Inside*. The player is essentially moving along one axis; either the Z axis (forward into the game) or the X axis (moving to the right on one plane). Although this may change a little for variance's sake the player is moving in one direction for the vast majority of the game (Kremers, 2010). The advantage to linear levels from a designer's point of view is control. If the level designer knows that the player is going to be moving in one direction it is a lot easier to add trigger points for events, to steer the player, control what they interact with and what they see.

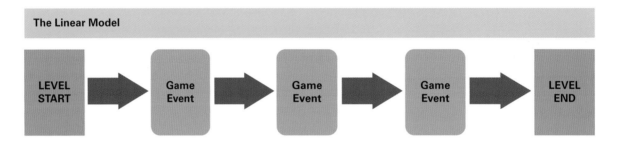

The Linear Model

LEVEL START → Game Event → Game Event → Game Event → LEVEL END

5.12
This is linear level design and often reflects not just the level but the linearity of the whole game. Many popular games use this approach—it is especially useful when a designer wants to control a narrative or path toward the end of the game. It is much easier to plan the level beats and pacing in a linear game than in a more open or multi-path game.

5.13
Uncharted 4: A Thief's End, Naughty Dog, 2016. *Uncharted 4: A Thief's End* is a linear game—the player always has one entry and one exit point. There are different traversal options in this part of the level but the player is always moving forward and the structure of the geometry supports that. The player cannot go up over the buildings or enter any of the doorways or windows.

The downside is that the player may feel those constraints, they may feel confined by the linearity and frustrated that they are unable to go off and explore on their own. These shortcomings can be overcome by good pacing in the levels and encouraging the player to choose how they move through the level (Ellis, 2016). This can be achieved using multiple approaches such as the placement of enemies, cutscenes for exposition and pacing, action sequences (for example, chase scenes), or timed events that can move the player on quickly. Action games rely on fast pacing and are well suited to linearity, but it is rare to find this model in an RPG game. A large part of what defines the RPGs is players becoming invested in exploring the world and becoming a "citizen" of it. Linear RPGs do exist, but they are rare (*Final Fantasy XIII* is one example). The advantage of using a linear style if you are working on a shooter or action game is that they have always tended to be linear so there is a built-in expectation (and probably acceptance) from the players. That is not to say these expectations cannot be challenged, but they are an established model for this type of game (Ellis, 2016).

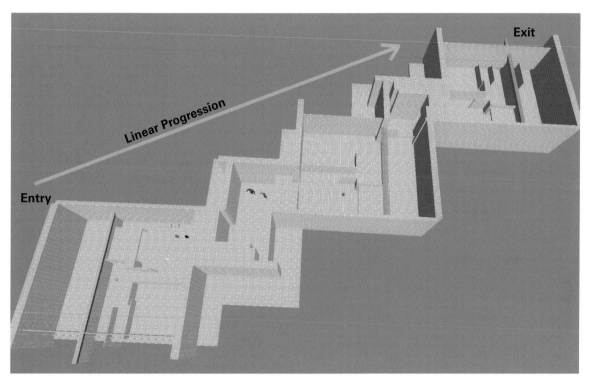

5.14
Linear progression offers little opportunity for exploration or deviation from the critical path. Most action games using this model focus on combat and narrative to engage the player. The linear model pushes the player through the level, giving it a different momentum and speed compared to other models.

The Branching or Nonlinear Model

If the game design requires a less-linear experience the level designer may consider a branching-linear approach (also known as semi-linear design) (image 5.15). In this kind of level a player may be able to branch off and explore or choose different paths towards a goal, but there are clearly defined points where those branches merge back, which then moves the gameplay forwards (Kremers, 2010).

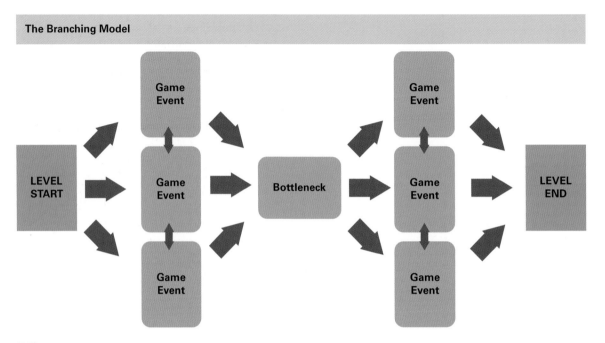

The Branching Model

5.15
This is an example of a branching design model. What the player does in the branching game events is usually interesting but minor in regard to the larger game. The events could be pickups or puzzles or discovery of the game's lore. The bottlenecks are to ensure the player receives the gameplay elements that are vital to the overall experience, such as a boss battle, major narrative exposition, being awarded specific loot, and so on.

Branching linear design can appear in a variety of combinations. It could be that in an otherwise linear level the player is given options that are nonlinear. For example, the player may be given some time to explore the environment after clearing an area of enemies or be given side missions by NPCs. In *Rise of the Tomb Raider* the game allows the player to take a direct route through the game or pick up side quests in caves that contain treasure, game lore, or interaction with NPCs. Players can spend as much time as they want exploring each level (which could be a village, military complex area, or temple) before moving on with the main quest. *Rise of the Tomb Raider* is nonlinear but also uses a hub-and-spoke model where the player can use a fast-travel mechanic to return to specific safe areas in the game world (Kang, 2016).

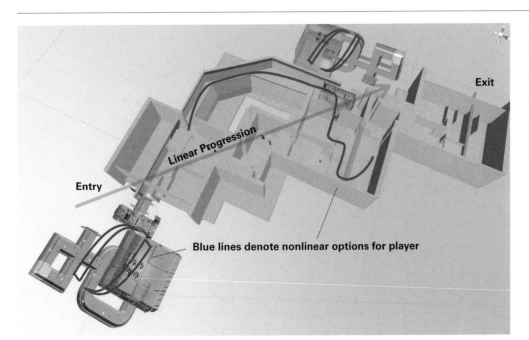

5.16
A (simple and small) example of a nonlinear level, the player can still follow the critical path but is also given options to explore. There are areas of traversal that bypass rooms entirely which could be used to strategize an ambush or could be used to draw the player towards specific narrative elements.

Unity 2018, additional asset from Modular Sci-Fi environment by Ogasoda.

The advantage to the branching-linear approach is that it offers variety to an otherwise linear game but without having to be completely open. It offers some freedom and choice for the player and allows them to feel that they have more control over their experience and can become more immersed in the environments or worlds.

The Hub-and-Spoke Model

This level design mode is most often seen in role playing games (RPGs) and action/adventure games where a player is offered mini-quests or side quests to be able to open up another part of the game. For example, in *The Talos Principle* (image 5.17) players can access a series of puzzles to solve the mystery of the game. To access each area the player has to return to a central plaza and then access one of the main buildings that houses the portals to the other puzzle areas. This is similar to hubs used in games such as *Lego The Harry Potter Years 1–4* (which uses Hogwarts as a hub) and *Psychonauts*, which has a "collective unconscious" that is used to access other levels in the game. When tailored to the game style hub games usually enable the player to choose which levels they want to attempt in whatever order they want to; if unsuccessful they can return to the hub and try a different one. Hubs can also be part of the nonlinear model; a hub does not have to be central but instead could be more of a "base" that a player can fast travel to in a larger open-world game.

5.17
The Talos Principle, Croteam, 2014. *The Talos Principle* is a puzzle game that uses the hub-and-spoke model for traversal. Each level is accessed through a building and portal and if the player cannot solve the puzzles they return to the hub and can attempt another one. There is no set order in which to complete the puzzles but each successful level completion unlocks another part of the game world.

The Open or Emergent Model

Emergent gameplay, sandbox, or open-world games fall into the nonlinear category (Kremers, 2010) (image 5.18). Emergent gameplay is best exemplified in MMOs (massively multiplayer online game), sports, fighting, or driving games. Although there is a clearly defined goal (beat the other team), getting to that goal is different almost every time the game is played. The changes come from player ability, strategy, team rosters, and even weather effects. MMOs such as *World of Warcraft* are the closest to truly nonlinear games, especially when part of the game is socializing or being in the game but not actively taking part in a quest. The disadvantage to nonlinear games from a design point of view is that they are so much harder to test because of the nature of their openness. Players will always find exploits or tunnel underneath areas they're not supposed to see, and in a linear game it is much easier to find these glitches in testing.

Emergent games are living games—rather than being a singular experience from A to B they are virtual worlds and offer deeper experiences because of the freedoms and play combinations they offer to the player. Nonlinear and emergent games can be played for months or years, giving the player an enormous return on their initial investment in the game.

5.18
The Legend of Zelda: Breath of the Wild, **Nintendo, 2017.** Nintendo's *The Legend of Zelda: Breath of the Wild* is a large open-world sandbox that has been designed for normal RPG questing but also player experimentation. The physics and mechanics of the game are such that players can find multiple approaches to problem solving (Hernandez, 2017) and this emergent gameplay adds depth to the player experience.

These are the dominant models used in level designing but multiple models can be used in a game. A game might have linear areas but also use the hub-and-spoke model (*Shadow of the Tomb Raider does* this as does *God of War* to a lesser extent). Using these models is a place to start when developing an early level. The design team will have input on the constraints that will certainly influence the type of level design being implemented. The next chapter explores the more advanced aspects of level design, including how to pitch design ideas to the team as the level increases in scope and detail.

Summary

There are no rules for design that are guaranteed to work with a wide range of people. This is true for video games. In the same way that advertising agencies spend a lot of time talking to their audiences to find out what works and what does not, as a designer it is critical to put the effort into running your concepts past the design team and others. Even then, no one really knows what will make one game successful and another one not (*I Am Bread* and *Goat Simulator* are testament to games that connected with the zeitgeist and sold very well for minimal production costs). Video games can be expensive and time consuming to make, which is why they are increasingly under analysis by their creators. Part of this process is being inspired by what has worked in other games and iterating on that (*Call of Duty* was not the first shooter-focused game but it has developed and expanded the genre considerably).

INTERVIEW: FILIP COULIANOS, LEAD LEVEL DESIGNER AT HAZELIGHT GAMES (STOCKHOLM, SWEDEN)

Filip has worked professionally in the Swedish game industry since 2010 on action and adventure games such as *Syndicate, Mirrors Edge Catalyst, Brothers: A Tale of Two Sons* and *A Way Out* on teams ranging from 10 to 120 people.

What was your route into the games industry?

I started making levels for games at around 10 years of age when I found that the level editor, then named Worldcraft, was shipped on the disc for *Half-Life*. It was during the age when the internet was still pretty young and finding information and tutorials was quite hard. I joined a Swedish online community where hobbyists would share information and feedback on how to make levels for *Half-Life* and its various mods. I became an active member releasing a series of levels and worked on different projects within the community up to the point where I went to university.

I studied 3D art at the university of Skövde (Sweden) for three years and received a bachelor's degree and ready to take on the industry I started applying for jobs, that was much easier said than done. My job search started right after the ripples of the financial crisis of 2008 had started hitting Sweden which heavily affected two out of the four big game developer companies Sweden had at the time. One company went bust and a major project was cancelled which led to quite big layoffs. This flooded the work market with very senior game developers of all disciplines making it impossible for me as a young unexperienced graduate to find a job.

I decided to continue my studies and improve my portfolio in the wait for the situation to calm down and started study at a vocational school called FutureGames Academy. During my studies there

I kept applying for jobs at all big Swedish game studios and finally managed (after applying about 10 times to the same company) to land a job at Starbreeze as a level designer a year later. Even though I had worked towards becoming a game developer my entire life, getting a foot in the door was hard back then. I realized early it wasn't good enough to just have a good portfolio, I had to be better than a senior designer to have a chance. On top of that I probably sent applications to the same studios over 10 times each (the people in human resources started remembering my name) before I got a chance to get an interview and land my first job.

Are there "golden rules" for pacing a level?

When doing my research at university I had hoped to find a "golden pattern." Perhaps unbeknownst to Valve there was a secret to their balancing between puzzles, arenas, boss-fights, pickups in *Half-Life*. I did not find such a pattern immediately, but looking through the data there was one rule that most successful games in the action adventure genre seem to follow:

Rarely does one type of gameplay work for longer than five minutes before the player starts feeling exhausted or bored. By "type of gameplay" I refer to a defined type of sequence within the game. It could be a boss-fight, a puzzle, a chase sequence or whatever type of encounters your game has.

You can play through any of your favorite games with a stopwatch and you are likely to find that your game will follow this rule more often than not. At Hazelight we live by this rule through and through. Print this out and put it over your bed!

You wrote an in-depth article on pacing a level through analysis for Gamasutra.com; is this an approach you have used in designing levels yourself? If so, could you go into some specifics?

When defining the groundwork for a title that has a serious publisher, it's common to agree on a play-time in the very early stages of signing the contract. If the title is going to be long (3+ hours) it helps to work backwards. What's the story like? Which areas, settings, types of encounters do we know are going to be in the game? We then write all this down on the paper and space it out by thinking about how many hours of gameplay content makes sense for each chapter. Once this is settled and everyone's happy with the math it's time to break it down even further.

If you're creating a level with 40 minutes of gameplay which ends with a boss-fight, and you follow the golden 5-minute rule (see above), you will need to make 35 minutes of content plus the boss-fight. 7×5 is 35 so it would make sense to start from there. How many great ideas do you have for this section right off the bat? More than 7? If so we're in a good place.

In general to simplify the pacing process we focus on high-paced sections and low paced sections, again breaking the content down into 5-minute chunks. Golden rule here; don't put two high-paced sections of five minutes right after each other. This is true for the other way around too. Don't have very slow puzzle solving without any progression or sense of achievement for longer than five minutes at a time.

What do you feel are the critical "pillars" of pacing in level design? How would they differ from an open world game to an action game?

Games are a medium where the players often expect very long play sessions and adventures that last far longer than 8 hours. This is a massive challenge. Variation, timing, and intensity are my critical pillars. Essentially, they are different tricks the designer will need to use to keep the players engaged to avoid repetition and eventually boredom.

Variation comes in making sure there enough mechanics in the game to keep it feeling fresh even if you're cycling through them at a high rate. Long gone are the days where you could just give the player a gun and still be considered a good designer.

Timing is linked to the golden rule of five minutes. Never allow a section to drag on for too long. Players are super-sensitive to timing, make sure you are too.

Intensity this adds a dimension to your already established mechanics. A car-chase and a calm drive along a beautiful boulevard are very different experiences but make use of the exact same driving mechanic.

How does player testing and feedback inform your process when designing a level?

Play testing and feedback are mostly useful to gauge where players are not able to follow the intent of the level as we have planned it out. For example: when playing through an intense part of a level we want the player to be completely focused on what's going on and not be disturbed or distracted by miscommunication between the game and the player. If there's a huge chase sequence and the player doesn't understand they need to shoot a red barrel at a critical moment and instead the player is constantly getting killed by the evil antagonist, the whole suspense of the moment falls to pieces.

If this would become a problem in several playtests the correct course of action is for us to ask ourselves questions like: Has the game informed the player that red barrels explode? When and where did the player do that earlier? Where is the player looking at the critical moment? Is the composition and focus of the scene somewhere else than on the red barrel? If the answers come up short, we know we have to make adjustments.

The Process of Level Design

Learning Objectives for This Chapter:

1) Level design as scaffold for the larger game

2) Iteration and level design

3) Making passes, procedural level design

6.0
Far Cry Arcade, Ubisoft, 2018.

At the beginning of this book it was clear that although most videogame industry people know what a level designer is in broad terms, when you get down to more specific definitions the role becomes less well defined (England, 2014). This is in part because every studio and every game is likely to use a level designer in a slightly different way. In this chapter we get deeper into the process of what a level designer's responsibilities are within the game designing process. The LD's focus is on creating the basic architecture of a level and then implementing interactions (combat, puzzles, player movement, pacing, pick-ups) (England, 2014). The LD is focused on how the layout and placement of game elements could make or break the level's impact on the player. This is the fundamental difference between level design and environmental design: a level designer focuses on creating the experience for the player from a gameplay point of view, while an environmental artist will add assets and aesthetics to a level that enhance and inform the visual and immersive experience for the player (Doetschel, 2015).

Level Designers Are Gatekeepers

Level designers are given a lot of responsibility for the game's success. At the core of their discipline is the principle that a level designer must stay true to what the game is and serve the player (Doetschel, 2015). A good LD will look to accentuate positive interactions and remove any encounters that may undermine the core of the game. In the production of a game it is possible for any member of the development team to add elements into a level that do not serve the overall game. A good level designer will act as a gatekeeper in these matters: if the feature adds value to the game it should stay,

if it does not it would get cut. Steve Lee, level designer on *Dishonored 2* and *BioShock Infinite* sums up his approach to thinking about level design by quoting from an architecture book by Matthew Frederick: "Beauty is due more to the harmonious relationships among the elements of a composition than to the elements themselves" (Lee, 2017). Lee approaches level design from the point of view that every aspect of the design, encounters, environments, and mini-games have to work in harmony to avoid pulling the player out of the experience. Inserting a questionable feature, even a small one, has a ripple effect on the overall game; this could be anything from a mini-game that breaks with the environmental aesthetic or a feature that seems out of context to the wider game (Lee, 2017).

Level design is focused on creating and maintaining the cohesion of the game not just in

6.1
Dishonored 2, **Arkane Studios, 2016.** In *Dishonored 2* there is cohesion between elements of mechanics, layout, and environment. Because the player can "warp" to higher spaces they are often looking up. The too-tall buildings in the background serve as obstacles that funnel the player towards the guards in the mid-ground. The guards on patrol will propel the player into movement (to avoid being discovered). The prominent awnings on the left of this scene offer a contrast to the flatter surfaces on the right enticing the player to move toward them. This is level design working on a variety of levels, teaching the player but also giving them options.

the individual levels but across the entire game. Steve Lee refers to this as "holistic level design" where the sum of the parts of a game (its levels) form the entirety of the experience (image 6.1). If one level is incoherently different from another, this can be jarring for the player. The same is true of transitions between levels. It can be problematic if the levels do not connect in a meaningful and cohesive manner (as is the responsibility of the LD). An example of a puzzling transition in level design is the Earthen Peak to the Iron Keep in *Dark Souls II*. On completing the Earthen Peak level the player uses an elevator to journey upwards from a maze of windmills and tunnels (which overlook the Harvest Valley) of the previous level. When the player exits the elevator they enter the grounds of a castle surrounded by moats of molten lava,

which would be sitting on top of the previous ground-based level. This odd choice of design does not break the game for the players, but it has caused head scratching on forums. The issue could have been solved by using a portal as a transition, which would have been more coherent for the player.

It could have been that the level designer just wanted to have these two cool-looking levels to connect and was not concerned about the lack of coherence, or the decision to connect the levels could have come from higher up in the design team. Either way, it is not the role of the level designer to put their personality into the game (Burgess, 2014); as with other design disciplines the work level designers undertake should be invisible to players.

The Iteration Process

When talking about level design to my students I have found it most useful to think of the process of iteration first. The level is not just a warehouse model, some enemies, some health pick-ups, and an entry and exit. To reach the point where the level works well and is enjoyable to the player takes multiple passes or iteration (Burgess, 2014). This is the same process in all design—moving from rough concept to final product takes multiple attempts whether the final product is music, a poster, or a video game. This may seem like stating the obvious, but often I find that students leave iteration behind, some tend to go with "first idea is the best idea" and never really tackle the process of iterating, changing up their concepts, and working through the problems. Sometimes this is due to time constraints and deadlines as well as pressure from other classes, but this is also where the real world meets the academic one. I can't imagine there is a designer in any discipline who thought that they had more than enough time and resources to finish their project (Sagmeister, 2016). What they do is work under pressure and iteration is a large part of that process. Look in any designer's sketchbook and you will see many steps in a process towards a final product, often with ideas being abandoned on the way (image 6.2). A video game studio (usually the game's producer) will build iteration into the timeline of the development process. It is not just preproduction but occurs all the way through until the point of a code-lock (when development has ceased and it's just testing and bug fixes). Sometimes code works and the models and animation look great ahead of time, but if planned properly the development process needs to allow time to enable the designers to find the game they want to make from within the concepts they started with.

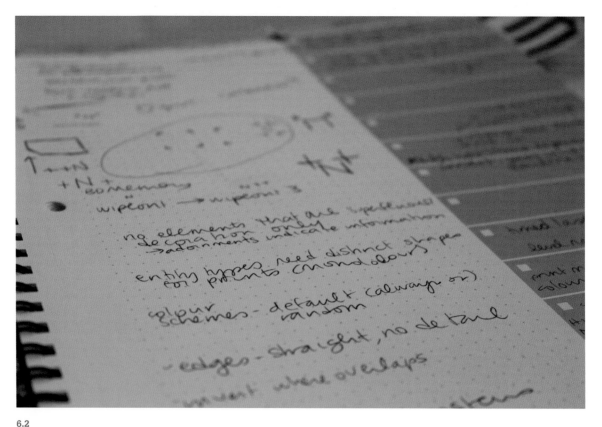

6.2

Metanet's iteration design process begins on paper. This method would be recognizable to designers working in web, UI (User Interface) and UX (User Experience) design. Paper wireframes are the fastest (and cheapest) way to iterate and because these early designs are paper, no one gets attached to them. An artist working on a character or an environment may spend many hours getting the aesthetics and proportions correct, and they are likely to fight hard for their design because it will become precious to them. Paper rough sketches and wireframes avoid that attachment.

Iteration has many benefits, as does soliciting feedback (although it can be painful at times)—it is all in service of making a better game. This is why designers and artists have critiques to offer the work up for feedback, which will inform the work or justify the design choices. Feedback can be personal and subjective, but that's part of the process of creativity. Showing work as early on as possible and inviting feedback is not just beneficial to the game but to the studio and development process (Luton, 2009). Making changes to a gray box level is much easier than a finalized level with complete assets, AI bots, and so on. Early play testing of prototypes enables for the integration of new features. As the level develops a feature can be introduced, tested, kept, or eliminated based on feedback (Baker, 2017). There are always deadlines but as with most of the design process the worst approach is a blinkered one where you just crank out level after level without garnering feedback and allowing for iteration to take place. This is especially difficult for independent developers; sometimes the teams are incredibly small, only one or two people (Metanet games for example), so they need to solicit outside feedback to maintain any sense of objectivity around their game.

The process of iteration is different at every studio depending on the culture. In 2014 at the Games Developer Conference in San Francisco, Bethesda's senior designer Joel Burgess outlined the level design process they used to create *Skyrim* and *Fallout 3*. The level design team split their development into a series of passes:

Pass 0: Pitch

Pass 1: Layout

Pass 2: Encounters

Pass 3: Core Complete

Beauty Pass

Final Pass: polish

(Burgess, 2014)

This is not a process restricted to Bethesda. The development of *We Happy Few* has been documented on Compulsion Games' blog and follows a very similar pattern. Compulsion Games is a much smaller studio than Bethesda, so they are using early access to the game (which provides playable builds to players) in order to solicit feedback from their community (Abbot, 2015). The core principle of the story-based survival roguelike has changed dramatically over the year and a half of development (the early access beta was made available in July of 2016), and there have been several changes to encounters and level design directly based upon community feedback (Abbot, 2017). Bethesda's iteration model is a solid basis from which to build a process because it is general and would scale to different sizes of games and teams.

The Pitch

Once the pitch for the game concept has been green-lit a level designer will be given a list of level requirements for the game. This could be thirty different dungeon levels, or three lava levels and five ice levels. At this point the level designer would sketch up some ideas of what the level could look like, how it could work, and what would be in it and then bring that back to the core development team for feedback. This can be short and should be focused because it is going to change over time. In order to sell the concepts of the levels they should have some form of unique selling point (USP) (Burgess, 2014). In a game such as *Skyrim* or *Fallout 3* there are a lot of levels (crypts, dungeons, buildings, subway stations) and the game is going to be played across many hours so each level needs something unique about it to make it memorable to the player. This could be the setting, the enemies, a puzzle, or an encounter that makes each level distinct (Taylor, 2013) (image 6.3).

6.3
Unravel, EA, 2016. *Unravel* has a compelling art style and each level is quite different in direction and aesthetic. The level design is based around problem solving with each level having its own novel solution that suits the style of the game play and adds depth to the game (MacDonald, 2016).

Burgess proposes that each level should also have its own story; this might not be anything the player ever sees, but it's the reason the level exists within the wider context of the game. An example of this is the inferred narrative in encounters during *Dishonored 2*. In the Dust District level, if you choose to take on the Overseer's outpost there is a small scene in which a player comes across an Overseer grieving for a fallen comrade lying on a bed. It's not important to the overall game (and could be easily missed), but it does humanize the NPCs who up until this point are seen as mindless zealots or thugs. This encounter, like a few others, informs the wider narrative of the game and its dystopian undercurrent and underlines the no-kill option that players have available to them. That is a very specific example and may not be suitable for most games, but just being able to think about "why is this here and what story does it tell?" is a useful part of the process. "Environmental storytelling is always important and making an aged leathery chair showing signs of use rather than a brand new one can contribute a lot to the mood of a scene" (Rosin, 2017).

Pass 1: Layout

Early prototyping is key; getting some form of playable content into the team's hands as quickly as possible moves the process from paper to a finished game. Some larger developers (such as Bethesda) use "kit artists" or modular design (this is addressed in detail in Chapter 7). These are designers who create simple models (usually in a 3D application such as Maya or 3d Studio Max) that can fit together easily and be used over and over again to create interesting environments (Mader, 2007). The real world uses these tools too—if you've ever seen an apartment complex being built, almost all of the components are modular; the walls are similar sizes, pipes are standard sizing and so on, and they can be oriented to create variations that differentiate them from other complexes. Kit artists will create a basic modular set of rooms or other environment assets that can be easily incorporated into the game engine by the LD using set measurement grids. These grids ensure that layouts translate and map correctly between software (from 3D application to engine). An initial layout can be completed using a modular kit (especially straightforward models such as interiors, dungeons, caves etc.) and then the level designer can start to build in unique features that allow the level to stand out (Burgess, 2014) (image 6.4).

The kits are also used for stress testing and refining the player's movement and general level layout. Even though the kits are low-poly and are not the final environment aesthetic, testing at this point in development sets a benchmark for what needs to be optimized before adding in richer textures and environmental models (Burgess, 2013). Player movement (the rhythm and flow of the level) can be locked down early on using kits. The models will change later in the game, but a corridor is a corridor and a room is a room. Working from the requirements given to the level designer, the kit layout may not change drastically as the game develops. It is the goal to add complexity to the level not to continuously rebuild it from scratch after the kit prototype has been used and iterated upon. The kit is employed to offer a playable version of the game quickly so that mechanics can be tested and the player experience begins to be mapped (Burgess, 2013).

6.4
An example of modular design using Unreal Engine 4, these hallways are created to snap together like a LEGO kit and can be used to make a playable level quickly (these model have textures and animations on them which you would not have this early in the process).

UnReal engine 4, Sci-fi Hallway asset.

Even when using kits and modular design the LD has to remember that every level is connected to every other level and is part of the larger game world. It can be a trap to think that each discrete level is its own small world (because of its uniqueness) but thinking like that can lead to a disconnect for the player. Connectivity between levels, NPCs, items, and assets must form a coherent internalized understanding of the game for the player. For example, in *Fallout 4* there were a few subway-based levels that the player had to traverse and flush out of enemies. Upon exiting a subway, the player's placement in the overworld had to make sense geographically.

Pass 2: Encounters

Once a solid layout for the levels has been established the LD will work with the programmers and kit modelers and move into testing encounter mechanics using primary enemy types and weapons (if applicable). The core mechanics of the game will be in place at this point—running, jumping inventory systems, and so on. (Burgess, 2014) The game is still rough, but it's playable and will start to get shared around the wider development team for testing and feedback. In a first person or third person action game this pass will introduce simple enemy animation and behavior routines (sometimes referred to as artificial intelligence or AI but the scope in games is too limited to be called "intelligence") such as path finding and patrolling routes (what areas the player can traverse versus areas enemies can traverse) (image 6.5), attacking, death-states, and spawn-states (the placement of enemies when entering the level and where the player character reappears when they die).

Pathing for enemies or NPCs can be created in a variety of ways; Bethesda uses their own engine's "Creation Kit" and a NavMesh editor (which Unity and Unreal Engine also have). A NavMesh is a visual representation of areas nonplayer characters can navigate (Pignole, 2015). NavMesh editors are used to draw paths onto the level that an NPC or enemy can follow and can be used to control how far an enemy can move (for example, can an enemy follow the player out of one room into another?). In addition to the enemy path finding other encounters would be added such as the barks (audio cues from enemies that alert the player to their location, such as "searching area now"—no guard would ever say this) and audio any player might need to listen to that's important for the mission; this would not be final audio and often it's the developers' own voices or sound library audio clips. This will flesh out the level as an encounter space as well as a storytelling space.

6.5

This is a very simple NavMesh working in the Unreal Engine 4; the green space is the area an AI character (the Troll) can move and act within. The player can move around outside of the NavMesh because the NavMesh is used primarily as a restriction on enemy character movement and behavior. In this case the Troll could not follow the player outside of the room it is in. The small semicircular black dots are target points. These are used to designate a path a patrolling enemy would take, or just a walking animation route so that the player could sneak past the enemy (or whatever the encounter requires).

UnReal Engine 4, assets from Infinity Blade Adversaries and Warriors packs.

Another form of encounter could be a puzzle or an NPC conversation, which would also be placed into the game in this second pass. The level designer is looking at multiple elements in the level now such as;

- Which enemies and objects need to be placed in the player's sightline (image 6.6)?
- What important elements will the player see when entering the level?
- What assets could be used to draw the player around the level and explore more (image 6.7)?

At this stage the focus for the level designer is purely on the optimal path (also known as "golden path") of the player (introduced in Chapter 4). The optimal path is the most direct path for the player from entry to exit with the required encounters in the middle. In effect, it is the ideal playthrough: there is no concern for how player X might approach the level different to player Y; that comes later in the testing process. The caveat is that all of these elements do not have to work completely, the puzzle could be as simple as "player walks onto pressure pad, door opens" and the enemy behaviors and patrols do not need to be working 100%. All of the encounter assets are to prove that the concept for the level is sound and that it fits into the overall game design.

6.6
A simplistic example of paying attention to sightlines. The LD will be looking at the level based upon the desired outcome. The game may want the player to enter the room and be surprised by the enemy, which could be a learning moment for the player, teaching them to be cautious and listen for any enemy to increase tension. Or the play style could be to wade into every room with guns blazing.

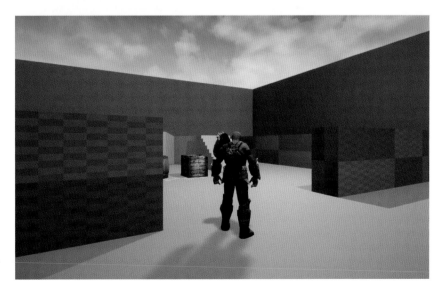

6.7
In this scenario, the LD has placed the enemy out of sight, which could lead to the player feeling that they have been ambushed. This line of sight implies that the most important object for the player is the staircase, however immediately when the player walks in they will be unprepared for combat, which may seem unfair (audio barks could alert the player to the enemy presence).

In the preproduction phase the game designers will have made decisions on what needs to be in the game beyond combat, story, and exploration. This second pass is an opportunity to invite other team members who are working on other mechanics to see how they work in the level (Burgess, 2014). This could be anything from a crafting or a cooking mechanic or other interactions such as puzzles, lock-picking, or mini-games. As much of the list as possible would go into this "what works and what does not" pass.

First Time Optimization

Pass two would also contain some optimization. If the levels are kits/modular design the polygon count should be low; what the camera "sees" and draws architecturally will be the same at low and then higher resolution with textures (walls, buildings, rooms etc.). Most AAA titles (*Fallout*, *Mass Effect*, *Gears of War* etc.) require extensive graphical power to run. Part of the LD's job is to make sure that the graphic processor (GPU) is used as efficiently as possible. A large open world or highly detailed level is going to have a lot of polygons (GPU Intensive) and animation (GPU intensive) as well as visual effects

(GPU intensive). There are many optimization techniques an LD can employ, the first one being to make sure that the 3D modelers are keeping their polygon counts as low as possible (whilst also looking good) and using occlusion culling and level of detail (LoD).

Game engines use a function called occlusion culling to optimize graphical rendering power. In essence, this means that what the camera (the player in first person games) can see is drawn, but what they cannot see (what is behind the player or beyond a door) is not. As this second pass is beginning to lock down the level layout it is a good time to optimize culling because once the art assets and "expensive" GPU–heavy models become finalized the culling will more or less be set. This means that if there are issues with frame rates or GPU overhead the LD will know it is not due to bad culling draws. Game engines have manual and automatic culling settings, but the larger the game the more this needs to be tweaked and optimized to ensure that the GPU is not being overloaded but also that the player does not accidentally get to see empty spaces that should contain models (the culling is too high) (Burgess, 2014).

6.8
This is a screen from my first-person exploration game *The Diaries of Professor Angell: Deceased*. This is the entirety of the second level, a house interior, without any occlusion culling. It is not a huge level, but there are a lot of rooms and models that tax the GPU.

6.9
This is the same level with occlusion culling on. The basic point of culling is that there is no point in showing the player what they cannot see. This is not an overly optimized scene but does convey the concept. The GPU renders what the player is looking at and then most likely to see, rather than the entire level constantly.

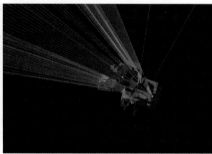

6.10
This is the same culling scene with "visibility lines" showing. A level designer can use these lines to fine tune the culling process and ensure that the GPU is only having to render what the player can see.

Another graphical optimization technique is level of detail. This works from the perspective that if a player is far away from an object it does not need to be rendered to full quality (in much the same way the objects that are far way in our world seem out of focus to our eyes). As the player approaches an object the game engine swaps out different levels of detail (which are incorporated into the model when imported) in the object so that more detail is effectively added the closer the player gets to the object. This technique is employed by the environment modeler based partly on predetermined requirements and restraints of the levels as well as the intended platform (console vs Pc, hand held vs mobile etc.). There will be back and forth between the LD and the modeler to tweak elements and get the best initial optimization pass which sets a baseline for performance early on.

  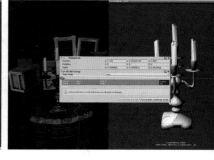

6.11
This is an example (in the Unity engine) of how level of detail (LoD) can work in a video game level. Dependent upon the game, a model could have several LoD settings from three to nine or more. In this first image the candelabra model has only three LoD levels. This is the lowest used when the player is farthest away from the object and has a polygon count of 956 vertices and 673 tris (triangles in the mesh). It is effectively a low-resolution image.

6.12
As the player gets closer (a distance determined by either a script or the LD setting it) the next LoD is triggered. In this case the count has gone up to 1395 vertices and 1119 tris (triangles). A significant jump in detail, the arms of the model are more curved and less jagged.

6.13
In this image the player would be very close to the object triggering the highest LoD. Here the model now has 2003 vertices and 1824 tris. We can also see the Unity inspector property that shows the level designer the distances at which the different LoDs are triggered. This can be set individually to every object or en masse through scripts.

Optimization is often a long process that occurs more than once as the game becomes more complex. Not every optimization problem can be solved so there are often compromises. Even AAA titles running on consoles (which have rigidly defined GPUs as opposed to PC platforms where a player can be using a graphics card that is average or incredibly powerful) still experience the phenomenon of bad draw distances (also known as "pop-in"), which is textures or LoDs visibly switching into the player's view as they approach an object. Optimization is used to decrease level load times and is a major factor in maintaining steady framerates (the more the GPU has to render the slower the game will run), which are critical for video games to run smoothly. As an example it would be painful to watch a film at a fraction of its framerate (films run at 24 frames per second or fps, games ideally run between 30 fps and 60 fps) and film is a static medium where the audience has no control over on-screen movement, unlike video games. This is part of the more technical aspect of level design, but "On some level, part of your job as an LD in this case is to help push the limits of the tech, and discover what it's capable of as well as what you would LIKE it to be capable of" (Seifart, 2013). High framerates are needed for a smooth, realistic aesthetic, and graphical fidelity. Any reduction or slow-down is very visible to the player (the game becomes "choppy"). Optimization is a large subject and it is also dependent on the format of the game being made. A low fidelity 2D game would not require LoDs and occlusion culling; the simpler graphically the game is and the more powerful the system it is going to run on, the less optimization needs to occur.

Pass 3: Core Complete

This third pass focuses on not a final, great looking level but one that is complete enough to be able to move on to a final polished state. At this point most, if not all, gameplay systems (crafting, combat, pathfinding, behaviors, puzzles, conversations, encounters, quests) are complete and most environmental art is in the level. The third pass is an opportunity to clean up anything that's been left behind from earlier passes such as temporary assets that remain in the level but now need to be updated or removed (a placeholder graphic or character) (Burgess, 2014). Third pass is also useful for making sure that all the assets and required gameplay elements that should be in the level, are in the level.

This is also the time to use feedback from early testers and the development team to tweak any elements that the level designer feels should be addressed. This can be a dangerous time for a level designer. By the third pass the LD will have been working on possibly a hundred levels across a game and there is the outside chance that the LD will revisit earlier levels and want to make significant changes in an attempt to tighten up the level or make it "perfect." As a designer, all the LD can see are the imperfections and issues, and this is where all the feedback and data is useful. A level designer may dislike an encounter or a puzzle, but if the feedback did not raise this as an issue, they know not to make changes:

"the longer you work on something [a level], the more you hate it. . .you tend to want to get rid of it. So, what you'll often end up with is something that is different, but not necessarily better. We look for trends in the feedback and reacting to those things specifically"

(Burgess 2014)

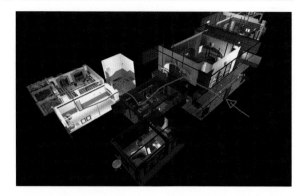

6.14
Player testing has a direct impact on level design. For example, in the third level of my *Diaries of Professor Angell: Deceased* game the interior level exits to an exterior level. As one would expect it to and when designing the placement of the exterior door I wanted the player to arrive in what would be the middle of the garden level. This would give the player an opportunity to take in most of the level at once and they would also be able to move quickly towards the puzzle areas.

6.15
However, when I created the layout of the interior the player takes a north to west path through to the garden exit. It did not occur to me that the player would actually end up at the north aspect, the rear of the house. In testing the players were confused. This was momentary and did not break the game, but a few testers mentioned it as odd and disorienting.

6.16
As part of the iterative process, the solution was to put the door where it "felt right" to the player, at the side of the house. As a level designer this somewhat spoiled the "big reveal" I had wanted, but it was more coherent for the player and made architectural sense to them so was in the final game.

Data from tester feedback is used to address specific issues raised during the game tests. It could be that eight out of 15 people felt lost in the level; how could that be addressed? Perhaps adding some signposts or on-screen prompts or making the player's position on the map clearer. It does not require rebuilding the entire level as this would take a lot of time and effort (and money).

Testing would have addressed any major mechanics issues in the second pass so this is a time for refining the levels to optimize the experience for the player as much as possible (image 6.17). Refinement depends on the game, for example in an RPG it could be tightening up some of the activities the player does to make them more meaningful or accessible (buying a house, mini quests, storing inventory items) or looking

at scenes that involve dialogue with the player. NPC and enemy behavior refinement happens in pass three too; in the previous iteration the LD may have been fine with two guards seeing the player and attacking them when they enter a room because it proves that the recognition, movement, and combat systems work. As the game has developed, custom scripts could be added to make the game seem more realistic, perhaps a guard who is asleep when the player enters a room wakes up if the player makes a noise. Or a guard could see the player and run to get help. Along with refinement to behaviors any puzzles would also move from being rough to final, they might be small in the scope of the game, but if the player cannot pick the lock to get the key they need to get a quest item, the game is essentially broken.

6.17
This is a level shown in Chapter 2; here it is more fleshed out with materials and textures. In this third pass the LD and encounter designer will be testing and tweaking player and enemy behavior. How soon do the guards spot the player? What happens if they chase the player up a ladder and fall off? What unexpected behaviors have come from the data through testing and how can those issues be addressed? Is the level too easy or too hard (based on behaviors)?

Because a video game is a system with many moving parts that all need to talk to each other, it's in this third pass that a holistic view can be taken of the game. Do all the systems work as required by the game design specification, and is there good balance between mechanics and systems? The final pass is an opportunity to reconcile the systems (lock picking, cooking, power ups, combat, player levelling etc.) and make sure that if a system was removed, its "child" attributes are removed too (for example, removing a cooking system means the mini quests to find specific ingredients need to be removed too). The feedback from play testers will make sure there's enough reason for a mechanic or system to exist in the game. Lock picking might be an interesting mini game, but is it used too little or too often? How useful a skill is it for the player to learn in the wider game and is it a good use of their time? Those questions along with performance issues and playability are addressed in this pass because at this point the game is playable from start to finish even if it is still rough in some areas.

Beauty Pass

This is not what is sounds like. This is a "final touch" process, not an opportunity for an LD to introduce new art and new content. As Burgess says, "Beauty for a game designer is not aesthetic, it's mechanical." The beauty pass addresses the question "does the game work and work solidly?" (image 6.18). This is the time to lock down as much of the game as possible for wider testing— the programmers need to know that if a tester finds a bug it's there because of a coding error not because there's a hundred new torches in the dungeon level. In previous iteration processes most of the testing will have been undertaken by the development team with a few outside testers; in this pass the testers will be from the outside, often playing the game for the first time (Collins, 1997). At this point the testers will be giving feedback to the developers and the level designer will usually work on finessing the level by looking at lighting, visual effects, and audio (no new encounters or unique visuals that might affect framerate). This pass is an opportunity to add minor art assets, usually referred to as "flavor" assets or props. These are incidental models that fill out the back story or provide the player with context on the level, from coffee cups to clip boards, logos, posters, or decals (images such as graffiti or signage that can be layered onto surfaces but require almost no graphical processing). Visual effects could include elements such as "god rays," smoke, water sprays, particle effects, electrical discharges, and so on, all of which could be refined to communicate the correct level of atmosphere in this pass (adding new particle effects is unlikely as it could have an impact on framerate) (image 6.19).

6.18
This subway level now has a functioning combat system, inventory, health, and enemy behaviors. It also has particle effects (smoke, gas, etc.) audio and flavor items such as trash, posters, and graffiti. Sound effects and animations of trains have also been added along with NPCs—all of which need to be closely monitored by the LD to check for GPU strain.

Audio is an important element which is used to sell the game's emotions and environments to the player (Bridgett, 2013). In earlier passes "place holder" audio would have been used (developers using their own voices of sound effects from libraries). Dialogue, event music (music that denotes an enemy is close by or character-specific theme music) and ambient or interactive music will have been professionally recorded and would be added into the levels at this point. The beauty pass may also include finalized sound effects on switches, hisses for the steam and anything that's required to make the level feel more real to the player. Audio and prop items are not usually the role of the level designer, it's the environmental artists and sound artists who are working on these last passes but the LD will still be keeping an eye on performance by testing the latest build of the game on the lowest playable specification of PC, or across different consoles. Once all of this has been achieved to a satisfactory standard of performance the game goes into code-lock (no new systems added or mechanics added) and gets passed onto the final polish pass.

6.19
Here the graffiti and "flavor" assets are more visible and the materials are now in place. The missing element is now lighting (this scene is too flat and lacks depth) audio and visual effects and optimization or polish.

Final Pass: Polish

In this pass the focus is on optimization. The game is complete and close to complete lockdown for shipping. All the development effort is on polishing the game as much as possible; no one is making any changes to the game (unless a critical bug is discovered). Effectively the level designer's job is done, there are no more edits or changes to make at this stage. This is a critical juncture to get as much feedback from play testers as possible. They are now playing what is effectively the final version of the game and the team is looking for game-breaking bugs and programmers are scrambling to fix as many bugs as possible (Zoss, 2009). It is incredibly hard to fix all the bugs in any game, especially games that are sixty or ninety hours long. Testers work incredibly hard to "break" games for the developers, but it is only when the game is released to thousands of players that some bugs will be discovered. That's what patches are for and this is not usually something that a level designer would be involved with.

As part of the development team every member takes on responsibility for the successes and failures of the game. No matter how great the wayfinding is or the behaviors and combat encounters, a game lives and dies on its overall performance. A great-looking game that runs sluggishly or one with a great concept that has bug-ridden mechanics will be remembered for those shortcomings not the efforts and hard work of the development team that went into creating the game. This is why the development process is so important and such incredibly hard work. The passes are an attempt to make the game as great as possible and to work through design problems before they become major issues. Instigating a process into your own workflow is a best practice that is worth adopting; even if the games you start to work on are small, you will be adopting habits and methodologies that can scale along with your ambitions.

Summary

Burgess sums up his experience in the design process as "Do the best you can, while you can" as there are diminishing returns to pursuing the creation of a perfect level. As a designer, you have to be happy that you have made the best possible product you could with the knowledge and tools you had at your disposal at that time. Every level, every game is an opportunity to learn and expand expertise. A theme that is repeated often in this book is that game design is hard, it brings together so many disciplines and is incredibly technical as well as being innovative. As a level designer you have to implement, use and trust in proven processes such as iteration and multiple passes. There is no standard practice across all game studios, but there is increasingly a common repository of knowledge and best practices (such as described in this book) that can help you become a better designer by adopting methodologies that have been proven to work across multiple games. In the next chapter there is a deeper dive into modular level design; not every game needs or benefits from this approach but it is a useful tool to know about. The chapter also addresses the role of the environment artist, a person who works closely with the level designer, as explored in this chapter. It is worth knowing what the role is and how an LD and environment artist work together to create engaging content.

INTERVIEW: STEVE LEE

Steve Lee has 10 years of level design experience in the AAA games industry, including working on *Dishonored 2* and *BioShock Infinite*. He has spent the three years since as a freelance game and level designer and occasional consultant.

Video games, like most design, is an iterative process. In your 2018 GDC talk "Creative Process for Level Designers" you use the term "design as exploration."

In the context of that talk, I describe design as exploration to emphasize the idea that design isn't something you do once at the start of the process, with the expectation that your first design will work, and be what you take to the final product. It basically never is, because there are so many moving parts and details to figure out, and so much unpredictability with how players will actually interact with it.

With experience you learn to make better initial decisions and assumptions about what a level should be, hopefully getting you off to a better start - but even then, you never know until you try things out, get people to play things, and repeatedly go back to improve it based on what you've learned along the way. It's a good instinct to respect the challenge of designing something good, and not assume that you've got it all figured out early on. Wisdom is knowing what you don't know.

You also mention your design approach of "designing vertically and horizontally"?

The idea of working vertically versus horizontally is derived from the idea of the Vertical Slice, which is a game development milestone typically marking the end of preproduction, where the team takes a small part of the game (a thin "slice", maybe a level or two), and pushes themselves to make a demo of it executed to as close to shippable quality as possible.

For level design, working vertically means focusing on a part of the level - perhaps a key gameplay sequence or area—and focusing on that to figure out exactly what it takes to do it at high quality. Working horizontally would be blocking out the entire level with basic geometry and placeholder content, so that the entire level can be tested from start the finish and being able to evaluate how everything works in context and fits together.

Crucially, this isn't a matter of which one is better—the point (in my opinion) is that it's important to alternate between the two of these modes of working. This way, you allow the two perspectives to inform each other, helping you keep an eye on all aspects of the level - quality, detail, polish (*vertical*), and composition, pacing, structure, how everything fits together and feels in the bigger picture (*horizontal*).

***Dishonored 2* has an abundance of environmental story-telling. How does this fit into and inform the level design planning process?**

It's there from the beginning in the sense that every level is set in a specific place, and you're always thinking about how to make the player feel like they're really there, and that the place has meaning.

As well as satisfying our gameplay goals, level designers should collaborate closely with artists to make believable architecture, interiors, and street layouts, so that everything fits together, and both sides are happy. And beyond that just creating fun gameplay that looks nice, both designer and artist on this kind of game have to be mutually interested in storytelling, through gameplay and art.

6.20
Dishonored 2, Arkane Studios, 2016. The level design in *Dishonored 2* goes to great lengths to empower the player to play in their own way, whether it be through stealth or combat, lethal or nonlethal. The player's choices and play style influence characters and scenes in later levels and the outcomes of the game's interactive narrative.

You worked on the Dust District level in *Dishonored 2*. What was the process for creating that level?

I was assigned to the mission (along with a level artist, Christophe Lefaure) early in the process, and after the key elements and constraints of the mission had been established by the level design leads. There was little concept art for the level, I only had some reference images gathered by the art department as a form of moodboard that outlined the level's setting.

As the level designer, the key elements and constraints are the most important thing for me to consider in our initial discussions. The main elements we had to work with were elements such as the general story behind The Dust District as a location. We also knew that this mission revolves around two factions and two targets, which is different to a typical *Dishonored* mission.

That difference brought a lot of implications and new design elements to consider in the level. Other design issues to solve were that the goal of the mission is to acquire a way into Stilton's bunker, which can be done by helping either of the factions or by solving a very difficult puzzle to skip the faction stuff entirely, which was also a big deal.

Knowing all this up front, me and Christophe talked a lot and got to work on blocking out layouts and ideas for different parts of the level from scratch. We each thought about our own creative goals, often working on each little experiment separately before showing them to each other and discussing how to find good middle ground between the two. As a level designer, I'm not focusing on matching concept art or making things look beautiful. Of course, I care about those aspects, but I trust Christophe to have that covered and fight that fight. It's my job to approach level design layout in terms of structure, the presentation of choices, and the interactive player experience.

6.21
Dishonored 2, Arkane Studios, 2016. *Dishonored 2* takes place in the fictional city of Karnaca, rendered in detail to evoke not just a sense of place, but a place that is rich with story. The team's level designers and level artists collaborate closely to make sure that gameplay, art, and narrative are all working together.

What do you see as the biggest challenges for level design in the next 5 or 10 years?

For me, specifically relative to the kind of level design that I like, I think the biggest challenge is that the AAA industry is moving away from games that have the kind of level design that I'm most passionate about: single-player first-person games, with handcrafted level design that combines rich gameplay and storytelling.

At the time of writing (end of 2018), much of the buzz, and therefore the publisher interest and funding, is in multiplayer games, open-world games, and procedurally generated roguelikes - primarily because they offer much longer, even theoretically infinite playtimes as a product, relative to the amount of time spent handcrafting levels. This business or market-driven need to maximize content and playtime from the amount of work being done makes the traditional level design of games like *Half Life 2* and even *Dishonored* seem like a poor and outdated business model, to those who are business driven. For me this is a pity, because I want more of the opposite from games. As a player I don't want to spend hundreds of hours in a game. I would rather they are richer, more authored, and more artistically interesting instead of simply offering great value for a huge amount of "content."

More optimistically, I think there will always be demand for deep, narrative-driven, single-player experiences in games. Commercially speaking these trends come and go, and I'm fine with things that I like not being the most popular things in the world.

How do you see multiplayer level design as a discipline? Is it very different from the more "handcrafted" approach to level design?

To be clear I don't want to say that multiplayer level design is any less handcrafted, just that the experiences they generate are much more about the interaction between players, than a conversation between a level designer and the players. Storytelling and world building does tend to take a backseat in multiplayer experiences, but I don't think these things have to be mutually exclusive. Games such as *Left 4 Dead* and *Portal 2* from Valve are examples of multiplayer experiences that are strong and interesting in terms of narrative and world-building.

Recent indie co-op horror game *The Blackout Club* (made by various *BioShock* and *Dishonored* alumni) is another a notable example, both of world building and storytelling elements being emphasized in a multiplayer context, and also of multiplayer gameplay not focusing on combat (it's more of a stealth game where you play as a bunch of kids uncovering weird things going on in your neighborhood). With games being such a broad and (relatively) new medium, I like to think that there is a lot of new ground still to explore, when we find the right ways to step away from traditional templates and assumptions about genre.

Modular Level Design and Environment Art

Learning Objectives for This Chapter:

1) An overview of modular level design

2) The rationale and process of using modular design

7.0
Prey, Bethesda Softworks, 2017

This chapter covers the practice of modular level design. Although not used in every game it is worth knowing about how to plan and use modular (or kit) design. It is a very useful approach, especially for new designers who may have a limited asset set and still want to create a large world for the player. This chapter also examines a complementary discipline to level design and one that is very much adjacent: the environment artist. The role of the environment artist is to not just tell the story of the world but to ensure that the player is being consistently visually reinforced as to the world's function, its history and its connection to the player

Why Use Modular?

Game development is a long and iterative process. Modularity enables expensive and time-consuming assets to be used in a variety of ways that will just "fit" into the environment without having to spend time recreating assets every time the layout changes. The advantages of modular level design are;

1. Customization: working with moveable geometry that locks together allows for easier revisions; moving a door in a modular system is a menial task compared to moving a door in a custom-modeled (and doubtless gorgeous) environment. It allows for faster iteration; a corridor might be better with a right turn rather than left and changing custom models would take a considerable amount of time.
2. Performance: being able to use a "kit" where each model is an instance of an original prefab (a corridor is the same model used 10 times) leads to lower performance hits. The game engine effectively sees one model mesh and moves that into memory; if that same asset is used multiple times the engine sees that as only a slight addition to its load. If all the assets in a level are unique that's a considerable strain on the processor as it has to keep all those pieces in memory at once.
3. Consistency: it may seem obvious but using the same models over and over will create a more uniform look and feel to the game. Of course, that can also be boring but most underground stations look the same on a single network with variations, most big cities in the US follow similar grid patterns, and skyscrapers are mostly just big rectangular slabs with varying textures and window configurations. It's the smaller details we notice and that stick with us that an art team can focus on. We're used to seeing this repetition in the real world, so we will accept it in a game world too. The same is true for the natural world in a video game; unless you're a geologist or fauna expert it's unlikely players will care about the reuse of limestone and granite models or the wrong type of ferns in a large cave system.

"Modularity allows team members to concentrate on doing what they are best at. Level designers with strong gameplay skills needn't worry about creating the loads of details required in high-end graphics. With a modular construction set they can focus on laying out the game and not get bogged down trying to create what should be considered art assets."

(Perry, 2002)

7.1, 7.2

These images are two different levels from my game *The Machine Stops*. The levels are based upon converted underground subway stations inhabited after a calamity. The change in textures and lighting give the player visual cues as to how one area differs from another even though the architecture is so similar. A sense of place is communicated through different posters and signage as well as audio cues.

Unity 2018, assets from modular sci-fi environment C by Ogasoda.

4. Mods: if your game has a modular system it's easier to create a standalone level editing tool for players to use (*Doom* and *Fallout 4* do this). This can extend the life of the game and enables players to create their own variations on a game, often for others to play, which leads to a creative and vibrant community.

The downsides are that modular construction is necessarily restrictive, and its use will depend on the type of game being made. If it's a small team and a small game every level and environment can be lovingly unique and hand crafted (depending on budget of course). A larger game may need the modularity to even be feasible to make in a realistic timeframe.

Another downside is that if applied poorly modular design can lead to "art fatigue" in the player. That is, a game with the same tunnel after tunnel and door after door (even with solid enemy or exploration mechanics) is going to become boring. In the design process this is compensated for by the introduction of unique pieces or unique rooms and different lighting and textures to break up any monotony. Adjusting scale, even if it is the same walls and doors will help too; verticality and breaking up the flow (corners, turns, looping architecture) all aid in preventing art fatigue. Reusing the same parts of

the kit in interesting ways is built into the design process (an interesting doorway can become a window or alcove) and is known as kit bashing or kit mashup. Kit bashing is a term that comes from physical model making in film. For example, when making the *Millennium Falcon* for *Star Wars* the modelers did not start with a completely unique model; much of the iconic space ship is made up of parts from other kits. "I had the idea that if I bought scrap junk airplanes I could break it down and build the sets, that was key to making the Millennium Falcon" (Guerrasio, 2018). This is where imaginative leaps from the art team and LD are important in service of the larger game. The main point of modularity is that it creates a system for designing levels.

Modular Level Design Is a System

In large open-world games (and some smaller games), modular level design is key to achieving large levels that will run on consoles as well as lower-powered PCs. An earlier term for what

LDs now call modular or procedural level design (procedural means that the levels are built on the fly by code and may be different every time the player encounters them) which is still in use is the "game kit."

Kits are a repository of environment parts from walls to stairs, doors, and windows that can be snapped together by a level designer like LEGO to create a scene or level. Many early games' level designs were essentially corridors, doors, and rooms snapped together, oriented in different ways and then dressed up slightly differently. From *Morrowind* (2002) and *Bloodrayne 2* (2004) up to *Fallout 4* a series of kit parts were used to snap to a predetermined grid in order to create a variety of levels. One of the bigger pushes towards the adoption of modular design began in 2002; Lee Perry, who was working at Epic Games at the time, published an article in *Game Developer Magazine*. He sums up the case for using modular level design with a simple series of questions that designers were asking him: "How do we quickly generate enough consistent quality content to fill a highly detailed world? How do we make sure those worlds can be easily modified and made flexible to design whims?" (Perry, 2002). Games were becoming more and more visually complex and the hardware was being released that could better realize the vision of game developers. The issue was that as a rule, level designers are not 3D artists and 3D artists are not level designers so there was a lot of back and forth between the two when creating a level. If an LD decided that a winding corridor needed to undulate more, they would have to go to the 3D artist and wait for them to create the model. Conversely (in general), 3D modelers are a product of their craft: the idea of creating a series of featureless boxes just to test the player flow is an anathema to them. They want to create amazingly realized visuals. This would be time consuming and could get in the way of rapidly prototyping a layout.

Modularity is a bridge between these disciplines. It uses a set of art assets repeatedly but with a high range of combination options. An LD can quickly sketch the layout of a level from predetermined and agreed-upon key assets. Designed properly an entire "organic-looking" city can be built up by reusing the same assets. For the LD the challenge is in connecting the mechanic and type of game with the required environment.

7.3
This is the "Ruined Building Kit" from Jason Wong (on the Unity asset store). These individual pieces can become an entire city that is much easier on the graphics processor than individually detailed unique buildings. By default Unity has a grid and snap function that can be used to align models. There are also scripts and assets available that will make the aligning process easier.

Unity 2018 assets from Ruined Building Kit by Jason Wong.

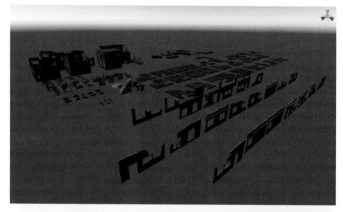

7.4
This is the same game kit in a playable first-person prototype in Unity. Players expect architecture in a ruined city to follow similar patterns and aesthetics and this expectation lends itself well to modular level design. Variation is key, as with a few musical chords making up a great song, repeating assets in an imaginative way will create an engaging level.

The examples Perry uses are that in a driving game you may use large building modules that do not need to be varied that much or deeply detailed because the player never gets close to them. In an RPG or action game a player is going to be exploring the environment up close so the level of detail of the models must be that much higher and the individual models are likely to be smaller and more intricate.

The Grid

Grids are pervasive in all design disciplines, from graphic design to architecture. The base concept for modular building is the use of a grid and a bit of math. The grid is dictated by the scale of the character, as mentioned in previous chapters. If a character is 128 units tall and 32 units wide (a standard in Unreal Engine) the grid could be in units of 128 or 256 or 64. The idea is to scale based upon a primary unit and everything flows from that measurement.

The math is important as the LD develops a footprint for each modular piece of the kit. For example a $512 \times 512 \times 512$ room will tile/snap with a $256 \times 256 \times 256$ corridor. However, if the room is $384 \times 384 \times 384$ that's not going to fit as well. That's not to say rooms can't be unique sizes; the point is to minimize their use. The kit doesn't have to fit on all axes either, as that would make for a lot of very square rooms and corridors. A corridor may only snap on two axis and a room only one but a junction may need to snap on three axes. Using grid paper to plan the individual models is a good place to start for the LD and environment artist. Even though the measurements might not convert one to one it will give the teams a good concept of how the modules will need to come together. If you've ever designed a dungeon in D&D it's a surprisingly similar process. It's also worth mentioning that not all models need to be uniform. There might be an alcove or recessed door, but that recess has to be figured into the sizing of the footprint of the model for the grid. So if a footprint for a model is $256 \times 64 \times 128$ that includes the recess or alcove.

Signing off on the measurements, footprint and axes will make the modelling and implementation of the level design that much easier. It is a constant refrain, but planning is a key component in all forms of design and given how complex video games are it's especially important.

7.5
This is an example of a modular kit on a grid that has been calculated for recessed doors. The models exist within the footprint of the space and do not overlap—or worse, exist on the same plane (co-planar). Planning in advance, knowing the units of measurement and having a solid sketch of how the models will be built are necessary for successful modular implementation.

Unity 2018, assets from modular sci-fi environment C by Ogasoda.

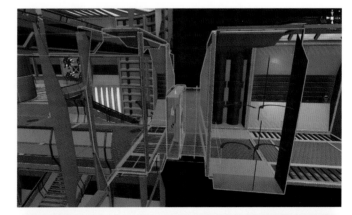

7.6
This is part of the footprint grid for this level. In this example you can see that the modeler has made room for recesses (as with the doors in Figure 7.5) so that the kit can still be built without overlapping (which leads to clipping issues as two textures vie to be seen by the player camera and will strobe).

Complexity through Simplicity

As mentioned earlier, a modular level design starts with conversations between the game's lead designer, the LD and the environment artist or modeler. Modular designs can become boring if applied in a too-uniform and unimaginative way. Most levels or areas within a level will need unique features (as discussed in Chapter 6) so the team will map out the repeatable parts as well as any unique assets (a fountain, specific building or grand architecture) and a plan for transitions between assets that make sense. The key to modular is to reuse as much as possible. This is one reason caves and corridors are so popular in games; a cave ceiling can become a floor with slightly different texture. The same is true of bulkheads inside spaceships or in underground bunkers. Variations on a central theme are important; one stairway can be resized to add visual interest and flexibility for the LD, but it will contain the same number of polygons and so is good for performance.

Planning for performance is part of the level designer's role. With modular kits early decisions can be made to set which elements inside a structure may not need to be back-facing. This is a common approach as it reduces the drawing load on the GPU. If a player never sees the other side of a hallway, why model and texture it? This again is part of the planning. Having a sketch or detailed design that shows where the player can and can't go informs these LD and the environment designer's decisions.

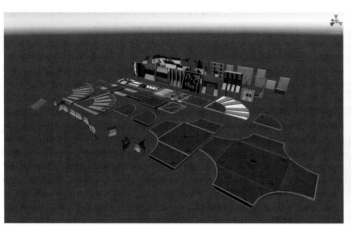

7.7
This modular sci-fi kit is another example of how a designer can build out a complex interior using a small set of well-planned models.

Kit from Ogasoda (Unity asset store)

7.8
In this prototype the models have been repeated but as this is what a player would expect from a space station or underground bunker so it does not come across as incongruous. Also note the use of one-sided models. As the player will not step outside of the interior there is no need to model or texture both sides.

In many games you can see use cases for modular systems as well as how the LD and environment artist have used elements to work around the limitations of a snap-to-grid system. This may be to make a cave read as more organic or to avoid repeating the same models too often. There's a reason so many walls that meet have a beam partitioning them or a level may have statues placed in alcoves or in transitional spaces. It's often for practical purposes, to hide seams as well as to break up the monotony of reused models (images 7.9 & 7.10). Foliage is another good way of hiding seams or breaking up the design flow. The LD will find uses for a lot of these models often in ways that were originally unintended. A doorway could become a window in another part of the level. Ductwork in one area (that hides seams) could be retextured to be a unique wall or ornamentation, and so on.

7.9, 7.10

This transitional archway model is from my game *The Diaries of Professor Angell: Deceased* and is a good example of how assets can be used to hide mismatching seams. This is especially useful when using assets where only one side is textured. As long as the asset fits into the environment in a way that makes sense, the player will never think about it.

Models from Artur G's "Abandoned Manor" Unity store asset

Stress Testing and Prototyping

As with all creative endeavors, problems are born from miscommunication. With modular design this most often occurs between the art team and the level designer. As stated throughout this book, planning and clear communication are imperative. Setting a form of standardization early on will prevent problems later in the development. For example, if every doorway is proposed to be 1.5-character widths wide this sets down a standard across the game. Once these standards have been established a kit can be created that will work as a proof of concept and the LD can work on the placement of the kit parts into the level.

This is where stress testing can begin. The LD will be looking for issues that can't be anticipated from a sketch. Ideally the kit art assets are delivered quickly in a raw form, so they can be placed and tested in-engine by the LD. Effectively the LD is putting together a jigsaw puzzle with only a rough idea of how the final level will look. The modules cannot support every use-case and the LD will not be able to anticipate every need and this is embraced as it is part of the iterative process. As an example, it may be that in a combat scenario the LD sees that it could be useful to have a player exit one door and

then run around a loop to ambush the enemies from behind. This would add to the combat depth and introduce the concept that this is a possible strategy in lieu of a frontal assault. However, when the corridor is placed the measurements are off. It would make sense to make a smaller section or "patch" corridor to make them meet, but this only works in this one instance; the modular way is that it may well be used multiple times in the game. That's a lot of patching. Early on this can be fixed by a quick remodel and made to work within the game engine (image 7.11).

Stress testing the rudimentary kit focuses on all aspects of game play, from placing out architectural elements to making sure that cover sections are the right height. The LD is making sure that player sightlines make sense and that corridors and rooms meet up among a host of other elements dependent upon the needs of the proposed level design. As the level begins to come together the LD will be able to see which modules are used the most and which parts of the kit will define the building blocks of the level. Placement also informs decisions on which pieces only need to run one way or can be connected two ways, which modules work as junctions or transitional elements and so on. Once the most practical pieces have been agreed upon, sub-kits (kits that might only occur in temples or bandit camps) can be discussed and introduced into the gray-box level. As this phase is completed the artist can start to create more detailed, texture-rich models for the level

7.11
In this example a miscalculation on sizing means that a looping corridor meets at one end but not the other. A small patch could be applied to bridge that gap, but that might be noticeable to the player and only addresses this instance. Remodeling and addressing this issue early on will fix it for the entire game.

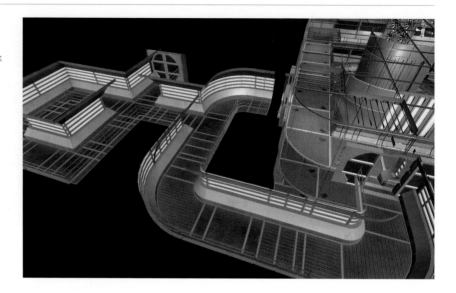

knowing precisely how the level fits together and works for the player.

Working in modular or unique game settings, the LD will be in constant communication with the environment artist in the planning phase and beyond as the game takes shape. In some smaller game companies, the level designer and environment artist are the same person, but these are most often seen as separate and individual skill sets (for example on *Tacoma* Nina Freeman was the level designer and Kate Craig was the environment artist).

Surfaces, Shaders, and Materials

An environment artist needs to understand color, interior design, architecture, landscape design, and the theories of the visual arts, but they also need to gain knowledge of lighting and the game engine's shader scripting language and process. On larger games lighting is often a specialized role but can be tackled by the environment artist too. Lighting is not just about placing lights in the game so the player can see where they are going; it is about understanding how the engine's shaders work. The unity manual defines shaders as: "small scripts that contain the mathematical calculations and algorithms for calculating the

colour of each pixel rendered, based on the lighting input and the Material configuration" (Unity, 2017).

Depending on the game engine or 3D modeling program the definitions for materials, shaders, and textures can be different. In general terms (the way they are defined in the Unity engine):

Shaders determine how the lighting system in the game visualizes the surfaces of models. A shader is a script that tells the lighting system how to represent the materials and surface of a model. For example, a textured material assigned to a car could then have a cartoon-style shader attached to it which would keep the colors and textures but ramp up the color reflection and make it much brighter than a more standard shader.

Materials are used to map colors or images onto a surface (a cube, robot, or wall, etc.) and have settings that determine how those aspects react to light in the scene.

Textures are bitmaps that usually contain normal maps and lightmaps, which allow the engine to understand how light reflects off the model. Normal maps and lightmaps add depth to a model from a flat 2D image. A surface material could be highly reflective but also have a texture that gives it a beaten or mottled look. This means that a perfect sphere could appear to be uneven or dimpled based purely on the material and texture.

7.12
This interior scene (in the Unity game engine) has materials and textures assigned to all of the models. The lighting is for an interior room with most of the light coming from outside the room. This scene uses the standard Unity shader.
Unity 2018, assets from Brian's house by Gabro media.

7.13
In this version of the same scene the only setting that has been changed is the shader. Here it is set to the *"Toon, Basic Outline"* shader. This dramatically alters the aesthetic of the models and is a good example of the effect that a shader has on the appearance of the level. Nothing else has been altered, the lighting and models are the same. Shaders are an important factor in locking down the aesthetic of the game environment and can be applied to single or multiple game assets.

Game engines have default shaders but often the game will require custom shaders to be written. This task falls on the lighting artist or the environment artist. As with all aspects of game design, the shaders are used to create the desired visual connection with the player. Although consistency is important, so is variety; a nuclear fallout–ruined environment can be contrasted against a pristine modern one for great effect (such as in *Fallout 4*). Opulent textures and models in one level can reinforce the degradation visuals in a poorer part of a level and underline the plight of the population to the player. These are all methods an environment designer can use to relate the player to the world without having to be too explicit. Working closely with the LD the environment artist will be creating the models necessary for the LD to work into the game and those which will communicate the best possible experience for the player.

Summary

As with all the principles and practices outlined in this book, the application of them depends on the game being created. One of the difficulties in defining level design and game design practices is that they evolve and have different applications within each game. Video games are experimental spaces and can use a variety of methods to express themselves to the player. The aesthetics may be rich, detailed immersive simulations of our own world or 8-bit pixelated fantasy environments that have no relation to our world at all. The amount of variance in video games far outweighs any other entertainment medium, from 2D to 3D to isometric viewpoints and games that mix between those viewpoints. Video games do need to follow a coherent visual and mechanics-based rule set to be enjoyable to play but as with music, from a few notes an almost infinite range of possibilities can be created.

INTERVIEW: PETE ELLIS, SENIOR DESIGNER

Pete Ellis is an experienced level designer who worked at Guerrilla Cambridge and now works for Naughty Dog in California, where he worked on *The Last of Us: Part 2*. He has experience working on first-person shooting games, having worked on *Killzone Mercenary* for the Playstation Vita. He was a speaker at GDC Europe 2016 where he discussed how the layout of an environment affects the difficulty of combat encounters. He has spoken at many other events, such as Eurogamer EGX 2015, as well as at many universities across the UK. He has been a mentor for student game jams, judged student game development competitions, and has also written many articles on games industry websites.

How did you get into the videogame industry?

In 2003 I went to the University of Teesside in the north of England to study for a BA (Hons) in computer games design. The course concentrated mainly on art and animation and we didn't get to experience working in an engine so I assumed I wanted to be an artist. After I graduated I had an unfocused portfolio full of all the art and animation I had done in my modules and I attempted to get a job as a 3D artist. However, I wasn't successful as I had crammed my show-reel with every piece of work I had done, rather than only including my best work, and when it comes to your portfolio 'you're only as good as your worst piece of work.'

Unsuccessful but undeterred, I went back to Teesside to do a master's in computer games art. In this course we got to use the Unreal Engine and it was then that I found what I really wanted to do was create the game experience itself: I wanted to be a level designer. I focused all my effort on creating levels and "modding" Unreal Tournament 3. After my master's I was armed with a specialized level design portfolio, and within 2 weeks of finishing university I had started at Frontier Developments as a graduate designer.

Students always ask, "How do I break into the games industry?" What advice would you give them?

To work in AAA games you have to be specialized as they have big teams, whereas for indie companies the team sizes are much smaller so

it means you'd have to have a hand in multiple disciplines. I've only worked in AAA so can only comment on this area, but to successfully break into the industry with a job at a big studio you have to specialize. A CV or resume that says, "I'm an artist and programmer' risks saying 'I'm average at both, but not great at either." At a AAA studio, you don't have job roles that cover such vastly different disciplines so you have to be specific with what you want. I learnt that the hard way by using that first show-reel. When I was applying for an environment art job I once had a response saying they had no vacancy for an animator. I hadn't applied to be an animator, but it showed me that I needed to strip everything out that was confusing for the role I had applied for.

As for advice on how to break into the industry, I'd highly recommend modding a game or creating a level in a game engine. There's the catch-22 of "needing experience to get experience," but you can gain experience of creating a working level by building one in your spare time with a free game engine like Unreal, CryEngine, or Unity. This is so you can demonstrate to a company that you are capable of creating, and most importantly finishing, a project in a similar way to how you would do it at their studio.

7.15
Killzone Shadowfall, Guerrilla Games, 2013. Level designers are always looking for opportunities to direct the player without having to use signage or in-game UI. This main building in *Killzone Shadowfall* is a good example because it stands out with its unique shape, beckoning the player towards it. It also helps the player understand where they are within the larger map as it is easy to spot as it's taller than the surroundings and is silhouetted against the sky, so it's not lost against the background.

How would you describe the role of a level designer?

A level designer is the central node between all the disciplines. You spearhead and lead the development of certain parts of the game for which you are responsible. For example, you will have a level, or levels, that you are responsible for, and you will design and craft the experience you want the player to have. This involves communication and an understanding of all disciplines, such as art, animation, programming, and audio. The level designer will create the essence of what the player experiences in the form of simplified level geometry, or "graybox," and any placeholder animations or scenarios and will extensively play test the level and iterate on it. The reason why the geometry is simplified is so that the speed of iteration is much quicker than if they had invested time in the visual assets, as well as meaning they won't get too attached to work that can potentially change.

[In AAA development] . . . it's the art team, not the level design team, who are responsible for

taking the foundation of the level (the graybox) and finalizing the visual look and aesthetics to production quality. Other departments specialize in their key areas, so by providing the animation team with a simplified version of movement you need, say a wall falling down to reveal a new route for your gameplay; they can then invest their time to make the final piece look awesome whilst you focus on other gameplay areas.

Depending on your studio you might also be tasked with working on some of the gameplay systems and mechanics. The design team creates the core of the gameplay experience in all its elements, ranging from the layout of the environment, the mechanics and actions the player gets to use, as well as the scenarios the player will find themselves challenged by. This also includes scripting any actions or events, such as combat encounters against the AI, dramatic entrances of enemies, dialogue between characters, or exotic gameplay sections with vehicles or unique abilities.

What skills do you need to become a level designer?

A level designer needs a range of skills that enable them to craft the player's experience. This includes knowing 3D modelling software, such as Maya or 3DS MAX, so that they can create the environments that are played in. Within the crafting of the environment they need to know and understand the principles of composition and architecture so that they can create believable worlds that draw the player in. They also need to know scripting, be it visual scripting with something such as Blueprints in the Unreal Development Kit (UDK), or a versatile scripting language such as LUA. This is so they can create the events of the game, ranging from things like enemy AI entering an arena and fighting the player through to setting up puzzles.

Good interpersonal skills are also important for a level designer to have as they will be communicating with each discipline. Different personality types should be dealt with accordingly and it's important to get a good working relationship with your colleagues as you want the whole team to be enthusiastic about the area of the game you're working on in order to get the best out of everyone.

How much does a level designer need to know about the technical aspects of game development such as system hardware, programming and so on?

A level designer needs to have some knowledge of each discipline, not only so they are effective communicators with those disciplines, but also so they know how they can leverage those aspects to their full potential in their designs. For example, I really like to use audio to its full potential to help highlight to the player where enemies are in the environment: are they running through water or on a different surface? Are their voices echoing inside a cave? Can the player use these audio cues to their advantage? This makes it a much richer experience for the player.

It is important for a designer to know the fundamentals of coding as they will be expected to be able to script the gameplay events, either in a scripting language such as LUA, or by using a visual scripter such as Blueprints in UDK. Different companies have different tools for this so it can vary, so having a fundamental understanding of coding will help. It is also important to know limitations of the hardware so that they can avoid highlighting them in their designs. For example, when we were developing *Killzone Mercenary*

7.16
RIGS: Mechanized Combat League, Guerilla Cambridge, 2016. Multiplayer games such as *RIGS: Mechanized Combat League* (Playstation VR) make use of boundaries that contain the action for the player and focus the conflict. The construction of physical boundaries is key in designing a level or map that defines the field of play.

on the Playstation Vita we found that the frame rate would chug if there were too many elements of alpha or transparency layered over the top of each other. This was because the rendering engine would have to do multiple draw calls per frame. One of the aspects I had to consider when creating an office space that had many windows was that there weren't any lines of sight with multiple windows overlapping each other. Without this knowledge we might have run into frame rate problems further down the line when it would have been much tougher to change the environments once they'd had a final art pass.

What is the production process for you when working on a game project?

We usually get a simple brief of what the game director wants to happen in the levels we are working on. From here we'll plan out on paper what the gameplay beats for the level will be. For example, if the brief specifies that there will be a tank battle then we'll need to figure out where we should teach the player how to use the weapons or elements they will need to defeat it. We'd then need to decide how to teach this in isolation, during a period of calm. Many designers will then plan out on paper how they want the level to be formed, but I prefer to get into a 3D modelling package as quickly as possible to start creating the space. This is because I find if you create from a 2D drawing the levels tend to end up very flat and uninteresting, whereas when you build the world from the player's perspective it can harness verticality a lot better and feel a lot more natural.

Once we've made simple grayboxes of the whole level we can test size and scale and make any adjustments we see necessary without losing too much work. It's then time to start throwing in enemies and scripting the combat encounters we want to have, as well as even prototyping any set pieces we want. When the level begins to get fleshed out we can start iterating on it with the other disciplines; the artists start to make the graybox look nice, the animators make final versions of the prototyped set pieces and the audio team setup the level to work with proper reverbs, echoes or moments of music.

Which game engines have you worked with? What was your approach to learning them?

During my professional career I've only ever used in-house engines that aren't commercially available but are specific to those companies. It doesn't really matter which engine you use as long as you know it well; it's better to know one engine in depth than multiple engines at only a shallow level. Don't spend your time trying to learn, say, CryEngine, UDK and Unity to a basic level, but instead invest more time in learning one of these to a state where you can create something quite impressive in it. Whatever engine you end up using at a game studio you'll be able to pick it up pretty quickly if you know a 3D package or a game engine really well. For example, I had never used Maya before I started at Sony, however I had used 3DS MAX for over 10 years and they are very similar programs, so when I started it was more about learning where all the buttons were rather than trying to understand how a 3D modelling package worked.

Designing Nonplayer Behaviors and Encounters

Learning Objectives for This Chapter:

1) Understand the use of artificial intelligence and behaviors in level design

2) How behavior systems have developed over time to create more realistic worlds

3) An introduction to combat design and how it affects level design.

8.0
Watchdogs 2, Ubisoft, 2016.

This chapter will examine some of the more specialized facets of level design, specifically working with nonplayer behaviors and introducing combat design. One will often see the term "artificial intelligence" being used to describe NPC behavior, or even to describe the role of an "AI Designer." However, AI is not really what is happening when a guard in a game seems to "decide" to investigate a sound made by the player throwing an object. These are scripted behaviors based upon environmental cues. The video game industry uses the term AI because it's been widely adopted by media and the public understands what the term represents (to a degree). Although increasingly there are games which go deeper into machine-learning algorithms and take onboard some of the depth of true AI research, for the most part video games use complicated scripts to imbue their characters with behaviors in service of displaying "natural behavior."

One use for AI/behavior design is in combat encounters or NPC encounters in-game. In larger studios combat and encounter designer are often roles that are separate from that of the level designer. They will work closely together but in large AAA titles there could be dozens of encounters, missions or technical issues with multiplayer that do not fall directly into the remit of the level designer role. Behavior design is usually a separate discipline as it's programming based and applied in a variety of ways throughout a game. AI development is usually separate from level design, but the systems (such as enemy combat or quest givers) are implemented into the level by the LD.

Artificial Intelligence, Bringing the World to Life (Sort Of)

True AI is used in video games such as *AlphaGO* and *Chess* to beat masters who have spent a lifetime learning their strategies. The algorithms used in those programs adapt and learn the more it plays, drawing on a huge array of moves and countermoves in milliseconds. In most video games the NPCs react to the player but along pre-scripted lines, which is why the term behavior design or algorithms is closer to what players interact with. When we think about artificial intelligence in film the AIs always seem to be smarter than humans and often homicidal

(Hal in *2001: A Space Odyssey*, Skynet in *The Terminator* franchise). AI in games, along with graphics, have come a long way, but at a basic level it consists of emulating behaviors of other players ("Bots") or objects (systems that place health packs or decide where and when enemies spawn in a level). Behavior algorithms are used in many ways but are mostly used to simulate the behavior of another player within the rules of the game's systems. The behaviors can be a set of simple rules such as "if you can see the player, track them; if they get too close, activate" (a sentry turret), or far more complex rule sets such as an enemy commander in a war simulation (track the players' moves, use game logic to strategize against those moves based upon a library of previous players).

Algorithms in video games are not the same as the AI research being undertaken in other industries and research areas, so much so that at the Game Developers' Conference talk AI programmer Alex J. Champandard said that, "the next giant leap of game AI is actually artificial intelligence" (Graft, 2015). Outside of videogames AI is being developed to learn by itself and be creative. AI researchers are attempting to create computer systems that can interact socially with humans and learn emotions or ethics. The goal of some researchers is to program a system as sophisticated as a small child. This level of sophistication is not what video games focus on—developers are not attempting to make a self-aware NPC or a sentient Orc. AI algorithms in video games are focused on the scope of the gameplay. It is there to simulate "intelligent-enough" behavior, which provides the player with a believable opponent or challenge.

Choice Architecture

To simplify the role of behavior systems in level design, most algorithms in games focus on decision making. A programmer will organize the decision process into two forms: "AI push" or an "entity pull" (Kehoe, 2015).

Push systems are most commonly used in real-time strategy games (RTS) and work outside of the game's architecture and environment. When a player is making a move (for example, moving troops to take over a village) the algorithm will spend its time calculating its best options based upon the game's rulesets (much like IBM's Watson AI playing against a human chess master). The AI will make a decision based upon the player's tactics and moves and will then tell its entities (troops, NPCs) to act accordingly, or as former *Sims 4* programmer Bruce Hill puts it: "For many games, this means the AI should behave in predictable and barely intelligent ways, like the enemies in a Mario game or most first person shooters" (Graft, 2015).

Pull systems are most commonly seen in games with simple enemies or NPCs. They may self-monitor and move based upon predetermined animations that update themselves based upon certain feedback (for example, guards who will go through a programmed routine of "stop and scratch" or "talk to another guard" then continue with their patrol route). The algorithm reacts to the player's interactions; for example, guards can move from patrol system to combat system when they spot the player and each has its own behaviors based upon the behavior system. When the guard's behavior system moves from "patrol" into "combat" the algorithm will tell the guard when to dodge, move forward or hide dependent upon those rules. An example in some first-person shooters, such as the *Gears of War* series, is that if the player stays in one place for too long the enemies will begin to throw grenades at the player to facilitate more engaged combat. The enemies have not learned this as a strategy from playing millions of hours of the game; it's a preprogrammed part of the algorithm: "if the player does X and Y is in play, do Z" and so on.

Most video game–based algorithms are not intelligence but instead are a series of rules that NPCs or entities follow. The trick is that from a relatively simple set of instructions, seemingly complex play can result. For example, a classic application of this system is *Pac-Man*. The movement of the ghosts in *Pac-Man* is based upon the concept of a target tile. The ghost knows where it is: "not on target tile," and most of the time it is trying to reach a predetermined tile from wherever it currently is.

The ghosts are given three behavioral modes: chase, scatter, or frightened.

Chase is the default mode in pursuing Pac-Man. Each ghost has a target tile they need to get to and uses Pac-Man's position as a factor in selecting the target tile so that to get to that tile they have to go through Pac-Man.

Scatter mode is instigated at the beginning of the level and is based upon a timer or is a re-spawn rule after a ghost has died. The ghosts will "scatter" towards their target tile, which are always at the furthest corners of the map.

Frightened mode is instigated when Pac-Man eats a power pill. This removes the target tile focus and gives the ghosts a simple random direction decision at every intersection they encounter.

There are some more subtle elements to the "AI" of Pac-Man, but these modes cover the majority of the ghosts' behavior. When listed out it does seem simple and one could assume the game would be easy to beat and offer little challenge. Instead, complexity arises from these simple rules because of the human interaction and decisions the player makes, which when set against the changing modes of the ghosts add almost infinite variety to the game. Experienced *Pac-Man* players found it hard to achieve very high scores when the game was released in 1980; it took nineteen years for Billy Mitchell to achieve the perfect score (Ramsey, 2015). In an ironic twist, it took a real machine learning AI system to complete the perfect game of Ms Pac-Man (which contains a more complex behavioral system) in 2017 (Liszewski, 2017).

Regardless of how simple or complex the behavior system is for the game is, the LD will integrate the systems into their level, so they must understand what it does and how it operates. *Pac-Man* is a good example of complexity from simplicity, but most open-world or larger AAA titles today use complex algorithms to make their worlds seem believable (and predictable when required) to the player. As with Liz England's door problem, the same process of "what if?" can be applied to an NPC's behavior when developing a behavior system:

Game developer: "We need an enemy that shoots at the player and then after X amount of damage dies."

AI developer: "Sure thing, just a few questions: can the enemy dodge the player's bullets? Will it look for cover? Will it hide or run away under certain conditions (if so what are they)? Can it call in aid from other NPCs? If it looks for cover how does it know where the cover is? Does the enemy track where the player is? How does it aim? Is the enemy a good shot?"

One example of these more complex systems is the use of the finite state machine (FSM) (image 8.1). They are a method of conceptualizing and implementing a behavior system attached to an NPC that has distinctive states in the game. These states are representative of the physical or emotional states that the NPC is in or can exhibit. The "emotional states" are not NPCs crying or empathizing with the player (which true AI would want to do) but instead are predetermined

behavior models that fit within the context of the level and the game: for example, a cowardly orc who runs away when the odds are against it (*Middle Earth: Shadow of Mordor*), or an inquisitive guard who will investigate a noise (*Hitman*), or an angry and aggressive elite soldier who will attack the player on sight and never back down (*Metal Gear Solid V: The Phantom Pain*).

In an article for Gamasutra.com, Donald Kehoe explains a more complex version of an AI system by applying an FSM to guards in a stealth game:

Idle. The guard is passively standing around or walking along a predetermined path. Perception/awareness of player is low. Player sounds (footsteps) are not checked for very often. If the guard is attacked by the player or the player enters their predetermined "cone of vision" the guard AI mode will switch to Aware or Aggressive state.

Aware. The guard is actively searching for the player, checking often for player sounds (footsteps, noises). The guard's "vision cone" is enhanced and can see further and wider than in the idle state. If, when moving around, the guard notices something out of place (system checks against a list of predetermined objects such as a body, an open door or object out of place) it will switch to Intrigued state.

Intrigued. The guard knows that something has occurred. To demonstrate this behavior to the player the guard will abandon its normal post or patrol path (possibly along with an audio bark) and move to the area of interest. If the guard spots a player it will move into the Alert state; if it does not it will return to Idle state.

Alert. The guard is fully aware of the player and will go through the predetermined activities of hunting down the player. This could include the guard moving towards the player to engage in combat or alerting fellow guards, sounding alarms and so on. When the guard is within a predetermined range of the player it switches to the Aggressive state. If the player escapes (moves out of sight/hides), the state will return to Intrigued and eventually Idle.

Aggressive. This is the guard's combat mode. The guard will attack the player when it can (has the ammunition and health) and will seek cover between rounds of attack (based on attack cool-downs or reloading times). The guard will leave this state if the player is killed (return to Idle state), if the player moves out of firing range (return to Alert state), or if the guard dies (go to Dead state). The AI monitors the amount of hits the guard takes and when it becomes low on health, it will switch to the Fleeing mode, depending on the courage rating of the guard (or amount of guards remaining in the level).

Fleeing. The guard will run from combat; there may be a secondary goal of restoring

health or leaving the combat area (to fight another day). When the guard finds health, it may return to the Alert mode and resume combat if the player is in pursuit. Otherwise it returns to Idle mode.

Dead. Once damage has reached beyond a certain limit the guard may just drop to the ground or it could make a noise alerting other guards, or go into an unconscious state, where it can later be revived by a medic (and returned to Alert mode).

Finite State Machine

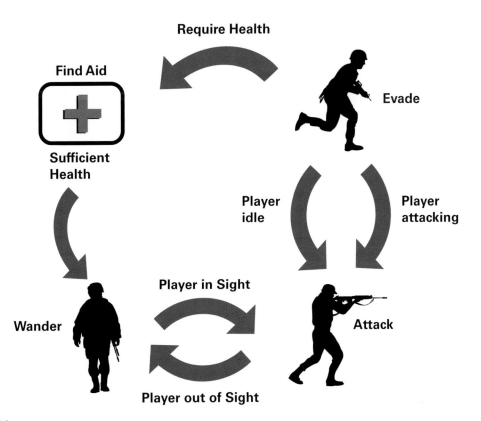

8.1
This finite state machine (FSM) describes a typical video game guard's behavior loop. Dependent upon the actions of the player the guard will move into different states before defaulting back to idle.

Predictability behaviors are ultimately unrealistic, but within the context of a game it creates achievable objectives and states for the player to overcome. If true AI was used the guards would stalk a player endlessly or call for backup and create impossible odds for the player to beat, which while more realistic would not be fun to play against. Additionally behaviors can be ramped up based upon the difficulty settings of the game. In a "veteran" mode an enemy could be more aggressive, find cover more often, or flank the player to increase the challenge. In most combat scenarios, the behavior system only needs to follow fairly basic rule sets, there are some games which do use player's moves and behavior against them to add tension or to increase the challenge (for example, some fighting games "watch" the players moves in order to better counter them) (image 8.2).

8.2

Alien: Isolation, **Creative Assembly, 2014.** In a reversal of the typical guard or NPC behaviors, the Xenomorph alien enemy in *Alien: Isolation* continuously hunts the player. More akin to the ghosts in *Pac-Man*, the alien's only goal is to get to the player and dispatch them. This makes for an intense experience as the player has no idea when the alien will appear and is not equipped to engage it in combat (unlike a regular FPS). The behavior set of the Xenomorph is always in "alert" mode and a positioning system ensures that the alien is always in close proximity to the player (often unseen).

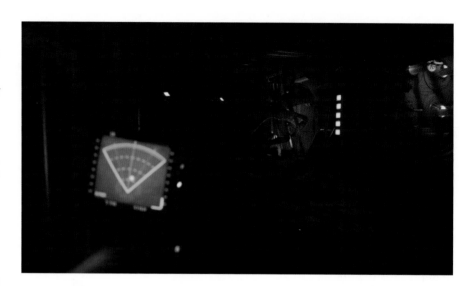

Adaptive and Predictive Systems

The FMS system works well in games that require an amount of predictability in the actions of the NPCs. A player needs to know that if they watch a guard on patrol and when they perform certain actions the guard will reliably react in the same way. This is so the player can strategize based upon those states; real-life guards would display a wide variety of unpredictable behaviors that would make a stealth game incredibly difficult. In a fighting game or an RTS game predictability would have the opposite effect. If *Street Fighter V*'s Chun-Li always performed the same moves in the same way when attacking the player, that would not be much of a fighting game. The same is true for an opposing general repeating the same tactics in *Command and Conquer: Tiberium Alliances*—predictability would ruin the experience. However, using deeper AI techniques such as "machine learning" is likely to create very unpredictable results (in the same way that humans are unpredictable). "It's not that we can't get good behavior out of machine learning techniques . . . it's that it may not be the behavior we want for the game experience we are looking for" (Graft, 2015). Instead the way that programmers approach AI to be more unpredictable is to use predictions and adaptation to add to the game's challenge. In a fighting game it is critical that the system be able to effectively anticipate the player's next move so a predictive system will use past-pattern recognition to predict a player's next move (player favors low leg sweep, use jump) and an adaptive system will alter the NPC playstyle if the player changes their style (player has switched to more punches, block more often) to determine the best action.

One algorithm used in strategy games to react to player's input is the Monte Carlo tree search (MCTS) algorithm (image 8.3). "MCTS embodies the strategy of using random trials to solve a problem. This is the AI strategy used in Deep Blue, the first computer program to defeat a human chess champion in 1997" (Lou, 2017).

This approach is for the system to track and evaluate the choices players have made in the past (remember that computers are really, really fast) against all the possible moves it and the player can make next. This creates a "tree" of possible outcomes and the system then "decides" which move or behavior is likely to have the best outcome. The next player decision is then evaluated against a set of criteria such as a previous advantage gained, or lost health based upon a series of moves, along with other

information gathered from other systems in the game (player health, moves available to the NPC, who is winning or losing). This data is then used to determine the success of previous actions and is set against an algorithm that evaluates if a change in tactics is required. The system is building a "tactics sheet" based upon the player's actions using a set of default general tactics (if player punches, NPC block) and then tries a random set of actions to see how the player will respond. In a strategy game such as *Civilization* there are so many variables that the system will choose at random a starting position and then react to the player's moves. In essence the player is playing against themselves when up against the "computer player" (using a similar system in 2008 the British Illusionist Derren Brown was able to beat ten chess masters in lightning-round games. What Derren was actually doing was mirroring the moves of a previous master on different boards; they were effectively playing each other with Derren acting as an intermediary).

Monte Carlo Search Tree

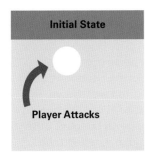

Initial State

Player Attacks

I.D. Possible Actions

Defend   **Attack**
Get Help

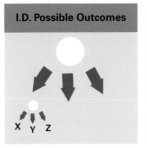

I.D. Possible Outcomes

X Y Z

Calculate Payback per Action

Payback

Hi   Lo

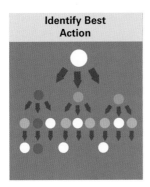

Identify Best Action

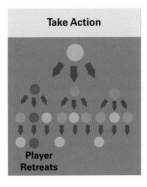

Take Action

Player Retreats

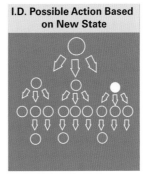

I.D. Possible Action Based on New State

8.3

This is a simplified MCTS algorithm structure, but it does demonstrate the more sophisticated decision possibilities available to the NPC or game. The advantage with this algorithm is that it can allow for "emergent" NPC behavior as each reaction could be different depending on the circumstances. The same NPC may react in entirely different ways dependent upon a multitude of factors within the current game state.

As with the ghosts in *Pac-Man* there are only so many moves available for each character in a fighting game, and although real-time strategy games can seem complex the rule set is still constrained (Chess has a strict rule set with a massive amount of possibilities, but they are finite). The video game AI system learns how the player plays and then adapts its actions according to preset rules, which in turn are based upon balance (the AI cannot cheat or use exploits like a human player could). The behavior system has to be balanced to the player's ability and against their style of play too. If, in the first few battles of an RTS level, the algorithm always wiped out the player because it is too aggressive, the player is likely to feel upset and will probably stop playing. A well-designed system of behaviors will adapt and grow along with the player, being "dumber" in early levels and then ramp up in complexity as the player learns the intricacies of the game. This behavior system balance is important because when playing against "the game" it is easy for a losing player to feel that the game somehow "cheated," a very different emotion to losing against a human player.

Knowledge of how these systems are being implemented into a game have a direct influence on the level design. If a guard's behaviors are more expansive, from taking cover to pursuing a player over a longer distance, the level's layout must reflect that. If there are doors or areas guards cannot enter, how does this effect the NPC? For example, in *Resident Evil 7 Biohazard* some enemies cannot pursue the player through any closed door (and return to their original area when encountering this) but other enemies can. This ramps up the tension for the player and they originally learn one set of enemy behaviors but then are surprised by a change. The only refuges for the player are the "safe rooms" and when pursued there by an enemy they will wither or melt away or wait for a short time before moving on.

AI Director Systems

If a game requires NPCs on a large scale but needs them to have some individual traits the system most commonly used is called a Director. The role of the AI or behavior Director is most commonly to control the flow and pacing in a cooperative multiplayer game. The game most famous for defining the AI Director was the *Left 4 Dead* series (image 8.4). *Left 4 Dead* had a specific issue—it was a team-based game that required one to four people. If there was only one human player the other hero characters had to work as human proxies. These behaviors were not inconsequential to implement as it includes the NPCs keeping close proximity to the real-life player and being able to decide when they should fight The Infected or heal the player based upon the situation. It could be a frustrating game to play as a sole human player as the decision trees of the NPCs could sometimes butt against the interests of the player.

The Infected horde had aggressive path finding based upon player noise (The Infected are in a continual listen state and if the player made too much noise a large horde would form and come toward the players, scaling obstacles and buildings if necessary). The Director system also places player-useable items in the level (ammo, molotovs, medpacks etc.) and it would "decide" on where The Infected will spawn, in what numbers and if any special options should be implemented (for example, an Infected "rush" which is a lot of Infected that overwhelm the player's position and would spawn a "special" Infected such as a Bloater). What is different about this Director system is that the encounter pros and cons are not based upon preset conditions but instead are based on how the player is performing in the game. The Director will check to see how long it's been since the last

Infected rush or special Infected has spawned, as well as the last time the player came across a health station and then react accordingly.

As well as creating encounter scenarios for the player, the Director is used to balance the game for the player. It can track factors such as the overall health of the players, which difficulty setting they have set and how close they are to the safe house at the end of the level and then add Infected or health items depending on the player's condition. If the player has low but not critical health, being chased by a horde of Infected is going to be a much more adrenaline-rush experience than strolling to the safe house with a high stock of ammo and health pick-ups, picking off a few Infected on the way. The Director is effectively monitoring the player's stress level and adjusting the game (more stress on harder difficulty settings or at the end of the level) to make the game that much more exciting. *Left 4 Dead* was designed with a high replay value (the levels are short, but intense) and because of the Director each play through would be different. The level's designer had to accommodate these systems and scenarios. There is a balance between larger open areas where enemies can swarm and come at the player from a variety of angles and smaller more intense indoor areas where the player is less likely to be overwhelmed by numbers but also cannot easily disengage. The levels also had to feel "real" in the sense that the game is set in a city and its surroundings.

8.4
Left 4 Dead 2, Valve Corporation, 2009. The AI Director in *Left 4 Dead 2* is able to create a dynamic game that is never the same twice. The director adjusts the game based upon the player's skill and progress in the game. This enables highly skilled and lesser skilled players to have a similar experience but also one that is different on each playthrough.

AI Directors have been used in games outside of *Left 4 Dead* and *Left for Dead 2*'s survivor-based combat games; for example, the *Binding of Isaac, Driver: San Francisco* and *Payday: The Heist*. For the level designer, a game such as *Left 4 Dead* is a mix of single-player and multiplayer skill sets. The design has to not only incorporate opportunities of traversal for the player but the AI Director's Infected horde, too. The level designer is looking for choke points (such as the bridge area in Figure 8.4) as well as wide open areas (which are harder to defend) to add variance and game play options for the player.

Emergent Behaviors

The opening image for this chapter is take from *Watch Dogs 2*, which may not seem to be the most obvious game to focus on when talking about AI and behavior systems. In fact, games such as *Watch Dogs 2* and other large open-world games rely heavily on these systems, not just for enemies and quest givers but for crowds. When attempting to simulate a world that appears to be "living," robotic people walking around in obvious loops doing the same task over and over again twenty-four hours a day ruins that immersion. Crowds should react to the player, positively or negatively; they need to reinforce the environment for the player in much the same way that the buildings and signs do. In creating *Watch Dogs 2* the drive was to create NPCs that were not player-centric. The crowds would be living their own lives and the player would walk through them much as we do in real life.

At GDC 2017 Roxanne Blouin-Payer of Ubisoft talks about the teams' use of an algorithm they used called an anecdote factory. The concept was to setup a series of NPCs "stories" that the player could watch or interact with and these added flavor and depth to the game. In an example a player takes a selfie close to a marriage proposal and the NPCs react to the player in a humorous way and this then ends in a verbal and physical fight between the lovers. Roxanne's team created a series of scripted events called "attractors" that could draw the player into an interaction. These are specific events in specific areas; other dynamic attractors were spawned randomly or based on circumstances and the NPCs would interact with each other or with the player. The concept behind these systems was to create emergent scenarios in the game, that is, behavior

or instances in the game that feel unique to the player. This was an attempt to move away from the canned, scripted environments of previous open-world games.

To further develop the immersion, the team built an NPC reaction system that could chain behaviors together, as in the example of the marriage proposal. The system uses a complex algorithm to string together reactions for the NPC which is initiated either by the player or other NPCs. For example, an NPC walking in front of a car which leads to a fist fight and bystanders taking video footage of it all. That feels "natural" to the player (image 8.5). It is still a system: the NPC takes a stimulus, makes a decision and then picks a reaction from a list of behaviors. The system uses "fuzzy logic" which somewhat randomizes different NPC reactions so one character may laugh whilst another becomes aggressive. The success of the *Watch Dogs 2* system was in the interaction between NPCs. Players can watch and react to behavior that may never occur in the same way again even in multiple playthroughs (as opposed to those guards on their set patrols who never deviate from their loop). As one might imagine, it does not always work, but emergent systems are good for creating those "water cooler" moments when discussing the game between friends or on community boards.

8.5
Watchdogs 2, Ubisoft, 2016. In *Watch Dogs 2* the design team created multiple behaviors for the NPCs that would "emerge" based upon different in-game stimuli. These actions could be caused by the player or by other NPCs. In this scenario the NPCs could react in several ways based purely on the reactions of the other NPC gang members which creates different experiences for the player each time.

Summary

Behavior design (or as it's still often called in the games industry, "Artificial intelligence") in games is an area that continues to develop and is beginning to open up possibilities across all game genres. Although this chapter has focused on the "guard" and "enemy combatant" behavior systems, algorithms and behavior systems are used in driving games, simulations or management sims in interesting ways. It is difficult to balance a predictable experience that a player can "know" over one that is more human and therefore unpredictable. This is the essence, in many ways, of the single player versus multiplayer approaches to game design. AI is useful when attempting to simulate aspects of the real world, but there are limits to that because of the artifice that is the video game itself. As with the AIs that beat humans reliably at *Chess*, a game system that could always outsmart the player removes that player as the hero of their own story. The player must be central to the game world and although they must feel challenged they should not be made to feel stupid. The challenge for the level designer is to be able to seamlessly incorporate these systems into the layout of the game. This is especially difficult when considering emergent behaviors that are different every time. An enemy who has the choice of cover, shoot, dodge and die is complex enough when planning a combat arena. Designing for the complexity of a variety of chained behaviors becomes all the more difficult as it's increasingly hard to test against an unpredictable outcome. The next chapter has a deeper exploration of the complexity of designing for combat, behaviors and human players.

INTERVIEW: ZI PETERS, LEAD DESIGNER, SILVER RAIN GAMES

Zi studied Creative Digital Media (Game Design route) at The University of Teesside (UK), and joined Codemasters's QA department soon after graduating. He was later hired into his first game design role at Frontier Developments, and since then has held design roles at Born Ready Games and Creative Assembly. His design credits include *Kinect Disneyland Adventures, Strike Suit Zero, Halo Wars 2, Hitman 2*, and *Spyder* on iOS for Apple Arcade.

How do you feel that the industry has changed since you began your career?

The craft of level design has become more refined industry wide. The market for games has become increasingly competitive with less room for lower quality titles to be shipped and earn moderate or high commercial success. We're fortunate enough to be seeing a higher standard of games across the board, where everyone is being pushed to get a better understanding of what creates a great player experience and improve their processes to facilitate that. I think this is in part helped by having a slightly more open development community to share approaches and best practices. There is also a more widespread approach to getting quantitative and qualitative player data on the games we're making during production and addressing that feedback back into the game before release.

There has also been an industry wide shift to more systemic approaches towards game design in order to increase player agency. We're seeing more games where the dynamics from the interplay of systems creates interesting and rewarding emergent results, for richer player experiences (the *Hitman* games being a great example of this interplay).

What are the main misconceptions about level design?

As a profession, I would probably say one of the main misconceptions is where the typical boundaries of responsibility lie for a level designer. Some people think that a level designer is responsible for the visual side of the level. Although they will have an influence on this, it is usually an environment artist who will oversee the aesthetic. The range of responsibilities can vary dependent on the scope of the production: indie versus AAA, or on studio culture. I think this is an important point for prospective level designers when creating portfolio pieces, in that they focus on showcasing their thinking about the design of a level, as opposed to the "beauty" of it. Otherwise you can start to create a confused message as to what you think the role entails and as to what your primary skills are.

Could you give a brief overview of your process when designing a level in a game?

In a professional environment you aren't usually beginning the level with a blank sheet. There tends to be some high-level direction that will determine the desired general type of gameplay experience, that is usually driven by the directors and associated department leads. This will include information such as the level duration, any critical narrative beats, what gameplay elements are available during this point in the campaign and what ones are being introduced here for the first time.

The first step is ideation, to generate as many interesting ideas that might be worth pursuing for the level that fit within the given remit. It's good practice to explore the possibilities early on and not get immediately attached to an initial idea and just proceed with it. It's also beneficial to get the input of others during the ideation phase. You don't have to come up with the best ideas for the level as the level designer, but you need to be able to identify them regardless of where they come from.

The next step is the level design document, to establish a loose framework before beginning to create anything in the editor. This distills all the created ideas to the most fitting and promising ones which deliver most on the level's direction and presents them in a cohesive format. This usually includes creating a diagrammatic map of the layout, along with icons placed to represent the spatial layout of gameplay elements and annotations. Documentation in the games industry is a contentious topic, but it is often used at many studios as part of the development process. It can be very useful for communicating the level design to other stakeholders quickly, and areas of critique can be raised early and reworked before valuable time is spent in the level editor.

Once the document is at an acceptable stage, it's time to try and prove the concept by implementing it into the game engine and testing it out. This will start with creating the layout, where you can begin to get a feel for things like scale, line of sight, landmark locations and camera compositions. It is good to place objects, such as a character models, around the map for scale reference. Then it's time to start implementing some gameplay, starting with critical components such as the main objectives, the introduction of new mechanics and enemies and the creation of any unique gameplay or narrative events. Once the larger key parts get implemented, it is then time to look at layering in the ancillary components of the gameplay such as more general encounters, item locations and so on.

How is designing for a game such as *Hitman 2* different from *Halo Wars 2*?

There's a considerable amount of crossover in the experience of designing for each from a high-level perspective. Firstly, they are both based on pre-existing IP, so there is a lot of learning of what has come before these instalments within the franchises and what the brands stand for. It's important in this scenario to get an alignment with these values, so that the designs you present are suitable. In terms of gameplay, both games strongly support player agency, which

requires designers to consider the multiple varied ways a scenario might play out and how their setups will handle that.

However, there are also some fundamental differences as you start to look at the low-level aspects of each game. The genres of each game are quite different with one being Real Time Strategy (*Halo Wars 2*) and the other a Third Person Action Adventure game (*Hitman 2*). The perspectives of the cameras that are typical of these genres are vastly different, with *Halo Wars 2* having a free independently moving camera from an aerial view and *Hitman 2* having a third person "follow" camera. It greatly changes the way you approach the layout of a level and consider elements such as composition, sightlines and vistas. It can be easily underestimated how even small differences in the way a game camera operates can have an effect on the level design.

The general process for creating levels for each game was quite similar, in that there was a "paper" design phase used to plan the flow of events and the layout before implementation began. In both cases this was then followed by whitebox/ graybox for blocking out the level geometry, before adding gameplay entities and volumes, and scripting gameplay logic. In regards to the player experience, they do both involve a lot of strategy. It's helpful in both cases for the player to be able to easily assess a challenge presented before them and quickly determine their options available to overcome it.

How do you approach scope and feature creep when planning levels for the game?

If you are working on a pre-established series, it's worth looking at the best levels in the games that have come before the one you are working on. If not, you could use another well-received game that might be comparable to yours as a point of reference. If possible, compare the size of the level geometry of your level with the reference. Time how long it takes on average to complete those levels, and also break them down to their constituent parts. This helps you to begin to answer questions such as; how many combat encounters are there? How many puzzles must the player solve? How many enemy types are used? There isn't a mathematical equation for creating a level because the makeup of a level should be dependent on the overall goal for the experience that the level is supposed to provide.

8.6

Halo Wars 2, 343 Industries, 2017. The camera design in *Halo Wars 2* required restrictions to the height of the camera plane and the camera's boundaries in order to limit the extents to which the player can move around the map. In *Halo Wars 2* the player determines what units they build to control on the battlefield and how many of them, which means you take a more general approach as to the requirements for the metrics of space.

8.7

Hitman 2, IO Interactive, 2018. In *Hitman 2* the player is controlling Agent 47. He has a fixed standard set of mechanics at his disposal with accompanying metrics (*the camera is fixed to third person, there is no "hover above" mode or birds eye view etc.*)

This approach can provide a rough benchmark as a starting point, plus it helps to highlight abnormal extremes that you may have in your design.

It is easy to become tripped up by generating lots of cool ideas and wanting to get all your best ideas into a level. You have to be able to edit those ideas and provide sufficient focus for the level. There are a number of ways in which to determine what you should include. Check your ideas against the high-level goal for the level and see if they support it. Don't be afraid to cut ideas that don't end up working as well as you thought, as they'll only bring down the quality of the rest of the level. Seek the feedback of peers who are removed from any personal attachment to your work, for what may be a more unsparing and honest opinions.

Consider the resources at your disposal. Are you going to be able to afford the environment art, animation, vfx (visual effects), technical gameplay and audio support to execute the idea to a high level of quality? Answering questions such as these early on, can save you a lot of heartache and anguish later. One approach to overcoming this is to aim for your ideal, but to also conceptualize an MVP (minimal viable product) specification as a fallback. The MVP is a more constrained and attainable version of what you would like to achieve that will deliver a lot of what you are attempting, but not quite to the same extent. Design is often a series of compromises, where you must decide what those compromises are.

How do you feel AI in games has evolved and become more sophisticated?

The expectations of players for AI has increased over time, and the games development industry has had to continually try to meet those expectations. Most of the modern major action games have embraced AI with that facilitate both stealth and action approaches to encounter setups. We're also seeing enemy AI being given greater capabilities with how they interact with the environment. Some people never notice, but enemy AI are often limited with things like traversal.

A lot of the "AI" design in games is modelled on providing defined and predictable behavior. Different enemy archetypes are created to present a specific type of challenge, where the player understands the required use for a particular type of approach to defeat them. I don't know if it is necessarily true of all games though. In *Alien Isolation* the Xenomorph learns from the player's actions and adapts accordingly so it is "learning" rather than just reacting to preset behaviors.

Red Dead Redemption 2 has taken things to a new level with how the AI of general NPCs respond to the player character, based on his appearance or the actions he has made. This results in a stronger simulation of people and for a more believable and immersive world. Companion AI in games has also improved greatly, not just in their implementation but also their design. Often companion AI would be a hindrance to the player, but I think we are getting better approaches to how they can support the gameplay experience now. Companion AI has become kind of a hallmark of Naughty Dog games, featuring heavily in both the *Uncharted* series and *The Last of Us* series.

All types of NPCs are being used to greater effect at supporting the narrative in the games we play. We are seeing NPCs who garner quite a following due to not just the writing of the character, but also how well the AI helps to support that to make them believable.

The implementation is getting better too. Good AI is easily readable by the player, so that they can determine what state the AI is in and how to act accordingly. When players act the AI should react in a way that makes sense to the player. In addition to that, the AI needs to support the overall goals specific to the game it is built for. I've always really liked how the enemies in the Predator encounters of the *Batman Arkham* games would express an increased level of fear when they noticed that other members of their group had been subdued. It strongly supported the psychological theme associated with the character, and therefore the fantasy of being Batman.

Developments in video game AI is being set with the likes of *Red Dead Redemption 2* and *The Last of Us Part 2*. Expanding the numbers of responses and actions the AI can make with the player and the environment to make for more believable NPCs. I think the challenge will be in maintaining that players only get surprised by their capabilities in positive ways, and not in a way that seems unfair.

How do you work with AI developers/ programmers on planning and integrating NPC's/Enemies into a level?

In my experience it has largely been about using them as a resource for understanding the capabilities and the restrictions of the AI and be able to build and markup the level for the NPCs to act effectively. Level designers later find issues with this initial design which only become apparent in a production level as opposed to a test level because of the AI This may then feedback into the design of the AI to improve it.

The integration really depends on the requirements of a level and the intended capabilities of the AI There are normally a fairly large number of requirements of scripted setups for the AI, where the level designer will want the AI to do something specific. This may include elements such as a patrol which would require level markup of waypoints or a spline (a model in the level) for the

AI to follow. In addition to this you might want them to perform specific animations or speak an exact line of dialogue at designated points. The level designer may also need to use trigger volumes, referencing either the AI in question, the player character or another NPC, to initiate required scripted responses.

For the more systemic behaviour the AI may only need minimal bespoke level markup, such as attack and defend zones or cover planes, which could be applicable to any number of objects or level geometry, but aren't necessarily a strict requirement. Otherwise the level designer will be using a lot of standard gameplay entities (normally created by a technical designer) that they can drag drop into the level, such as a door. If the AI needs to have some sort of interaction with it, then they'll respond accordingly.

How do you design levels for emergent gameplay (such as in the *Hitman* series)?

When designing levels for a game with generously sized sandbox levels or large open worlds, an approach where you plan for a strong critical path serves as a good starting point. With the intention that this is how majority of the players will experience the content. A clearly defined objective is key to keeping players from getting lost in the options presented to them. Along the critical path you will be able to identify parts that are compulsory for the flow of events to still be logical, and those that are optional. If there is an action that deviates from the critical path, you can then design for it to loop back in at specific points. The critical path then acts as a strong spine for the rest of the design, to help keep the player anchored to their goal.

It is good practice for any game you're working on to build profiles of the main player types that form the intended audience of your game. For example, a stealth player who tries to progress through the space undetected, an action player who goes in guns blazing for a full-frontal assault etc. Then as you go though your level or mission, you can adopt those play styles and see how it holds up and make changes accordingly which better support those approaches. Having a set number of player types will help to maintain a relative amount of focus for the level designer. Playtesting is also crucial for finding out how players react to the situations you present and what their expectations are.

When supporting alternative options for the player, you really need to ask yourself how meaningful a choice it is and what it will cost in resources to fully implement. If an option you're creating isn't supporting one of your intended playstyles, is it really the right fit for your game? If it doesn't add something different in comparison to other options you already have, then is it worth adding? If the player can't ascertain the difference between two different options that are presented to them, then is it adding value to the player experience? Is an option you have in mind going to require significant resources from art, animation, audio, code and narrative? If so, is it really worth their time and effort? Questions like these will really help level designers be able to self-edit their designs to what really matters and prevent it from becoming needlessly bloated.

Is there a future for linear based level design now that the open-world model has become so popular?

I think, and hope, there continues to be a market for linear level design. I don't believe one supersedes the other, rather that each have their own benefits as well as drawbacks. Each type of design appeals to people with different preferences, and for some just at what specific mood they are in at any given time. Linear level design had grown a negative reputation, which I don't think necessarily holds true for many games that would be categorized as such. Linear games have been evolving for a long time to embrace more player agency while still holding true to the values that are have been very effective in that structure.

One part of the challenge lies in finding the right balance between player agency and the need to direct the experience for narrative and pacing. When Bungie created the Halo series, they coined the term "wide pipe" level design, which proposes level layouts that provide multiple avenues of navigation. Many *Halo* levels throughout the series have been characterized by wide open landscapes, despite an ultimately linear trajectory. You will also find some levels with areas with nonlinear objectives. The *Gears of War* series proposed the idea of combat bowls, which were slightly more open spaces that allowed for more dynamic combat encounters. Naughty Dog have spoken about a similar approach that they refer to as "wide linear", that they have been practicing in the *Uncharted* series. This has become ever more apparent as the series has grown, examine

Uncharted 4: A Thief's End Chapter 10: The Twelve Towers. This is a great example of how they have pushed this concept within their framework.

Another important aspect of linear design is in the implementation of the gating. There is a difference between where gating becomes overly frequent and obvious and when experienced developers can get the most out of gating opportunity to enhance the pacing or a narrative beat. Matthew Worch (Design Lead, epic games) gave a great GDC presentation on the design of *Dead Space 2*, where he supports the linear level structure of that game and compares it to *Doom*. He promotes how both games deliver on player agency and meaningful choice due to their systemic combat regardless of the linear nature of the level layouts themselves.

Open world design has been very popular for some time now, and I think there are a percentage of player's that have grown tired with open world design. Or at least an approach to open world design. When you look at the design of missions or quests in many open world games they are as linear as content in the games that don't take place in an open world environment. A building in an open world may only have one entry point for example, and all the enemies may be instantly aware of the player's character's presence just as they would be in a linear designed level.

The conversation is far more nuanced than it has been presented by some of the games industry news media. We also need to remember that not all games are made the same, and we need to look at what the vision and pillars are of the game we are making.

What are the advances that have had the biggest effect on level design?

One of the most important is the improvement in the tools we now have access to. Design as a whole is often seen as the glue that binds the work of other disciplines together. Tools that can make level designers become more independent at the early stages of development, to implement any functionality that typically would have required a programmer, an artist, animator or audio designer, has really empowered level designers.

This allows for prompt whiteboxing, prototyping and playtesting of ideas, and the ability to quickly iterate on a design. This iteration cycle can then be completed more times within the same given timeframe, in comparison with less friendly tools. Ideas that don't work can be dismissed faster, and the ideas with potential can be polished enough to be proven to work. When it isn't too laborious to experiment with ideas, we don't have to be precious with what we produce early on. We can simply throw away what isn't working and make way for the best ideas to blossom and prevail. This allows more time to polish with less issues becoming apparent in the later stages of development, where it may be too late to do anything about them.

Combat Design and Multiplayer Design

Learning Objectives for This Chapter:

1) Explore combat design and its effect on level design

2) Introduce player types in relation to combat scenarios

3) Overview multiplayer level design

9.0
Fortnite, Epic Games, 2017.

This chapter rounds out this book by exploring combat design and its impact on level design. Combat design can also be seen as encounter design that does not have to be violent, it depends on the game. An encounter with an NPC or quest giver or a follow/ chase mission are variants on combat design. When designing for combat in a game's level the LD needs to understand (as covered in the previous chapter) that the combat designer and AI programmer will be bringing specific mechanics and behaviors into the level. The LD's job is to incorporate these into a coherent level design that fulfills the goals and objectives of the level. As with all game design, the layout and components must work not just for one style of play, but several. When designing for multiplayer, humans versus humans, there are strategies that an LD can employ to think through the design but ultimately players will always find a way to leverage some unseen advantage.

Combat and Level Design

The role of the level designer is to create the "combat zone" once they know how the combat and behavior systems work. As we saw in the previous chapter the same behavior questions come into play; for example, can the enemies flank the player? Can they use cover? How many hits can an enemy/the player take? Do they all use cover (soldiers do, but larger "tank" enemies do not)?

On top of the more obvious enemy or NPC behavior there is environmental feedback— perhaps when an enemy or the player throw an explosive there is "splash damage"? People outside of the main impact area can also be damaged or perhaps there is the need for destructible models (from walls to crates or windows). Other environmental feedback could come from other interactions. Some surfaces allow a bullet to pass through while some do not (and how consistent would this be? It seems common for bullets to be unable to pass through chain-link fences for some reason). Is there a mechanic or physics that allow for bullets to ricochet? Even a "simple" combat scenario runs into England's "door problem." Once these questions have been answered the LD can take these factors into account when designing the level's layout (if splash damage is allowed it would be a good idea to make sure enemies can stand close to each other, so the player can take advantage of this feature).

In a 2015 Gamasutra article Zi Peters (Creative Assembly) wrote an excellent breakdown of the *Gears of War* level "knock-knock" and how the designers of that game moved the concept of third-person combat forward. The level designers created what Peters refers to as an hourglass structure of "combat bowls" followed by tight corridors.

9.1

The hourglass design of *Gears of War* is repeated throughout the game. The combat bowls are intense so the corridors are used to break up the action, slow down the pacing and to introduce exposition or limited exploration for pick-ups. This design format was also used on a larger scale in the *Doom* reboot.

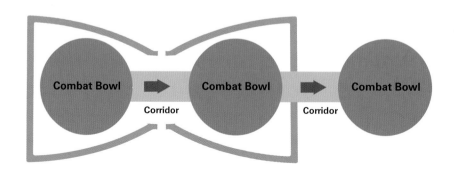

Combat can occur in any of the spaces, but the "bowls" are reserved for the larger battles. The corridors act as pacing elements slowing down the player movement (sometimes considerably if there is narrative exposition). When entering a combat bowl the player is given enough time to take in their surroundings, which adds to the immersion and also allows them time to strategize (scope out cover areas, note where enemies are most likely to appear, look for ammunition, etc.). The larger bowls will usually contain a special architectural feature, such as a fountain or sculpture; this is used to direct the player's eye and can trigger a cutscene when approached or show the most likely emergence position of the enemy.

9.2
God of War, SIE Santa Monica Studio, 2018. *God of War* (2018) uses a version of the "combat bowl" (also called arenas) model. The game switches between more open combat scenarios and combat arenas. One of the earliest combat scenarios has the main character drop into a circular space that is closed off and inescapable until the combat scenario is completed, after which the player can continue deeper into the world.

Combat bowls, arenas or large areas of open combat all rely on communication between the LD, AI and combat/encounter designer for their success. The LD has to remain the advocate for the player by testing and iterating on the amount of cover available for different play styles, on where items are placed dependent upon difficulty settings and making considerations for how the NPCs inhabit and navigate the level. Every game is going to approach and solve these problems differently, which is why a book that says "this is the only way to do level design" could not be written. As with all design, it is in the service of creating the best experience for the audience or player.

9.3
This image is from a prototype third-person game made using the Unreal 4 Engine. This combat zone contains the four main elements of a combat bowl: player territory, enemy territory, the killzone and a flank. There is also a clear player objective; the green-lit statue is a unique object and is "protected" by the enemies. To reach their goal the players must use strategy based upon the rules of the combat system.

UnReal 4, assets from *Infinity Blade: Ice Lands*.

Breaking Down Combat Design

Combat bowls are still very much in use and have become a blueprint in level design. Although they are unrealistic from a real-world point of view, they are useful for constraining the actions of a player, pacing (elevating action and tension) and force the player's progress. Level designer Pete Ellis (*The Last of Us 2, Killzone Mercenary*) breaks down the components of a combat bowl into five areas:

Player territory: this is the player's safe zone. The player is under attack but is far enough away that they will take lessened damage and are not fully engaged with the battle. There is more cover and this all gives the player an opportunity to strategize.

Enemy territory: the area from which the enemy launch their assault. Most of this area is hidden from the player (the LD may want to hide enemy spawn points). As it is the enemy territory it will have less cover options (multiplayer maps would balance this).

Player/Enemy front: this is the edge of the safe zone; crossing these puts the player/enemy into the full combat area.

Killzone: the area in between the player/enemy fronts; contains sparse cover and is not an area either side wants to be caught in. This is the area the player must traverse to get to the enemy front and beat the level.

Flank route: possible routes for the player/enemy that circumvents the killzone; can pose a higher risk as the route is tighter than the open combat bowl.

9.4
This is the same design as in image 9.3 from a higher angle and better shows the layout of the combat bowl. It would be immediately recognizable to anyone who has played *Gears of War*, *Uncharted* and *Mass Effect* styles of game. This area is much smaller than maps in a multiplayer game, but does have Pete Ellis's five combat bowl components.

A single level may contain several combat bowls but although the layout and assets may alter slightly the overall design must be able to accommodate different player styles. The designer should enable a creative a balanced experience for the player and enable them to experiment with different styles of play. Even if the player prefers stealth it does not mean that they should be encouraged to limit themselves to that one play style; offering variety is key to continual player engagement. Combat bowls can also be used to "teach" the player different tactics that might break them out of one style of play. This can be achieved through offering different weapons or styles of enemy combat and weapons.

Player combat types are most commonly defined as:

Run and gun: players who follow the most obvious path to the goal and are most inclined to run straight down the middle relying on aiming and fast reactions to beat the enemy.

Stealth: players will take time to strategize on routes that avoid direct combat and will take the least obvious path.

Sniper: players will hang back in the player safe zone for as long as possible and use ranged weapons to defeat the enemy; only engages in full combat as a last resort.

9.5

The combat bowl accommodates the three main styles of play. Each style can be disrupted by the enemy. If the enemy stay in place the sniper has an advantage, but if they advance towards the player to try to flank the run and gun model would have to be used. Stealth is dependent upon the behavioral intelligence of the enemy: are they on alert or passive? In this image there are three players so each of them could take up a different style of play.

UnReal 4, assets from *Infinity Blade: Ice Lands, Warriors* and *Adversaries* packs.

Players may switch between these combat types in a level so the design should accommodate that. The sniper player may be "flushed out" by enemy encroachment and would have to switch to "run and gun," and the stealth player may get ambushed and would have to forego stealth for more direct combat and so on. There are further variants of these modes covered in the multiplayer section of this chapter.

Detail Is Important, Even in Combat

In addition to considering player styles, there are other design elements that Josh Bridges (*Dead*

Rising 2) says are totally false constructs but do need to fit the "fiction" of the level design. He cites the use of crates, which are a long-time convention in video games but also one that shows a lack of imagination. They are useful as cover (hard or soft cover dependent upon their destructibility) but burned out cars, fallen masonry or militaristic style traffic barriers may better integrate into the environment and reinforce the narrative of the game environment as well as serving a function in the level. Cover and other assets can be used to add an amount of variety to the level's aesthetics but can also force the player into different modes of play. If a player's only option is to take cover behind a flammable barrel or a crate that can be destroyed this will expose the player to enemy fire and they are going to have to break out of their current play style and engage new tactics (for example, switch from sniper or stealth into run and gun).

9.6
Replacing the stone barriers with barrels and crates may break up the fiction of the combat space. Although they would work in the same way as the barriers, (and may be destructible, forcing the player out of cover) they do not always fit the fiction of the scene. This layout broadcasts "combat arena" in an obvious manner, as well as "why are all these barrels and crates in the middle of this space?"

Seemingly inconsequential design aspects, such as the placement and amount of cover, can have a tangible impact on the game experience. The combat arena is going to be significantly more difficult with less cover, or if all the cover can be destroyed by the player or enemy. Bridges summarizes the rationale for different uses of cover:

- *Amount*: more cover means more protection from enemy fire and more opportunities to use stealth. Less cover results in a larger killzone area increasing the challenge.
- *Spacing*: how far the player can run or roll is an important metric when designing a combat level. Cover that is spaced further than the player can sprint makes for a risky run through the killzone. Cover that allows the player to connect jumps facilitates a layered stealth path.
- *Size and Height*: big and wide cover assets offer comfortable cover while a narrow column would expose the player to multiple lines of enemy fire.
- *Density*: a cluster of small trees would break the sight lines of the enemy but offers no protection.
- *Temporary*: destructible cover will eventually become no cover, which exposes the player to the killzone.

(Bridges, 2009)

9.7
Wherever possible the level designer should enable different paths through combat to accommodate player styles and to afford the player the opportunity to attempt different tactics. This limited freedom can have a profound impact on the player and adds replayability to the level and game.

Affording the player options for traversal is an aid towards a deeper immersion as well as communicating the feeling of "outsmarting" the game. When a player can sneak around a combat arena and surprise attack enemies that strategy can have a deeply positive impact on the player's connection to the game. Because these combat arenas are relatively small, they are easier to test than large multiplayer maps and levels. Because of this a level designer can use tester feedback to iterate on the level quickly and improve it through multiple plays.

9.8
This image is an example of the Freeform model of a combat arena. Enemies and the player may start from different areas in the arena but quickly mix up because of the layout of the cover points and the centralized objective. Conversely the player may be "ambushed" in this style of arena and be surrounded by enemies they have to dispatch in order to progress in the game.

CHOKE POINTS AND FREEFORM COMBAT ARENAS

There is no set model for combat design but most of the current designs for bowls or arenas fall into two forms: Choke Point and Freeform. Choke Point design sets the player's objective at a fixed point behind the enemy. The player must move towards this objective and there are few paths. If there are flanks they will funnel back into the main arena at some point (popularized by the *Gears of War, Mass Effect* and *Call of Duty* series). Freeform has no explicit zones or territories. The combat may start with two sides facing each other but the cover is distributed. There may be an objective in the center of the arena or the goal is to defeat all the enemies to be able to move further into the level (popularized by *Sleeping Dogs, The Batman Arkham series*, and *Assassin's Creed series*).

It is worth mentioning that the images used as examples in this chapter of the combat arena are employing a camera angle that is more of a "bird's eye" overview, which would not be used in the game proper. A level designer would constantly change between an overhead perspective and the player's point of view. The LD is looking at general layout options, such as distances and distribution, but is also examining player sightlines that add to the intensity of combat (an enemy can sneak up on a player or the player can hide in order to heal up or restrategize). They are also ensuring that the player can see as much as possible in order to direct their role in the combat. Depending on the behavior algorithms or difficulty settings of the enemy the player can use the level design and enemy traits to afford a positive outcome in the combat. To balance this the enemy should also be able to surprise the player or prove a difficult enough opponent that the player can win with a sense of accomplishment.

9.9
In first- or third-person camera mode sightlines are an important part of the level design process. Cover offers protection but can also allow for stealth options. In combat arenas, there is a lot of visual and audio feedback for the player so they tend to have less ornamentation than other parts of a level. The LD has to balance visual richness with visual overload or confusion. If the player is constantly disoriented in combat, or cannot see a clear objective, it can lead to a frustrating experience.

Encounter or mission design is not limited to only combat of course, but it is a good example of how interactive space is designed for a specific purpose. These same rules could be applied to a variety of encounter scenarios in a video game. These are only outlines of the most general combat scenarios. With the advent of increased behavior algorithms and more "intelligent" enemies or NPCs the evolution of combat and encounters continues at a pace. As covered in the previous chapter, a surprising amount of complexity can be achieved with a simple rule set and minor variances and behavior chains. It is the same with combat arenas, changing up placement of cover and resources and varying enemy numbers and abilities can prevent every encounter from becoming a cookie-cutter version of itself. The other way of ensuring a level of randomness and chance into an encounter or combat scenario is to introduce humans. Unlike algorithms and scripts humans will always work on angles and look for exploits in order to "game" the level as much as possible and because of that level designers have to give up some of their control of the space to the players.

Level Design for Multiplayer

Much of what has been covered in relation to single-player level design and the combat arena model can be transferred into the design of multiplayer maps. But, unlike discrete battle arenas or bowls that are a part of a larger game, the entirety of the multiplayer level (or map) is focused on combat. The role of the level designer is to create affordances for the player that attribute positively to that goal. There are two common forms of multiplayer games: the first is best exemplified by games such as *Overwatch* or *Player Unknown: Battlegrounds* (image 9.11). These games focus completely on multiple human players in combat scenarios. The second are games that mix single player (usually referred to as "story" or "campaign" modes) with multiplayer modes. *Call of Duty, Uncharted* (image 9.10) and the *Mass effect* series all have single player and multiplayer modes.

9.10
Uncharted 4: A Thief's End, Naughty Dog, 2016.
Uncharted 4: A Thief's End extends gameplay options by including several multiplayer modes. The level design and character design is consistent with the single-player "story" mode and players can choose to play as one of the game's heroes or villains. There is an established language of multiplayer modes, king of the castle (Command in *Uncharted 4*), capture the flag (Plunder), escort, deathmatch and horde (Survival) and Battle Royale (*Player Unknown: Battlegrounds*).

One of the main differences between single player and multiplayer is in deciding how soon the player engages with the action (for example, entering into a combat scenario). In single player narrative-based games, or FPS games, the time it takes for a player to get into combat differs dramatically. For example, in *Rise of the Tomb Raider* and *Uncharted 4: A Thief's End* the games' introductions explore the movement mechanics, exposition and climbing well before combat encounters are initiated. In multiplayer-based *Overwatch* once a party is formed in the lobby, it's seconds before the player is engaging in combat. Most action games use narrative to contextualize the objectives and world for the player and to ensure that the player gets as much out of each level as possible because single-player games are designed in the knowledge that most players will only go through them once. With multiplayer it's the opposite; players will engage with the same level multiple times. To accommodate these different foci Elisabeth Beinke-Schwartz (*BioShock Infinite, Doom*) in 2017 outlined some of the challenges for a level designer when approaching designing for single-player or multiplayer games:

Single Player:	Multiplayer:
Sell the narrative	Narrative is low priority
Frame the gameplay objectives	Frame player routes/options
Design option routes for rewards and play styles	Design routes for advanced players and play styles
Play test less, polish more in between	Play test often and use repeat testers
Exploits are a low priority	Fix exploits and sightlines

In single player games the level design focus is on objectives, set pieces and player traversal as well as side quests, missions and encounter design. These aspects directly inform the size and scope of each level. In multiplayer games the objectives are very direct (beat the other team/players) and there are no set pieces or side missions. Being able to accommodate a set number of players is ultimately what dictates the level's size.

9.11
Player Unknown's Battlegrounds, PUBG Corporation, 2017. Making a large map for a handful of players equates to a longer time before combat is initiated. This could be a deliberate design choice, as is the case with *Player Unknown: Battlegrounds* where players drop into a large map unarmed and unprotected. The players are given time to scavenge for weapons and resources as well as work on strategy before entering into combat. In other games such as *Overwatch* the player will create their "load out" of weapons and enter into combat immediately.

Framing and Composition for Multiplayer

In a single player game the player is given time to look around, to take in their environment and the framing of each area of the level communicates to them by showing exits and entrances, story moments, a history of the level or environment and so on. Framing options need to occur much faster in multiplayer; the competitive nature of the action means that players are making split-second decisions on where to go and what options could aid them strategically. The level design needs to communicate entrances, exits, high ground and cover as quickly and as obviously as possible. There is no real need for barrels and crates, props or flavor items because the player is just not going to notice them or stop to pick them up (explosive barrels or traps would be the exception). When designing for multiplayer

it is important that the player knows where paths are going to lead as the pace is so much faster than in single-player. When designing the layout the LD will look toward buildings that have multiple entrances and exits (to facilitate player flow and allow for chance encounters, also to prevent too much "camping") and none of the stairs would be blocked. Dead ends are rare in multiplayer levels because they break up the flow of the game play; the player is always moving and relocating. This does depend on the game—*Player Unknown* is infamous for its "bathroom campers"—but compensates for this by a moving "dome of death" that forces players into an ever-smaller combat zone.

Multiplayer levels tend to have a much more circular or hub-and-spoke design to them to best facilitate movement and best lines of sight. The player must be able to see as much of the action at all times as possible but the LD will also place strategic cover options whenever possible and will minimize areas that a player could hide in (multiplayer games tend to have icons over the player's character identifying them as friend or foe which makes hiding difficult).

Multiplayer Definitions

As with all other aspects of video game design there is no one agreed-upon set of definitions for "types" of multiplayer games. There are variations on themes, and different modalities are being brought into play constantly. *Player Unknown: Battlegrounds* popularized and improved upon the Battle Royale mode that was already in place, but not in common use at the time of its launch. *Fortnite* brought a building mode into the multiplayer game, aspects of which already existed in a smaller scale in other games but *Fortnite* capitalized on it. No matter the mechanics of the game, the player is always the focus.

When approaching level design for multiplayer, no matter the genre of the game they are all developed with player archetypes in mind. These models of player types have been around since the earliest days of *Unreal Tournament*.

Bobby Ross, a world designer on *Star Wars: The Old Republic* has broken down multiplayer types into these archetypes:

Stealth (players who rarely take the direct approach to game play)

Sniper (players who like to keep their distance and protect themselves)

Roamer (players who let the action come to them as they explore)

Rusher (players who prefer the most direct approach)

Camper (the player everyone dislikes the most)

From these player types Ross infers types of cover and combat ranges that have become useful conventions in multiplayer games.

9.12
These are the most common types of cover a player would come across in a multiplayer game. There is "affordance" here, that is, a level designer can use the environment to afford the player different actions. Placing soft cover closer to enemies is a risk affordance; it offers some, but not total protection compared to a wall. But getting closer to the enemy affords a better chance of success. It sets up a risk/reward model for the players.

Unity 2018, assets from Ruined Building Kit by Jason Wong.

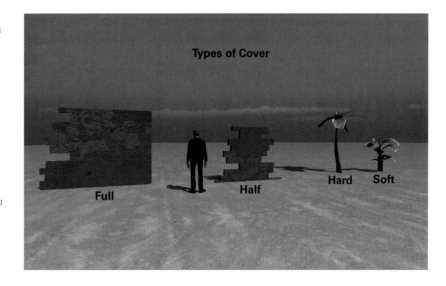

The same is true of how player styles inform combat ranges: stealth players will prefer close quarter ranges and snipers will prefer distance ranges. The LD has to be able to construct the level based around these factors and balance it so that each player style has an equal chance of success and failure. Snipers do not move much so can be ambushed by other players, stealth players can be discovered and dispatched and so on.

9.13
When level designers are discussing options with combat designers spacing is one of the main considerations. Players may have a dominant or preferred play style, but those preferences can be changed based upon the level design (less open spaces, corridors). The LD has to make affordances for a variety of combat ranges. The level layout must be able to work up close as well as for distance combat. These are all considerations for where types of cover, pickups and enemies would be placed.

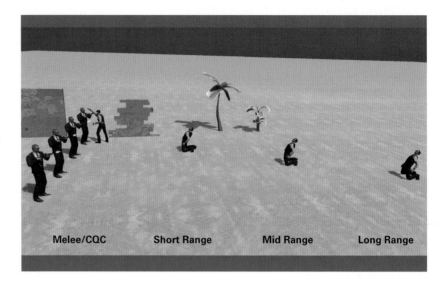

Melee/CQC   Short Range   Mid Range   Long Range

Thinking about the player style and ranges is the first step in developing a level design. The issue for level designers is that as the multiplayer genre has grown so too have the modes contained within them. Each mode has a different function for the level designer.

Team survival (popularized by in *Gears of War* and *Ghost Recon*): Each player has one life with no respawns.

Team deathmatch (*Halo*, *Quake*, *Unreal Tournament*): Same as team survival but with respawns, game ends after set amount of fatalities.

King of the hill (*Call of Duty*, *Black Ops*, *Halo*): players have to hold specific ground (a defensible position) and prevent it being overrun by other teams or players. Variants are Hardpoint in *Black Ops 2* where players would instantly respawn.

Capture the flag (*Halo*, *Quake*): teams or players "steal" an item or flag from the opposition and return it to their own position. Variants are escort missions, bomb missions.

Search and destroy (*Call of Duty*, *Counter Strike*): team survival but with specific objectives such as defusing a bomb or planting one.

All of these modes have variants, the multiplayer game has become increasingly deep and each level has to be created to best work with the mode of play. For example, in capture the flag the item (not always a flag) should be easy to see from multiple angles in the level. All of the modes that are going to be incorporated into the game will have been decided on well in advance at preproduction. Each mode will have its subtleties and affordances that are important for the LD to implement into the design. Once the gray box version has been built to suit the mode, the LD will explore the level looking to minimize exploits (not really a "cheat" but can give an unfair advantage to a player) in the level.

Sightlines and Exploits

Multiplayer maps are tighter in layout than single-player levels. In a campaign or story game the player is often free to explore and wander around taking in all the sights and talking to NPCs. If there is combat and it's hard for the player to see the enemy, the player can move to a better position because most of the time the combat is happening in front of them. The enemy behaviors will often be simple, the enemy may not be able to move up beyond a certain point or they will disengage if the player runs away and so on. This allows the player time to heal, restock or pace out their experience. In multiplayer it's human versus human, which means that the action is frenetic and being human the players are looking for the slightest advantage in order to win. Players will experiment with all kinds of mechanics, physics and layout quirks to gain an advantage (for example rocket-jumping, or blowing themselves up so their respawn point gives them a tactical edge), there are so many ways players use "exploits" or unintended quirks of the game to win. In single-player games finding a small window or unintended sightline where the player can get a drop on an enemy can be emotionally rewarding for the player. In multiplayer, the player needs to know where they are being attacked from so if a player is able to take out others through a small crack in a column, "[the other player] gets frustrated if they die and they don't know why . . . in a multiplayer game it's important to understand why you died. The player should feel like they made a mistake if they died, and not that there is some gaming of the system that feels unfair" (Beinke-Schwartz, 2017).

9.14
The sightlines in this image vastly prefer the player in the foreground; the player entering the building will never see or know where the shot came from. In a single player game this would be a very positive experience if the player is the one in the foreground. In multiplayer these forms of exploits must be addressed in multiple testing passes as they affect the balance of the game. A realignment of the storage crate would mean that the player in the foreground is going to have to move out of cover to shoot and the other player will see the movement and react or at least know where the shot came from.

Unity 2018, assets from Modular Warehouse by Adamations.

Another consideration when designing for multiplayer is that movement is fast and so traversal has to be fluid, with as many options as possible. Single player can have multiple paths through a level adding depth and variety, but it is not essential. In multiplayer, the player is going to be using the same map over and over again—multiple paths are indispensable. The paths need to directly map onto the expertise of the player, so there could be easy, medium, and harder traversal options. The more experienced player may be much more comfortable with wall running or using a double jump, and the traversal options should take that into account and offer as many ways for the player to move through the map as possible within the context of the mechanics and gameplay.

9.15

In multiplayer levels, multiple routes are an essential part of the design. An interior level (such as the garage in the image shown) that was mostly corridors with few entries and exits would be acceptable in single player, but in multiplayer it would become boring when played multiple times. This small combat-bowl style area has multiple traversal options for the players as well as clear sight lines, which will facilitate more intense combat.

PvP No AI Required

The advantage of multiplayer player vs player (PvP) games is that there is no need for artificial intelligence because that comes built into the human player. Players will always be seeking exploits and ways to "game the game" to their advantage, which is hard to compensate for or anticipate. Once the game is released, the fans will spend a lot longer playing the game than its testers. This is where the community surrounding a game becomes so important: the players become not just ambassadors for the game but often its police and jury too—reporting exploits, discussing strategy and coming up with myriad ways to use the mechanics of the game in unexpected ways. Unlike single-player experiences, multiplayer games are never finished, they are a work in progress and evolve along with their player base, which is one of the reasons they have such lasting impact as a genre of video games.

Summary

When you design and create the formation of a combat encounter the narrative is an important consideration to start with. Within a level, skillful placement of cover positions and other interactive geometry can influence how the enemies behave and thus how an encounter unfolds. This method of constructing a combat encounter is preferable over that of "area restricting" enemies where possible, as relying too heavily on the latter can lead to exploits by the player and worse still, can lead to the AI not behaving correctly.

A carefully considered level layout can also affect the difficulty without the need for altering an enemy's default numerics, such as health, damage or accuracy. Affecting difficulty through geometry placement also affects the way the player experiences your encounter. It is good to move the player around the environment to experience the combat in different ways, be it by moving the combat focus and direction the player fights toward, or by introducing flanking enemies that force the player to move. Moving the front and the combat focus can also help with navigating the player through the environment in the sequence you intended and help orientate them to be facing the exit or next objective when the battle ends.

Next Steps

We have reached the end of the level and the game. It's been an exciting and challenging journey for all of us. Originally in this book I wanted to gaze into the potential future of level design, to talk about new technologies and possibilities. The fact of the matter is, as I recall working with my students, the future is you. Every game you make moves the industry forward a tiny fraction. Every new designer with their own backgrounds, histories, sexualities, genders and ethnicities move the industry forward. We all stand on the shoulders of giants in the industry; so much has been achieved in such a short amount of time. The games industry is not static, it evolves every day and every game incorporates lessons from the past and, if successful, moves the industry forward and with it every discipline. The future of level design is yours to make. It will be a hard road, and at times you may want to give up, but the experience will be worth it.

Case Study
Pete Ellis. Level and Combat Design for *Killzone: Mercenary*

Creating Combat Narratives in *Killzone: Mercenary*

Combat narrative gives reason or pretext for what is happening in the environment and the state of the enemy characters when you arrive. For example, are they nervous and on edge and expecting the player's presence? Or are they relaxed and not expecting an attack? This can form the basis of how the setup is created.

Additionally, each combat encounter should relate back to the main story plot and reflect both its overall story arc and specific story beats. For example, is this a section where the player's character is supposed to be feeling powerful? If so, are there plenty of environmental tools for the player to use against the enemy in order to feel powerful? The considerations for combat narrative in KZM were mostly communicated through environment layout. As an example, the *Crysis* series utilized extensive traversal, speed, stealth and power skills. The player character has superhuman abilities and gameplay mechanics to match, so there are more obvious opportunities for creating an environment that makes the player feel powerful. A combination of ledges and climbable objects allows the player to climb up to spots with a height advantage, allowing them to either watch over the enemy while in stealth, shoot down onto them over the top of their cover

or even perform "death from above" jumps to take them out. Explosive objects can be littered around the environment to allow the player to either target them when enemies are nearby (a static barrel is easier to hit than the moving enemy), or pick them up to throw at targets. Players can crawl into hidden areas of refuge and then, by using the stealth cloak, get away from a threat. Alternatively, when a story beat intends for the player to feel weak and on the backfoot, there may be limited options for the player in that specific encounter, whereas the enemy AI might have more tools to fight the player with.

As the player character in *Killzone: Mercenary* was not a superhuman (but indeed a mercenary as the title suggests) he purposely didn't have such extreme speed and traversal mechanics as the characters in *Crysis*. The closest element to this was a "vanguard" system that allowed the player to purchase a variety of weapon systems ranging from destructive air strikes to invisible cloaking devices. We built environments that would support these exotic weapons but our main consideration for the game was to create combat narratives using the core weaponry and cover mechanics.

More subtly than the *Crysis* examples, the environments in KZM that promoted a feeling of power included lots of low cover options that allowed the player

to observe the enemy as well as offering a vantage point from which to attack. Being in low cover meant the player could still see over the top of cover from their first-person view, but enemies couldn't see them. This was because when the player was in low cover enemies checked that they could see the player's body, rather than their head. This was in the player's favor so low cover was still a defensive option, without the player having to be face up to a wall or being visible at all times. This gives the player a great advantage, knowing the enemies' location means a player can plan their strategy of attack, as well as not getting caught out by any potential flanking movements or unseen enemies.

Using Cover as a Superpower

Lots of high cover and elevated positions were used to make the player feel more safe and secure as they are completely blocked from any gun fire. It also allowed the player to run behind high cover to escape the enemy or block their line of sight, as well as allowing them to get into a stronger position or move closer to a foe without the risk of being shot. The player can get a better understanding of the arena layout from higher up which gives them a combat advantage. It is also easier for the player to target and shoot enemies who are below them.

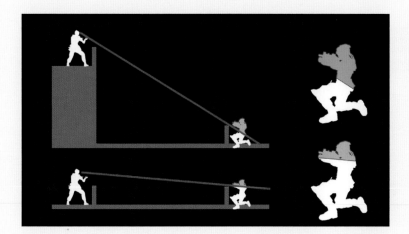

9.16
How much of an enemy is revealed from cover is affected by the elevation of the player; fighting down towards an enemy will reveal more of the enemy because of the height advantage, making them easier to hit. Additionally, less of the player can be hit from an enemy fighting upwards.

One specific example from a KZM level I worked on is the third combat area in the first level; "The Halls of Justice." Narratively, the player has just discovered the location of a hostage they are trying to find and they rappel down the back of the building to the floor she is being held on. The enemies on this floor don't know the player is approaching, but they are in a cautious state as they are occupying a building which they have taken by force and must remain prepared.

The player enters the environment undetected and in an elevated position so that they can watch the patroling enemies below and assess their options. Additionally, the enemies can be heard talking about the location of the hostage, which gives the player extra narrative information.

There are also explosive objects within the enemies' territory but none in the area around where the player enters. This gives the player the upper hand in the combat scenario, if we reversed this scenario and the player started close to explosive barrels instead, they would start the level with the feeling of being in danger and would want to move to a safer location.

9.17
Killzone Mercenary, Guerilla Cambridge, 2013. In this level the player enters at the back of the room with a wall behind them so there is no risk of them being flanked by the enemy. This is considered a position of power due to the elevation, as well as a position of safety, because of the secure boundaries.

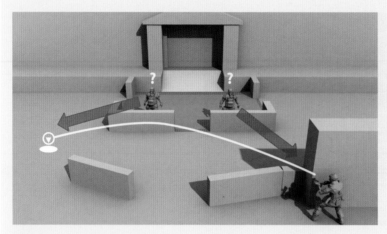

9.18
Guards can be distracted by throwable items and this tactical knowledge can be used when planning an attack. This kind of behavior is something we want to promote as it makes the player feel clever.

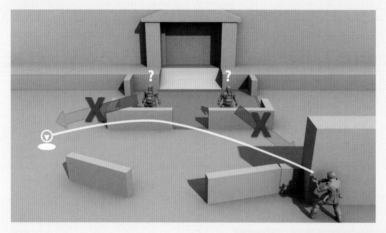

9.19
However, if in a situation the player tries to implement their plan and it fails because the enemies don't react accordingly then the player can feel cheated. They may have even used up a limited item to try and achieve their expected result, and in this case they might feel especially annoyed.

In the design of this level the entry point for the enemy reinforcements is higher than the player (a floor above), but when entering the arena, the enemies run out of the doors and vault over the railings and land on the floor below the player. This is a dramatic entrance, but it also means that the enemies don't occupy the upper floor and have a height advantage over the player. The player will always see the next wave of reinforcements entering the area and know the amount and location of the replenished enemy. If the enemy entered out of sight the player

may become overwhelmed or be taken by surprise when extra enemies reveal themselves in much more dangerous positions.

The Importance of Predictable AI Enemy Patterns and Environments

AI in games is all about player expectation and results. For example, the player might have been taught throughout a game that an enemy gets lured to a position by a certain tool in the player's inventory, such as using a brick or a bottle to create a noise distraction (*The Last of Us*), or they can bring the enemy to the player with a knock sound (*Metal Gear Solid*).

That is not to say that designers should never change up the rules of the game; after all, introducing something fresh will prevent the game from becoming repetitive. What you need to remember is to give feedback to the player that either those learned rules won't apply in a new situation, or if this isn't a valid option for your encounter then you must give feedback as to why the expected result hasn't occurred. For example, there might be times when you need to restrict enemies to certain locations in the level. Perhaps you have some enemies protecting the exit of an environment who you want to make sure the player must deal with before leaving the area, or maybe narratively these enemies were supposed to be protecting something. In these cases it's usual for a designer to restrict the enemies to certain

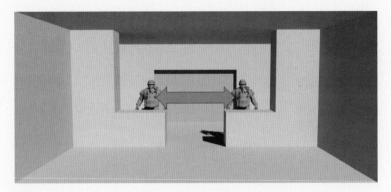

9.20
This is an example of corridor design where the enemies are kept within a tighter space with no options for movement (making them easy targets), but if the enemies are guarding an exit that could be a good challenge for the player.

areas or zones which they can't leave. How then do you give feedback to the player that trying to lure an enemy out of this zone won't work?

A great example of this was in *The Last of Us*; the designers had two systems for dealing with this situation. The enemy who was restricted and couldn't go to investigate a distraction outside of their zone would call out to other enemies asking them to examine the position giving the player feedback that the enemy wouldn't be leaving their area. The AI rule would then have an alternative enemy go to the location of the distraction. If there were no other enemies left they would shout out saying there was no way they were going to that location, reinforcing the restriction feedback to the player as well as giving narrative context for the situation the enemy found themselves in.

Using Geometry and AI to Prevent Player Boredom
A player will feel like they are in a shooting-gallery game if there is only one direction and location that a threat is coming from and the player can target and defeat this threat while staying within one screen.

Have multiple locations and directions that enemies occupying the level can combat as it provides different avenues of fire which promotes player movement and adds a variety of experiences in each combat encounter. When developing KZM we created arenas that incorporated multiple avenues of fire, which also meant that we had to make sure to balance the difficulty appropriately.

The arrangements of our arenas in KZM also incorporated complex circular navigability and opportunities for flanking routes for the player and the enemy.

These kinds of arrangements promoted movement around and through the combat arenas so that the player wouldn't be faced with a repetitive encounter of firing down single avenues but would experience dynamic combat from multiple angles.

Combat Fronts
Another method for supporting player focus change is moving the combat front. A "front" is the perceived line or boundary that faces the enemy and is the nearest position that combat should be engaged from.

Once they had successfully killed one of the two assault troopers, a "backup" trooper dropped into the environment in a different location to replenish the numbers.

The enemies coming from the left side of the arena redirects the combat focus towards the exit of the ground floor and the cover

9.21
Imagine if you had a situation with split enemies so the avenues of fire were more than a screen width apart, be it because a wall (a line-of-sight blocker) in the center split the enemies or there were spawn points at each side.

9.22
This is much harder to tackle as the player must divide their attention and balance their focus between two fights, allowing the "unseen" enemy to do what they want, such as fire at the player unhindered, or advance toward them without them knowing.

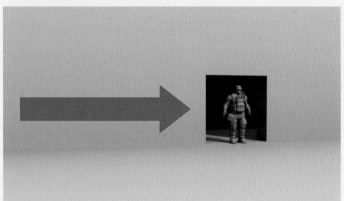

9.23
They could even move position altogether so when the player looks back they've completely gone and now the player has turned their focus away from an enemy they could see and were shooting at, to an empty space, now facing away from two enemies who can shoot at them unhindered.

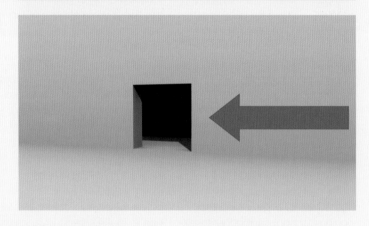

position of the troopers frames the exit for the player. When they take cover here this establishes a new enemy front, which creates a new front for the player (and the buddy character, Ivanov).

These kinds of techniques ensure that the player will move to different cover positions to fight different threats throughout the encounter. In later levels we designed multiple combat fronts and multiple locations that enemies enter from and occupy. As the player's ability increases we can balance difficulty using a variety of different methods, including spreading the avenues of fire wider apart, giving multiple options for movement within the environments and setting up contrasting combat fronts.

9.24
Killzone Mercenary, Guerilla Cambridge, 2013. In the tutorial at the start of KZM we wanted to promote the arena combat but had to keep it simple enough for the player to learn the mechanics and controls on the PS Vita. At the start of the first level I had the player enter a combat space facing where two enemies dropped down into the environment.

9.25
Killzone Mercenary, Guerilla Cambridge, 2013. The landing position of a new trooper then starts to shift the focus of the combat further toward the left of the screen and to that side of the environment. This is the first stage of "redirecting the front" toward the exit out of the first section (a climbable pipe at the left side of the arena).

9.26
Killzone Mercenary, Guerilla Cambridge, 2013. As this is the tutorial and the player's first experience of shooting, there is no immediate cover for the new trooper to use (as there was for the first two troopers) which makes him an easier target. If the player doesn't manage to take this trooper out at the start, the combat front begins to move 90 degrees to the left as the trooper begins to move to the closest available cover location.

9.27
Killzone Mercenary, Guerilla Cambridge, 2013. It is possible for the player to target this third trooper while remaining at their starting position, so to encourage player movement two more enemies are introduced who flank from the exit side (the left), forcing the player to move into a new cover position (the player does not have protective cover on their left side and is now vulnerable). Forcing the player to move ensures that the battle doesn't become static or repetitive.

9.28
Killzone Mercenary, Guerilla Cambridge, 2013. The player's new front becomes the line of cover which faces the new enemies' low cover, perpendicular to how the player started. There are now a few options for the player to position themselves along this cover and this determines how the enemies move and react to the player.

Bibliography and Game Credits

Introduction (Chapter 0)

Game Credits

Gone Home, The Fullbright Company. 2013.
Tacoma, The Fullbright Company, 2017.
F.E.A.R., Monolith Productions, 2005.
BioShock 2 DLC Minerva's Den, Irrational Games, 2010.
Call of Duty: Black Ops, Treyarch, 2010.
Assassin's Creed: Origins, Ubisoft, 2017.
Halo 5: Guardians, 343 Industries, 2015.
Fallout 4, Bethesda Softworks, 2015.
Super Mario Galaxy 2, Nintendo, 2010.
Sonic the Hedgehog, Sonic Team, 1991.
Super Mario Bros. 2, Nintendo, 1988.
Uncharted 4, Naughty Dog, 2016.
Gears of War 4, The Coalition, 2016.

Bibliography

Perez, Matt. "Inside The Mind Of Steve Gaynor, The Level
  Designer Behind 'Gone Home' And 'BioShock 2'."
  Forbes. November 22, 2016. Accessed July 09, 2017.
  https://www.forbes.com/sites/mattperez/2016/11/21
  /inside-steve-gaynors-mind-the-level-designer-behind
  -gone-home-and-bioshock-2/#5be4dc5858e8.
Sheppard, Mare, and Raigan Burns. "Empowering the
  Player: Level Design in *N++*." *GDC Vault*. March 2016.
  Accessed July 09, 2017. http://www.gdcvault.com
  /play/1023282/Empowering-the-Player-Level-Design.

Chapter 1

Game Credits

BioShock, Irrational Games, 2007
System Shock 2, Looking Glass Studios, 1999
Rocket League, Psyonix, 2015
Supersonic Acrobatic Rocket-Powered Battle-Cars,
  Psyonix, 2008
Journey, ThatGameCompany, 2012
Broken Age, DoubleFine Productions, 2014-2015
Firewatch, Campo Santo, 2016
What Remains of Edith Finch, Giant Sparrow, 2017
Red Dead Redemption 2, Rockstar, 2018

Bibliography

Finley, Alyssa. "Postmortem: 2K Boston/2K Australia's
  BioShock." *Gamasutra: The Art & Business of Making
  Games*. September 2, 2008. Accessed July 31, 2017.
  http://www.gamasutra.com/view/feature/132168
  /postmortem_2k_boston2k_.php.
Games, Zipline. "Get Started With MOAI." *Moai*. 2014.
  Accessed July 31, 2017. http://moaiwebsite.github.io/.
Mathieson, Lesley. "Building a Successful Production
  Process." *GDC Vault*. March 2008. Accessed July 31,

2017. http://gdcvault.com/play/304/Building-a
  -Successful-Production.
Schreier, Jason. "Inside Rockstar Games' Culture
  Of Crunch." *Kotaku*. October 24, 2018. Accessed October
  28, 2018. https://kotaku.com/inside-rockstar-games
  -culture-of-crunch-1829936466.
Sergeev, Artyom. "Who Are Level Designers?" *80 LEVEL*.
  Accessed October 21, 2018. https://80.lv/articles/who
  -are-level-designers/.
Vlaskovits, Patrick. "Henry Ford, Innovation, and That."
  Harvard Business Review. July 23, 2014. Accessed July
  31, 2017. https://hbr.org/2011/08/henry-ford-never
  -said-the-fast.

Chapter 2

Game Credits

BioShock, Irrational Games, 2007.
Pac-Man, Namco, 1980.
Tomb Raider, Eidos, 1996.
Sunset Overdrive, Insomiac Games, 2014.
Max Payne 3, Rockstar Studios, 2013.
Medal of Honor: Heroes 2, Electronic Arts LA, 2007.
Rise of the Tomb Raider, Crystal Dynamics, 2015.
Detroit: Become Human, Quantic Dream, 2008.
Far Cry 4, Ubisoft, 2015.
Uncharted 4: A Thief's End, Naughty Dog, 2016.
Madden NFL 16, EA Tiburon, 2016.
Metal Gear Solid V: The Phantom Pain, Kojima
  Productions, 2015.
Dishonored 1 & 2, Arkane Studios, 2012, 2016.
Hitman, IO Interactive, 2016.
Marvel's Spider-Man, Insomniac Games, 2018.
The Legend of Zelda: Breath of the Wild, Nintendo, 2017.
Gears of War 4, The Coalition, 2016.*Resident Evil 7:
  Biohazard*, Capcom, 2017.
Overwatch, Blizzard Entertainment, 2016.
Assassin's Creed Unity, Ubisoft, 2014.
Far Cry 5, Ubisoft, 2018.

Bibliography

Allison, Fraser. "The Game Narrative
  Triangle." *Kotaku*. July 23, 2010. Accessed
  July 31, 2017. http://kotaku.com/5594540
  /the-game-narrative-triangle—redkingsdream.
Bura, Stephane. "Emotion Engineering: A Scientific
  Approach For Understanding Game Appeal."
  Gamasutra: The Art & Business of Making Games.
  July 29, 2008. Accessed July 31, 2017. http://www
  .gamasutra.com/view/feature/132135/emotion
  _engineering_a_scientific.php?page=5.
Bycer, Josh. "How Game Mechanics Condition Us."
  Gamasutra: The Art & Business of Making Games.

October 26, 2016. Accessed July 31, 2017. http://www
.gamasutra.com/blogs/JoshBycer/20161026/284120
/How_Game_Mechanics_Condition_Us.php.

Duarte, Cristiane Rose and Ethel Pinheiro. Spatial
empathy and urban experience: a case study in a public
space from Rio de Janeiro. Nicolas R´emy (dir.) ; Nicolas
Tixier (dir.). Ambiances, tomorrow. Proceedings of 3rd
International Congress on Ambiances. Septembre 2016,
Volos, Greece, Sep 2016, Volos, Greece. International
Network Ambiances; University of Thessaly, vol. 2, p.
611– 616, 2016.

England, Liz. "Level Design in a Day: The Worlds of Sunset
Overdrive." *GDC Vault*. March 2015. Accessed July 31,
2017. http://www.gdcvault.com/play/1022114/Level
-Design-in-a-Day.

Kerr, Chris. "Creating compelling puzzles in Rise of the
Tomb Raider." *Gamasutra: The Art & Business of
Making Games*. December 2, 2015. Accessed July 31,
2017. http://www.gamasutra.com/view/news/260637
/Creating_compelling_puzzles_in_Rise_of_the_Tomb
_Raider.php.

Koster, Raph. *A theory of fun for game design*. p43.
Sebastopol, CA: OReilly Media, 2013.Mandryka,
Alexandre. "Fun and uncertainty."" *Gamasutra: The
Art & Business of Making Games*. January 29, 2014.
Accessed July 31, 2017. http://www.gamasutra.com
/blogs/AlexandreMandryka/20140129/209620/Fun_and
_uncertainty.php.

Moss, Richard. "7 introductory levels that all game
developers should study." *Gamasutra: The Art &
Business of Making Games*. January 10, 2017. Accessed
July 31, 2017. http://www.gamasutra.com/view/news
/287878/7_introductory_levels_that_all_game
_developers_should_study.php.

Palmer, Jack. "Time for a timer!—Effective use of timers
in game design." *Gamasutra: The Art & Business of
Making Games*. October 19, 2015. Accessed
July 31, 2017. http://www.gamasutra.com/blogs
/JackPalmer/20151019/256526/Time_for_a_timer
_Effective_use_of_timers_in_game_design.php.

Plunkett, Luke. "Uncharted 4 Has The Perfect Video Game
Ending." *Kotaku*. May 26, 2016. Accessed July 31, 2017.
http://kotaku.com/uncharted-4-has-the-perfect-video
-game-ending-1778806080.

Rams, Dieter. "Dieter Rams: Design by Vitsœ." Speech,
Jack Lenor Larsen's New York showroom, New York,
New York, December 1976. Accessed July 31, 2017.
https://www.vitsoe.com/files/assets/1000/17/VITSOE
_Dieter_Rams_speech.pdf.

Ray, Sheri Graner. "Explorative Acquisition." *Gamasutra—
Tutorials: Learning To Play*. October 6, 2010. Accessed
July 31, 2017. http://www.gamasutra.com/view/feature
/6160/tutorials_learning_to_play.php?print=1.

Remo, Chris, and Brandon Sheffield. "The Illusions We
Make: Gearbox's Randy Pitchford." *Gamasutra—
The Illusions We Make: Gearbox's Randy Pitchford*.
October 12, 2009. Accessed July 31, 2017. http://www
.gamasutra.com/view/feature/4158/the_illusions_we
_make_gearboxs_.php?print=1.

Schaffer, Tim. "Adventures in Character Design." *GDC
Vault*. March 2004. Accessed July 31, 2017. http://www
.gdcvault.com/play/1015300/Adventures-in-Character.

Schatz, Emilia. "Defining Environment Language for Video
Games." *80 level*. June 27, 2017. Accessed July 31,
2017. https://80.lv/articles/defining-environment
-language-for-video-games/.

Seppala, Timothy J. "The true story of the worst video
game in history." *Engadget*. July 14, 2016. Accessed
July 31, 2017. https://www.engadget.com/2014/05/01
/true-story-et-atari/.

· Stout, Mike. "Trinity, Part 7 - Ramps, Part 2." *Gamasutra:
The Art & Business of Making Games*. July 22, 2015.
Accessed July 31, 2017. http://www.gamasutra.com
/blogs/MikeStout/20150722/249134/Trinity_Part_7
_Ramps_Part_2.php.

Taylor, Dan. "Ten Principles of Good Level Design (Part
1)." *Gamasutra: The Art & Business of Making Games*.
September 29, 2013. Accessed July 31, 2017. http://
www.gamasutra.com/blogs/DanTaylor/20130929
/196791/Ten_Principles_of_Good_Level_Design_Part
_1.php.

Venturelli, Mark. "Difficulty Levels And Why You
Should Never Use Them." *Gamasutra: The Art &
Business of Making Games*. June 24, 2016. Accessed
July 31, 2017. http://www.gamasutra.com/blogs
/MarkVenturelli/20160624/275674/Difficulty_Levels
_And_Why_You_Should_Never_Use_Them.php.

White, Brian. "All Video Games Should Have a Difficulty
Option." *Talk Amongst Yourselves*. January 19, 2016.
Accessed July 31, 2017. http://tay.kinja.com/all-video
-games-should-have-a-difficulty-option-1753890139.

Chapter 3

Game Credits

Gears of War (series), Epic Games, The Coalition,
2006–2016.
Uncharted (series), Naughty Dog, 2007–2016.
Final Fantasy XIII, Square Enix, 2010.

Bibliography

Baron, Sean. "Cognitive Flow: The Psychology of Great
Game Design.*" Gamasutra: The Art & Business of
Making Games*. March 22, 2012. Accessed July 08,
2017. http://www.gamasutra.com/view/feature/166972
/cognitive_flow_the_psychology_of_.php.

Burgess, Joel. "GlitchCon 2014: Level Design by Joel
Burgess." *YouTube*. February 15, 2014. Accessed August
04, 2017. https://www.youtube.com/watch?v=EFJ5IE7
ud_s&feature=youtu.be&t=51s.

Burgess, Joel. "Skyrim's Modular Approach to
Level Design." *Gamasutra: The Art & Business of
Making Games*. May 1, 2013. Accessed August
04, 2017. http://www.gamasutra.com/blogs
/JoelBurgess/20130501/191514/Skyrims_Modular
_Approach_to_Level_Design.php.

Iwinski, Marcin. "Complexity of Open World." *Insights
from the greatest minds in video games*. September 30,

2016. Accessed July 08, 2017. http://www.criticalpath
project.com/video/complexity-of-open-world/.

Mullich, David. "The Objectives Of Game Goals."
Gamasutra: The Art & Business of Making Games.
July 12, 2016. Accessed July 08, 2017. http://www
.gamasutra.com/blogs/DavidMullich/20160712/276847
/The_Objectives_Of_Game_Goals.php.

Seifert, Coray. "Level Design in a Day: Your Questions,
Answered." *Gamasutra: The Art & Business of Making
Games*. March 13, 2013. Accessed July 08, 2017. http://
www.gamasutra.com/view/feature/188740/level_design
_in_a_day_your_.php.

Stout, Mike. "Learning From The Masters: Level Design In
The Legend Of Zelda." *Gamasutra: The Art & Business
of Making Games*. January 12, 2012. Accessed July 08,
2017. http://www.gamasutra.com/view/feature/134949
/learning_from_the_masters_level_.php.

Yee, Nick. "Unmasking the Avatar: The Demographics of
MMO Player Motivations, In-Game Preferences, and
Attrition." *Gamasutra: The Art & Business of Making
Games*. September 0, 2004. Accessed July 08, 2017.
http://www.gamasutra.com/view/feature/130552
/unmasking_the_avatar_the_.php?page=2.

Chapter 4

Game Credits

Uncharted 4: A Thief's End, Naughty Dog, 2016.
The Witcher 3: Wild Hunt, CD Projekt RED, 2015.
Everybody's gone to the rapture, The Chinese Room, 2015.
The House of the Dead, Wow Entertainment, 1996 .
Police 911, Konami, 2000.
The Legend of Zelda: Skyward Sword, Nintendo EAD,
2011.
Call of Duty: Modern Warfare 3, Infinity Ward, 2011.
Quake 3, Id Software, 1999.
The Division, Massive Entertainment, 2016.
Yakuza 0, Sega, 2015.
Shadow of the Tomb Raider, Crystal Dynamics, 2018.
Ryse Son of Rome, Crytek, 2013.
Batman: Arkham Knight, Rocksteady Studios, 2015.
Inside: Playdead, 2016.
The Legend of Zelda: Breath of the Wild, Nintendo, 2017.
Dead Space 3, Visceral Games, 2013.
Alice: Madness Returns, Spicy Horse, 2011.
The Last of Us: Naughty Dog, 2013.

Bibliography

England, Liz. "The Door Problem." *Liz England*. April 21,
2014. Accessed August 04, 2017. http://www.lizengland
.com/blog/2014/04/the-door-problem/.

Graft, Kris. "In open world game design, curiosity is key,
says Bethesda's Todd Howard." *Gamasutra: The Art &
Business of Making Games*. March 17, 2016. Accessed
July 14, 2017. http://www.gamasutra.com/view/news
/268274/In_open_world_game_design_curiosity_is
_key_says_Bethesdas_Todd_Howard.php.

Melendez, Clement. "The art of guiding players through
an environment." *Clement Melendez Level Designer*.
May 29, 2017. Accessed July 14, 2017. http://www

.clement-melendez.com/portfolio/articles/push-pull
/composition/.

Chapter 5

Game Credits

Doom, ID Software, 2016.
Borderlands, Gearbox Software, 2009.
X-Men Origins: Wolverine, Raven Software, 2009.
Batman: Arkham Asylum, Rocksteady Studios, 2009.
Little Big Planet, Media Molecule, 2014.
Final Fantasy XIII, Square Enix, 2009.
The Talos Principle, Croteam, 2014.
LEGO Harry Potter: Years 1–4, Traveller's Tales, Feral
Interactive, Open Planet Software, TT Fusion, 2010.
Psychonauts, DoubleFine Productions, 2005.
The World of Warcraft, Blizzard Entertainment, 2004.
God of War, SIE Santa Monica Studio, 2018.
I am Bread, Bossa Studios, 2015.
Goat Simulator, Coffee Stain Studios, 2014.

3D Models Credits

The bodyguard models come from Batewar.

The soldier models are from the Soldiers Pack by The
Avatar Studio.

The character animation (poses) comes from the Raw
Mocap Data for Mecanim by Unity Technologies. The
interiors are modified from the République Tech Demo
by Camouflaj, LLC.

Female character and the "general" are from the Third
Person Controller by Opsive.

These assets are available from the Unity asset store
https://www.assetstore.unity3d.com.

Bibliography

Bowen, Robert. "How To Convince The Client That Your
Design Is Perfect." *Smashing Magazine*. October
06, 2010. Accessed August 02, 2017. https://www
.smashingmagazine.com/2010/10/how-to-convince
-the-client-that-your-design-is-perfect/.

Coulianos , Filip. "Pacing And Gameplay Analysis In
Theory And Practice." *Gamasutra: The Art & Business
of Making Games*. October 3, 2011. Accessed August
02, 2017. http://www.gamasutra.com/view/feature
/134815/pacing_and_gameplay_analysis_in_.php.

Ellis, Peter. "Subverting Player Expectation by Using Level
Design." *80 level*. March 15, 2016. Accessed August
02, 2017. https://80.lv/articles/subverting-player
-expectation-by/.Hernandez, Patricia. "*Zelda Players
Have Found Wild Ways to Break Breath of the Wild's
Shrines*." Kotaku. April 27, 2017. Accessed August 02,
2017. http://kotaku.com/zelda-players-have-found
-wild-ways-to-break-breath-of-t-1794710556.

Kang, Jeremy. "World Building through Artifacts in Rise
of the Tomb Raider." *Gamasutra: The Art & Business of
Making Games*. March 3, 2016. Accessed August 02,
2017. http://www.gamasutra.com/blogs/JeremyKang
/201603.

Kremers, Rudolf. *Level design: concept, theory, and
practice*. p55. Natick, MA: A.K. Peters, 2010.Rogers,

Scott. *Level up!: the guide to great video game design.* p82. Hoboken: John Wiley & Sons, 2014.

Thorsen, Tor. "Behind Borderlands' 11th-hour style change." *GameSpot.* March 15, 2010. Accessed August 02, 2017. https://www.gamespot.com/articles/behind -borderlands-11th-hour-style-change/1100-6253257/.

Chapter 6

Game Credits

BioShock Infinite, Irrational Games, 2013.
Dark Souls II, From Software, 2014.
We Happy Few, Compulsion Games, 2018.
Unravel, ColdWood Interactive, 2016.
Fallout 4, Bethesda Game Studios, 2015.

Bibliography

Abbot, Sam. "Introducing We Happy Few." *Compulsion Games.* February 26, 2015. Accessed August 04, 2017. https://compulsiongames.com/en/news/6/introducing -we-happy-few.

Abbot, Sam. "Sneak peeks of our next and last major content update." *Compulsion Games.* June 30, 2017. Accessed August 04, 2017. https://compulsiongames .com/en/news/130/sneak-peeks-of-our-next-and-last -major-content-update.

Baker, Tim. "Upgrades and Playtesting." *Gamasutra: The Art & Business of Making Games.* June 19, 2017. Accessed August 04, 2017. http://www.gamasutra .com/blogs/TimBaker/20170619/300184/Upgrades _and_Playtesting.php.

Bridgett, Rob. "Why ambient sound matters to your game." *Gamasutra: The Art & Business of Making Games.* October 2, 2013. Accessed August 04, 2017. http://www .gamasutra.com/view/news/200150/Why_ambient _sound_matters_to_your_game.php.

Burgess, Joel. "GlitchCon 2014: Level Design by Joel Burgess." *YouTube.* February 15, 2014. Accessed August 04, 2017. https://www.youtube.com/watch?v=EFJ5IE7 ud_s&feature=youtu.be&t=51s.

Collins, Jeanne. "Conducting In-house Play Testing." *Gamasutra: The Art & Business of Making Games.* July 7, 1997. Accessed August 04, 2017. http://www .gamasutra.com/view/feature/131619/conducting _inhouse_play_testing.php.

Doetschel, Stefan. "Stefan Doetschel: The Principles of Level Design." *80 level.* July 21, 2015. Accessed August 04, 2017. https://80.lv/articles/stefan-doetschel-the -principles-of-level-design/.

England, Liz. "From Student to Designer." *Liz England.* May 23, 2014. Accessed July 30, 2017. http://www .lizengland.com/blog/2014/05/from-student-to-designer -part-1/.

Frederick, Matthew. *101 things I learned in architecture school.* Cambridge, MA: The MIT Press, 2007.

Lee, Steve. "Level Design Workshop: An Approach to Holistic Level Design." *GDC Vault.* March 2017. Accessed August 04, 2017. http://www.gdcvault.com /play/1024301/Level-Design-Workshop-An-Approach.

Luton, Will. "Making Better Games Through Iteration." *Gamasutra: The Art & Business of Making Games.* October 15, 2009. Accessed August 04, 2017. http:// www.gamasutra.com/view/feature/132554/making _better_games_through_.php.

MacDonald, Keza. "Unravel: The Kotaku Review." *Kotaku.* February 08, 2016. Accessed August 04, 2017. http:// kotaku.com/unravel-the-kotaku-review-1757752324.

Mader, Paul. "Creating Modular Game Art For Fast Level Design." *Gamasutra: The Art & Business of Making Games.* December 2, 2005. Accessed August 04, 2017. http://www.gamasutra.com/view/feature/130885 /creating_modular_game_art_for_fast_.php.

Pignole, Yoann. "The Hobbyist Coder #3: 2D platformers pathfinding—part 1/2." *Gamasutra: The Art & Business of Making Games.* April 27, 2015. Accessed August 04, 2017. http://www.gamasutra.com/blogs/YoannPignole /20150427/241995/The_Hobbyist_Coder_3__2D _platformers_pathfinding__part_12.php.

Rosin, Geoffrey. "Environment Storytelling in Dishonored 2." *80 level.* July 26, 2017. Accessed August 04, 2017. https://80.lv/articles/environment-storytelling-in -dishonored-2/.

Sagmeister, Stefan. "Make/Think | Stefan Sagmeister." *YouTube.* November 01, 2016. Accessed August 04, 2017. https://www.youtube.com/watch?v=7YQ1Y sf36vA.

Seifart, Coray. "Level Design in a Day: Your Questions, Answered." *Gamasutra: The Art & Business of Making Games.* March 19, 2013. Accessed August 04, 2017. http://www.gamasutra.com/view/feature/188740/level _design_in_a_day_your_.php?page=2.

Taylor, Dan. "Ten Principles of Good Level Design (Part 1)." *Gamasutra: The Art & Business of Making Games.* September 29, 2013. Accessed August 04, 2017. http:// www.gamasutra.com/blogs/DanTaylor/20130929 /196791/Ten_Principles_of_Good_Level_Design_Part _1.php.

Zoss, J. Matthew. "The Art Of Game Polish: Developers Speak." *Gamasutra: The Art & Business of Making Games.* December 22, 2009. Accessed August 04, 2017. http://www.gamasutra.com/view/feature/132611/the _art_of_game_polish_developers_.php.

Chapter 7

Game Credits

Morrowind, Bethesda Game Studios, 2002.
BloodRayne, Terminal Reality, 2004.
Dear Esther, The Chinese Room, 2012.
Killzone: Mercenary, Guerilla Cambridge, 2013.
Killzone Shadowfall, Guerilla Games, 2013.
RIGS: Mechanized Combat League, Guerilla Cambrigdge, 2016.

Bibliography

Guerrasio, Jason. "A Creator of the Original Millennium Falcon Describes How the Legendary 'Star Wars' Ship Was Made with Airplane Scraps and Lots of

Imagination." *Business Insider*, 22 May 2018, www
.businessinsider.com/how-the-millennium-falcon-was
-made-with-airplane-scraps-2018-5.

Perry, Lee. "Modular Level and Component Design." *Game
Developer*, November 2002, 30-35.

Technologies, Unity. "Materials, Shaders & Textures." *Unity*,
29 Mar. 2017, docs.unity3d.com/550/Documentation
/Manual/Shaders.html.

Chapter 8

Game Credits

AlphaGo, Alphabet Inc, 2015.

Middle Earth: Shadow of Mordor, Monolith Productions,
2014

Battlefield 1, EA Dice, 2016.

Alien: Isolation, Creative Assembly, 2014.

Street Fighter V, Capcom, 2016.

Command and Conquer: Tiberium Alliances, EA
Phenomic, 2012.

Forza Motorsport 7, Turn 10 Studios, 2017.

Left 4 Dead, Valve Corporation, 2008.

Binding of Isaac, McMillen & Himsl, 2011.

Driver: San Francisco, Ubisoft, 2011.

Payday: The Heist, Overkill Software, 2011.

Watch Dogs 2, Ubisoft, 2016.

Kinect Disneyland Adventures, Xbox Game Studios,
2011.

Strike Suit Zero, Born Ready Games, 2013.

Halo Wars 2, 343 Industries, 2017.

Hitman 2, IO Interactive, 2018.

Bibliography

Graft, Kris. "When artificial intelligence in video games
becomes . . . artificially intelligent." *Gamasutra: The
Art & Business of Making Games*. September 22, 2015.
Accessed July 16, 2017. http://www.gamasutra.com
/view/news/253974/When_artificial_intelligence_in
_video_games_becomesartificially_intelligent.php.

Kehoe, Donald. "Designing Artificial Intelligence for
Games (Part 1)." *Intel® Software*. January 01, 2015.
Accessed July 16, 2017. https://software.intel.com
/en-us/articles/designing-artificial-intelligence-for
-games-part-1.

Liszewski, Andrew. "Microsoft's AI Just Shattered the Ms.
Pac-Man High Score." *Sploid*. June 14, 2017. Accessed
July 16, 2017. http://sploid.gizmodo.com/microsofts-ai
-just-shattered-the-ms-pac-man-high-score-1796091352.

Lou, Harbing. "AI in Video Games: Toward a More
Intelligent Game." *Science in the News*. August 28,
2017. Accessed November 15, 2018. http://sitn.hms
.harvard.edu/flash/2017/ai-video-games-toward
-intelligent-game/.

Ramsey, David. "The Perfect Man." *Oxford American*.
July 1, 2015. Accessed July 16, 2017. http://www
.oxfordamerican.org/magazine/item/622-the-perfect
-man.

Chapter 9

Game Credits

Dead Rising 2, Capcom, 2010.

Player Unknown's Battlegrounds, Bluehole, 2017.

Sleeping Dogs, United Front Games, 2012.

Fortnite, Epic games, 2017.

Unreal Tournament, Epic Games, 1999.

Ghost Recon, Ubisoft, 2001.

Bibliography

Beinke-Schwartz, Elisabeth. "Level Design Workshop:
Singleplayer vs. Multiplayer Level Design: A Paradigm
Shift." *GDC Vault*. February 27, 2017. Accessed July 21,
2017. http://www.gdcvault.com/play/1024304/Level
-Design-Workshop-Singleplayer-vs.

Bridges, Josh. "Anatomy of a Combat Zone." *Gamasutra:
The Art & Business of Making Games*. July 15, 2009.
Accessed July 19, 2017. http://www.gamasutra.com
/view/feature/132469/anatomy_of_a_combat_zone.php.

Peters, Zi. "The Art of War: Gears of War—Knock Knock."
Gamasutra. August 21, 2015. Accessed July 17, 2017.
http://www.gamasutra.com/blogs/ZiPeters/20150821
/251625/The_Art_of_War_Gears_of_War__Knock
_Knock.php.

Ross, Bobby. "Visual Guide: Multiplayer Level Design."
Visual Guide: Multiplayer Level Design. May 06, 2015.
Accessed November 17, 2018. http://bobbyross.com
/library/mpleveldesign.

Index

A

AAA games, ix, 98–9, 105–6, 118–19, 124, 126, 134
Abandoned Manor asset, Artur G, 25, 115
ActionScript, 11
Activision, 44, 46
Adamations, 153
adaptive and predictive systems, behavior, 128–30
Adobe Edge, 6
Adobe Flash, 6, 11
aggressive, 126–7
alert, 126
algorithms
    behavior systems, 125–8
    Monte Carlo tree search (MCTS), 129
    video games, 124–5
Alice: Madness Returns (game), 61
Alien: Isolation (game), 128
AlphaGO (game), 124
Amazon's Lumberyard, 6
anatomy of level design
    breaking down, 72–8
    creating a playable blockworld, 75
    creating level "beats," 76
    defining and agreeing on each level's content, 74
    defining primary constraints, 73
    eliminating what is not working, 77–8
Ando, Tadao, 13
Andrew Pray, Victorian Interiors, 25, 36, 45, 57
Animation arts, 36, 45
Arkane Studios, 26, 91, 106
artificial intelligence (AI), xi, 28, 96, 120
    AI director systems, 130–1
    bringing world to life (sort of), 124–5
    in games, 137–8
    geometry and, 159
    player vs. player (PvP), 154
    term, 124
Artur G, Abandoned Manor asset, 25, 115
Assassin's Creed (game), 62, 147
Assassin's Creed: Origin (game), x
Assassin's Creed Odyssey (game), 71
Assassin's Creed Unity (game), 26
Audience Choice Award, 11
audio, level design, 103
aware, 126

B

backtracking, 29, 30, 43, 64
Batewar, 19, 24, 30
Batman Arkham (game), 137, 147
Batman Arkham Asylum (game), 4, 78, 79
Batman Arkham Knight (game), 64
"beats," creating level, 76
beauty pass, level design, 102–3
behavior systems, 133
    adaptive and predictive, 128–30
    AI director, 130–1
    choice architecture, 125–8
    emergent behaviors, 131–2
Beinke-Schwartz, Elisabeth, 149, 153
Belsay Hall, UK, 5
Bethesda, 36, 44, 60, 93, 95, 96
Bethesda Game Studios, 29, 61
Bethesda Softworks, 73, 109
bidirectional gameplay, 29, 30
Binding of Isaac (game), 131
BioShock (game), 2, 20, 21, 107
BioShock 2: Minerva's Den (game), ix
BioShock Infinite (game), 90, 105, 149
The Blackout Club (game), 107
Blade Runner (film), 4
Blizzard Entertainment, 22, 37
blocking out levels, 8–9
blockworld levels, 75, 76
Bloodrayne 2 (game), 112
Blouin-Payer, Roxanne, 132
Blueprints, 120
Borderlands (game), 77
Born Ready Games, 134
branching model, level design, 82–3
breadcrumbs, 60
Bridges, Josh, 145–6
Briner, Justin, 50
Broken Age (game), 6, 7
Brothers: A Tale of Two Sons (game), 86
Brown, Derren, 129
brutalism, 13
BSPs (Binary Space Partitioning), 8–9, 75
Burgess, Joel, 43–4, 93–4, 102, 104
Burns, Raigan, 11–15

C

Cage, David, 21
Call of Duty (game), 5, 85, 147, 148, 152, 153
Call of Duty: Black Ops (game), x, 152
Call of Duty: Infinite Warfare (game), 37
Call of Duty: Modern Warfare 3 (game), 58
Camouflaj, LLC, 65
camper, multiplayer type, 151
Campo Santo, 7
Candy Crush (game), 6
Capcom, 31
Captain America: Civil War (film), xii
capture the flag, multiplayer design, 152
Cartlife (game), 49
case study. *See also* interviews
    N++ case study: part one, 67–9
    Pete Ellis and design of *Killzone: Mercenary*, 156–61
CD Projekt Red, 57, 63
Champandard, Alex J., 124
character, movement, 41
chase, 125
Chess (game), 124, 133
Choke Point, 147
Cibele (game), 49–53
Civilization (game), 129
The Coalition, 1
CocoS2d-X, 6
coding, 52
combat arena, 133, 143, 146, 147
combat bowl, 142, 143, 144, 145
combat design, 142
    breaking down, 144–5
    cover in, 146, 151
    enemy territory, 144
    flank route, 144
    fronts, 159–60
    importance of detail, 145–7
    killzone, 144
    Killzone: Mercenary (game), 157–61
    level design and, 142–3
    multiplayer, 148–9
    player/enemy front, 144
    player territory, 144
    player types, 144–5
    run and gun, 145
    sniper, 145
    spacing considerations, 152
    stealth, 145
combat zone, 42, 142, 143, 150
Command and Conquer: Tiberium Alliances (game), 128
complexity through simplicity, modular designs, 114
composition, multiplayer, 150
Compulsion Games, 93

consistency, modular level design, 110
Coulianos, Filip, 78–9
    interview with, 86–7
Counter Strike (game), 153
cover
    in combat design, 146, 151
    Killzone: Mercenary (game), 156–8
Craig, Kate, 116
Creative Assembly, 128, 134, 142
critical path, level design, 43
Croteam, 84
CryEngine, 118, 121
Crystal Dynamics, 20, 60
Crytek, 6
Csikszentmihalyi, Mihaly, 42
cubes, as reference, 40
curiosity, navigating without maps,
    59, 60
customization, modular level
    design, 110

D

Dance Dance Revolution (game), 42
Dark Souls II (game), 91
Dark Souls III (game), 17
dead state, 127
Dead Rising 2 (game), 145
Dead Space 2 (game), 139
Dead Space 3 (game), 61
Deep Blue, 129
Detroit: Become Human (game), 21
*The Diaries of Professor Angell:
    Deceased* (game), 25, 98, 100,
    115
difficulty, level design, 28
DigitalKonstrukt, 19
Dishonored (game), 106–7
Dishonored 2 (game), 26, 37, 90–1, 94,
    105–6
Disney Interactive, 46
Disney parks, 60–1
Doom (game), 38, 43, 46, 73, 111,
    139, 149
door problem, 56–8
DoubleFine Productions, 6, 7
Driver: San Francisco (game), 131
Dys4ia (game), 49

E

EA, 46, 94
efficiency, in level design, 29
Ellis, Pete, 118–21, 144
    design of *Killzone: Mercenary*,
        156–61
emergent behaviors, 131–2, 138
emergent model, level design, 84–5
emergent narrative, 22
emotion, level design creating, 30–2
empowerment of players, level design
    principle, 27

encounters, level design process,
    96–100
England, Liz, 56, 66, 126
enjoyment, varying level for
    maximum, 45–7
Epic Games, 112, 141
Eurogamer EGX 2015, 118
Everybody's Gone to the Rapture
    (game), 58
explicit narrative, 21
exploits, 84, 130, 148, 149, 153–5
explorative acquisition, 23

F

Fallout (game), 59, 60, 98
Fallout 3 (game), 93
Fallout 4 (game), xi–xii, 18, 29, 61, 62,
    96, 111–12, 117
Far Cry 4 (game), 62
Far Cry 5 (game), 28
Far Cry Arcade (game), 89
F.E.A.R. (game), ix
feedback, 87, 103
The Fifth Element (film), 4
Final Fantasy Online, 52
Final Fantasy XIII (game), 81
finite state machine (FSM), 127, 128
Finley, Alyssa, 2
Firewatch (game), 7
First Person Exploration Kits, WhileFun
    games, 25, 36
First-Person Shooter (FPS) game, ix, xi,
    2, 28, 128
fleeing, 127
flow, level design, 42–3
Ford, Henry, 2
foreshadowing, 60, 64
Fortnite (game), 141, 151
framing, 61, 150
Frederick, Matthew, 90
Freeform model, combat arenas, 147
Freeman, Nina, 49–53, 116
frightened mode, 125
FromSoftware, 17
Frontier Developments, 134
Fullbright Company, ix, 27, 49, 50, 51
fun in navigation, level design
    principle, 19–20
FutureGames Academy, 86

G

Gabro Media, 25, 30, 42, 43, 62, 117
Gamasutra.com, 2, 18, 87, 126, 142
game design, xi, 33
    level design and, 14
    process of, 52
Game Developer Magazine, 112
game development
    modular level design, 110–11
    preproduction process, 2–3

GameMaker, 6
Gamesalad, 6
Gaynor, Steve, ix, xii, 27, 50, 51
GDC (Games Development Conference),
    10, 93, 105, 118, 124, 132, 139
Gearbox Software, 77
Gears of War (game), 28, 41, 43, 61, 73,
    80, 98, 125, 138, 142, 144, 147
Gears of War 4 (game), xi, 1
Ghost Recon (game), 152
GlitchCon, 43
goals, level design principles, 22–3
Goat Simulator (game), 85
God of War (game), 85, 143
golden path, 97. *See also* optimal path
Gone Home (game), ix, 27, 37, 38
Google Images, 4
Grand Theft Auto V (game), 18
graphic design, *N++* (game), 11
graphic processor (GPU), 29, 36, 98–9,
    102, 114
grid, modular design, 113
Guerrilla Cambridge, 118, 120, 157, 161
Guerrilla Games, 55, 119
Guitar Hero (game), 42

H

Half Life (game), 59, 86
Half Life 2 (game), 107
Halo (game), 28, 138, 152
Halo 5 (game), xi, 72
Halo Wars 2 (game), 134, 135, 136
Herngren, Max, 6, 8
High Impact Games, 10
Hill, Bruce, 125
Hitman (game), 23, 126, 138
Hitman 2 (game), 134, 135, 136
Horizon Zero Dawn (game), 55
The House of the Dead (game), 58
Howard, Todd, 59
How Do You Do It? (game), 49
hub-and-spoke model, level design, 83
Hutong Game's Playmaker, 7

I

I Am Bread (game), 85
IBM's Watson AI, 125
idle, 126
implicit narrative, 20
Independent Games Festival, 11, 49
IndieCade Collection 2015, 49
Infinity Blade: Adversaries (game),
    96, 145
Infinity Blade: Grasslands (game), 40
Infinity Blade: Icelands (game), 143, 145
Infinity Blade: Warriors (game), 38, 40,
    96, 145
Inside (game), 80
Insomniac Games, 44, 56
integration, 37–9, 42

intensity, level creation, 87

intensity ramping, 44

interviews

Burns, Raigan, 11–15

Coulianos, Filip, 86–7

Ellis, Pete, 118–21

Freeman, Nina, 49–53

Lee, Steve, 105–7

Peters, Zi, 134–9

Sheppard, Mare, 11–15

intrigued, 126

invisible design, ix

IO Interactive, 136

Irrational Games, 21

J

Java, 6

Journey (game), 6

jump height, 40

K

Kehoe, Donald, 126

Kickstarter, 50

Killzone: Mercenary (game), 118, 120, 144

level design of, 156–61

Killzone Shadowfall (game), 119

Kimmy (game), 49, 52

Kinect Disneyland Adventures

(game), 134

king of the hill, multiplayer design, 152

kits, 95–6, 98, 112–15

Kojima Productions, 23, 28

L

landmarks, navigating without maps,

59, 60–2

The Last of Us (game), 35, 62, 64, 65, 74,

75, 80, 158, 159

The Last of Us: Part 2 (game), 118,

137, 144

layout, level design process, 95–6

Lee, Steve, 90, 91, 105–7

LeFaure, Christophe, 106

Left 4 Dead (game), 107, 130, 131

Left 4 Dead 2 (game), 131

Legend of Zelda (game), 6, 31

Legend of Zelda: Breath of the Wild, viii,

31, 64, 85

Legend of Zelda: Skyward Sword

(game), 61

Lego The Harry Potter Years 1–4

(game), 83

level design, viii, ix, xiii. *See also*

anatomy of level design

analyzing for pacing, 78–9

applying principles of, 19–32

balancing the level, 44

challenges for, 15

combat design, 142–3

critical path, 43

as discipline, xi–xii

flow, 42–3

intensity ramping, 44

modular, 110–11

for multiplayer, 148–9

objectives, 46–7

preproduction, 2–3

principles of, 18

scale, integration, and proportion,

37–9, 42

technical constraints, 36

varying level for maximum

enjoyment, 45–7

level designer (LD)

blocking out levels, 8–9

composition skill, 5

focus of, 90

Freeman, Nina, 49–53

Freeman defining role of, 51

as gatekeepers, 90–1

preproduction, 2

role of, 48, 119

technical constraints, 36

level design models

branching or nonlinear model, 82–3

hub-and-spoke model, 83

linear model, 80–1

open or emergent model, 84–5

level design principles

creating emotion, 30–2

design driven by mechanics, 32

easy, medium, and hard, 28

efficiency, 29

empowerment of player, 27

fun in navigating levels, 19–20

level designer Dan Taylor, 18

surprise in, 26–7

teaching constantly, 24–6

telling what but not how, 22–3

visual storytelling, 20–2

level design process, 90, 93

beauty pass, 102–3

first pass and layout, 95–6

iteration, 92–103

level designers as gatekeepers, 90–1

pitch for game concept, 93–4

polish as final pass, 103

second pass and encounters, 96–100

third pass and core complete,

100–102

lighting, 60, 65

linear model

level design, 80–1

progression in, 81

Little Big Planet (game), xii, 80

Little Big Planet 3 (game), xi

M

The Machine Stops (game), 111

Madden NFL 16 (game), 22

Magic Kingdom, 61–2

Mandryka, Alexandre, 27

Marinello, Seth, 72–3

Mario series (game), 74

Marmoset's Skyshop, 7

Mass Effect (game), 73, 98, 144, 147, 148

massively multiplayer online games

(MMOs), 22, 84

materials, 116

Mathieson, Lesley, 10

Max Payne Chronicles (game), 60

Maya, 8, 9, 39, 95, 120, 121

mechanics, driving level design, 32

Medal of Honor (game), 46

Medal of Honor: Heroes 2 (game), 18

Menendez, Clement, 60

Metal Gear Solid (game), 158

Metal Gear Solid V: The Phantom Pain

(game), 22–3, 28, 126

Metanet

development of *N++*, 11–15

game development philosophy, 12–13

iteration design process, 92

Metanet Software, xi, 11

Microsoft, 1, 72

Middle Earth: Shadow of Mordor

(game), 126

Millennium Falcon, 111

Mirrors Edge Catalyst (game), 86

Mitchell, Billy, 126

Moai, 6

models. *See* level design models

modular level design, 110–11

advantages of, 110–11

complexity through simplicity, 114

grid in, 113

stress testing and prototyping,

115–16

surfaces, shaders, and materials,

116–17

system, 111–13

Mojang, 6

Monte Carlo tree search (MCTS)

algorithm, 129

Morrowind (game), 112

Motion++ (www.motionplusplus.com),

13

movement mechanics, 41

Ms Pac-Man (game), 126

Mullich, David, 46

Multiflag Studios, 24

multiplayer

capture the flag, 152

definitions, 151–3

framing and composition for, 150

king of the hill, 152

level design for, 148–9

player vs. player (PvP) no AI

required, 154

search and destroy, 153

sightlines and exploits, 153–4
team deathmatch, 152
team survival, 152
types, 151

N
N (game), 11, 13
N+ (game), 11
N++ (game)
    case study, 67–9
    development of, 11–15
    early design for ninja characters, 14
    early moodboard for, 12
    graphic design levels, 11
    level creation, 68
    level design, 14
    process, 67–8
    for PS4, 13
    testing, 69
    tools, 68–9
    wireframes of user interface, 69
Naughty Dog, 20, 22, 35, 61, 65, 75, 77,
    80, 118, 137, 138, 149
navigation
    curiosity, 59, 60
    denial and reward, 60
    foreshadowing, 60
    landmarks, 59, 60–2
    level design and fun, 19–20
    lighting, 60
    optimal path vs. exploration, 60
    without maps, 59–60
NavMesh, 96
nebulous objectives, 22
Nintendo, viii, 31, 64, 85
nonlinear model, level design, 82–3
nonplayer characters (NPCs), 27, 29, 38,
    94, 137–8
    behavior, 124–6, 128–30, 132
    combat and, 142–3, 148, 153
    design process, 94, 96–7, 101–2
    door problem, 57
    emotion of, 31
    level design and, 75–6, 82
    motivating, 58

O
objectives of level design
    challenging, 47
    clear, 46
    concrete, 46–7
    obtainable, 46
    principles, 22–3
    rewarding, 47
occlusion culling, 36, 98, 100
Ogasoda, 83, 111, 113, 114
onboarding, 24
open model, level design, 84–5
opportunity time, 36
Opsive, 30, 41, 42, 65, 76

optimal path, 76, 97
    vs. exploration, 60, 62–3
Overwatch (game), 22, 37, 148, 149

P
Pace University, 49
pacing, 32, 51
    analysis for Gamasutra.com, 87
    analyzing a game's level for, 78–9
    cutscenes for, 22
    environmental, 61
    flow and, 42–3
    golden rules for pacing a level, 86–7
    intensity of level, 44
    level, 45–6
    players, 59
    predictive, 44
    rollercoaster approach, 27, 44
    sense of, 5, 13
    types of, 68
Pac-Man (game), 18, 125, 126, 128,
    130, 132
Payday: The Heist (game), 131
performance, modular level design, 110
Perry, Lee, 110, 112, 113
Peters, Zi, 134–9, 142
PhyreEngine, 6
pitch, game concept, 93–4
platformer game, ix
play and learn approach, 23
player(s)
    curiosity, 60
    door problem, 56–8
    foreshadowing, 64
    immersion, xii
    landmarks, 60–2
    lighting, 60, 65
    motivating the, 58, 66
    navigating without maps, 59–60
    no straight paths and maps as
        reward, 62–3
    player vs. player (PvP), 45, 154
    psychology of, 72
    speed, pacing, and distance, 59–62
player empowerment, level design
    principle, 27
Player Unknown: Battlegrounds (game),
    44, 148, 150, 151
Playstation Vita, 118, 121
play testing, 44, 67, 87, 93, 102, 103,
    119, 149
Police 911 (game), 58
polish, level design, 103
Polybrush, 9
Portal 2 (game), 107
PowerPoint, 6
preproduction process
    level design, 2–3
    'safe space' to experiment and fail, 3
Prey (game), 109

principles, 18. *See also* level design
    principles
ProBuilder, 9
production process, video game, 10
proportion, 37–9, 42
prototyping, modular design, 115–16
psychology, 20, 26, 30–1, 48, 56, 66, 72
Psychonauts (game), 83
Psyonix, 3
PUBG Corporation, 150
Puchiwara no Bouken (game), 11
pull systems, 125
push systems, 125

Q
Quake (game), 152
Quantic Dream, 21

R
Rams, Dieter, 18, 33
Rapture, dystopia in *BioShock*, 2, 20
real-time strategy (RTS) games, 125
Red Dead Redemption 2 (game), 10, 137
Republique Tech, 65
research
    level design, 52
    video games, 4–5
Resident Evil 7: Biohazard (game),
    31, 130
RIGS: Mechanized Combat League
    (game), 120
Rise of the Tomb Raider (game), 20,
    82, 149
roamer, multiplayer type, 151
Rocket League (game), 3
rollercoaster design approach, 44
Ross, Bobby, 151
RPG (role-playing game), 2, 19, 81, 83,
    85, 101, 113
Ruined Building Kit, Jason Wong, 112
run and gun players, 145
rusher, multiplayer type, 151
Ryse Son of Rome (game), 60

S
Salmond, Michael, 25
scale, 37–9, 42
scatter mode, 125
search and destroy, multiplayer
    design, 153
semi-linear design, 82
shaders, 116, 117
Shadow of the Tomb Raider (game), 60,
    65, 74, 85
Sheppard, Mare, xi, 11–15, 45
SIE Santa Monica Studio, 143
sightlines, 97, 148, 153–4
Sims 4 (game), 125
Skyrim (game), 24, 43, 59, 60, 72, 93
Sledgehammer Games, 58

Sleeping Dogs (game), 147
sniper players, 145, 151
Sonic the Hedgehog (game), xi, 45
Sony, 6
Square Enix, 23, 74
Square Enix Montreal, 18
Starbreeze, 86
Star Maid Games, 49, 50
Star Wars (film), 111
Star Wars: The Old Republic (game), 151
stealth players, 145, 151
storytelling, in level design, 20–2
Stout, Mike, 44
Street Fighter V (game), 128
stress testing, modular design, 115–16
Strike Suit Zero (game), 134
Studio Max, 9, 95
Styncyl, 6
Sunset Overdrive (game), 32, 43
Super Bubble Blob (game), 11
Super Mario Bros. 2 (game), xi
Super Mario Galaxy 2 (game), xi
*Supersonic Acrobatic Rocket-Powered
    Battle-Cars* (game), 3
surprise, in level design, 26–7
Syndicate (game), 86
System Shock 2 (game), 2

T

Tacoma (game), ix, 49, 51, 52, 116
The Talos Principle (game), 83, 84
Taylor, Dan, 18, 22, 33. *See also* level
    design principles
teaching, level design constantly, 24–6
team deathmatch, multiplayer
    design, 152
team survival, multiplayer design, 152
teaser, 61
technical constraints, 36
10 Principles for Good Design, industrial
    designer Dieter Rams, 18
10 Principles of Good Level Design,
    18, 73. *See also* level design
    principles

The Terminator (game), 124
textures, 116
thatgamecompany, 6
3D Realms, 43
3DS MAX, 120, 121
Third Person Controller, Opsive, 30, 41,
    42, 65
343 Industries, 136
timing, level creation, 87
Tomb Raider (game), 18, 38
Tom Clancy's The Division (game), 59
Tony Hawk Pro-Skater (game), 43
tools, essential, for video games, 6–7
Train Yard, 24
Treyarch, x
2001: A Space Odyssey (game), 124
tutorializing, 24

U

Ubisoft, x, 26, 71, 89, 123, 132
Uncharted series (game), 73, 80, 137,
    138, 144, 148
Uncharted 4: A Thief's End (game), xi,
    20–2, 37, 61, 77, 80, 139, 149
Unity, 6, 7, 9, 36, 41, 96, 99, 118, 121
Unity 2018, 19, 24, 30, 41, 43, 62, 83,
    111, 112, 113, 117, 153
Unity Asset Store, Andrew Pray, 25,
    45, 57
University of Teesside, 118, 134
Unravel (game), 94
Unreal Development Kit (UDK),
    120, 121
Unreal Engine, 6, 8, 9, 96, 113, 118
Unreal Engine 4, 8, 9, 37, 38, 39, 40, 95,
    96, 143
Unreal Tournament (game), 151, 152
Urban Underground, Gabro Media, 30,
    42, 43

V

Valtameri (game), 50
Valve Corporation, 131
variation, level creation, 87

Victorian Interiors, Andrew Pray, 25, 36,
    45, 57
video game(s), 10
    creation of, xiii
    door problem in, 56–8
    essential tools, 6–7
    production, 10
    research, 4–5
    speed, pacing, and distance, 59–62
Video Game Design (Salmond), viii
Visceral Games, 72
visibility lines, 98
visual communication, 15
    navigation of levels, 19–20
visual storytelling, in level design, 20–2
von Moltke, Helmuth, 36

W

Walt Disney parks, 60–1
Watchdogs 2 (game), 123, 131–2
A Way Out (game), 86
weenie, 61
We Happy Few (game), 93
What Remains of Edith Finch (game),
    5, 58
WhileFun games, 25, 36
Witcher 3: Wild Hunt (game), 28, 43,
    57, 63
Wong, Jason, 112
Worch, Matthew, 139
World of Warcraft (game), 84

X

X-Men Origins: Wolverine (game), 78

Y

Yakuza O (game), 59
Yee, Nick, 44
YouTube DoubleFine Channel, 7

Z

Zbrush, 8
Zimonja, Karla, 50, 52